A Beginner's Guide to Lisp

Tony Hasemer

ADDISON-WESLEY PUBLISHING COMPANY

Reading, Massachusetts • Menlo Park, California • Wokingham, England
Don Mills, Ontario • Amsterdam • Sydney • Bonn • Singapore
Tokyo • Madrid • Bogota • Santiago • San Juan

The programs presented in this book have been included for their instructional value. They have been tested with care but are not guaranteed for any particular purpose. The publisher does not offer any warranties or representations, nor does it accept any liabilities with respect to the programs.

Cover design by Marshall Henrichs.

Print and binding Krips Repro Meppel Holland.

Library of Congress Cataloging in Publication Data

Hasemer, Tony
  Looking at LISP.

  Bibliography: p.
  Includes index.
  1. LISP (Computer program language) I. Title.
QA76.73.L23H37   1984   001.64'24   84-9323
ISBN 0-201-12080-1

BCDEF 8987

Contents

Foreword

About this book

This book is intended for microcomputer users. In the U.K., the term "microcomputer" tends to mean a very much smaller machine than it does in the U.S.A. Hence the occasional stress throughout the text on dialects of Lisp which are less elaborate than those normally available in America. This does not, however, affect the validity of what I have to say; and after reading this book the owner of a large Lisp should be able and eager to explore its extra facilities for him/herself.

The main use of Lisp, in higher education and in industry, is for the study of Artificial Intelligence. This is a fascinating subject, and the book considers quite a number of AI techniques, principles and problems. Where necessary to explain the workings of Lisp, the reader will also find information normally classed as Computer Science – simply explained and without recourse to abstruse mathematics. The book might well be thought suitable as a primer for undergraduate courses in programming or AI.

Choosing a Lisp for your computer

Microcomputer Lisps are almost invariably written for a specific machine and model. But of course it is the computer's Central Processor Unit which is important, and there are far fewer types of these than there are makes and marques of machine. A reputable dealer, or the software house concerned, will be able to advise you as to whether or not any particular version of Lisp can be used on your computer.

The various Lisps available for microcomputers are subsets of the full Lisp language, which is only available on mainframe computers (as yet!). Unfortunately, there is no generally-accepted standard for these subsets, and what one software designer sees as a highly desirable feature of Lisp may strike another as an irrelevance. On the other hand, there is necessarily a MINIMAL subset of Lisp functions – without which the Lisp would not be a Lisp at all – and that subset is far smaller than the subset available on any Lisp disc or tape that you will buy. For the purposes of this book I have assumed the existence of that minimal subset in your Lisp. Beyond that, should you find that I mention a function which doesn't exist in your Lisp, you have only to turn to the Appendix at the end of the book to find out how to create it. However, before buying any Lisp tape or disc, have a good look at its manual, and bear the following points in mind.

First, one of the most commonly-used functions in Lisp is called QUOTE. Now, it is a pain to have to keep typing that word in full, often several times on a single line of Lisp code. So any Lisp worth its salt provides what is called the QUOTE READMACRO. All this means is that instead of typing the word QUOTE (plus, as it happens, a couple of brackets), you simply type an APOSTROPHE – that is, the single-quote sign. My advice is: do NOT buy a Lisp which does not allow the single-quote sign in place of the word QUOTE, unless you have absolutely no alternative.

Second, check the following minimal subset of Lisp functions against those listed in the manual. The manual will certainly contain a number of functions not listed here, but it should include all of these. You could possibly do without the arithmetical functions PLUS, DIFFERENCE, TIMES, QUOTIENT, GREATERP and LESSP; but I wouldn't really advise it. There are occasions when even Lisp has need of a number or two.

APPLY
ATOM
CAR
CDR
COND
DEFUN or some equivalent, to create or "define" Lisp functions.
DIFFERENCE, DIFF, SUBTRACT or SUB (The function MINUS, if
      supplied, usually multiplies by −1, and is not the same thing.
      DIFFERENCE subtracts).
EQ or EQUAL
EVAL
GREATERP
LESSP
NULL and/or NOT
NUMBERP
PLUS
PRINT
QUOTIENT, QUO, DIVIDE or DIV
READ
RPLACA
RPLACD
SET and SETQ
TIMES

Third, find the section in the Lisp's manual which deals with the definition of new functions: functions not provided by the Lisp as it stands. (The key word to look for may be DEFUN, DEFINE, DEF or DE). Make sure that the manual mentions the possibility of creating at least the two major types of Lisp function, called EXPRs and FEXPRs. In top-class Lisps there may also be one or two further types. A Lisp which allows only EXPRs to be defined will be far from unusable, but you'll get a great deal more satisfaction out of it (and out of this book) if you're able to write FEXPRs as well.

Fourth, look in the manual for some mention of RECURSION. Recursion is the name given to a special way in which certain Lisp functions operate. And again a Lisp which did not permit you to define recursive functions would be pretty uninteresting to use. For the purposes of this book, the ability to recurse is essential. Some microcomputer Lisps specify a limit to what is known as the "depth" of recursion. If there is such a limit, it should be set at an ABSOLUTE MINIMUM of ten "levels" to be of much practical use. Large Lisp systems offer many hundreds of levels.

Fifth, the manual should have a section on PROPERTY-LISTS. It may well be quite a short section; but it should be there. A Lisp without property-lists would be not so much uninteresting as frustrating to use. One of the sections in Chapter 6 of this book shows you how to simulate property-lists for a Lisp which doesn't provide them. But, for a number of reasons, it is better to have the real thing.

And finally, it will be a great advantage to you if your Lisp comes complete with its own editor. An editor is used for putting right the (inevitable) mistakes in one's programs, and one of the nicest types to use is what is called a "structure editor". A structure editor understands, to some extent, the language for which it is designed, and can help you to avoid irritating, typing-mistake level, errors. Any type of editor, however, is infinitely preferable to no editor at all. It is possible to buy editors separately – on a different disc or tape from Lisp. If you contemplate doing this, you'll need to be sure that you have enough spare memory-space on your computer to be able to load both Lisp and the editor together. And, preferably, that your editor and your Lisp can be "interfaced" together: that is, that you will be able to use the editor from within Lisp, rather than having to exit from Lisp and re-enter it each time.

Lisp, being a more sophisticated language than – say – BASIC, does need a bit of memory space to work in. As examples, a Lisp towards the simpler end of the range may occupy around 10K, whilst a Lisp towards the more advanced end may need around 48K. This is a choice you must make, I'm afraid: there is obviously a one-to-one tradeoff between the amount of memory-space you have left after loading Lisp and the size of the Lisp programs you can then write. All of the programs in this book can be run using a 10K Lisp on a 32K machine.

There is nothing inherently "wrong" with a simpler Lisp, and throughout this book I've assumed that that is what you will have. As I'll show you, a simple Lisp can within very wide limits be extended and improved by its user so that it becomes comparable with the more sophisticated versions. Broadly speaking, a facility which exists in one Lisp can usually be duplicated in another. On the other hand, you may feel that a sophisticated Lisp will be a better buy in the long run, when you will have learned all that this book has to tell you and will want to progress further. Most of the existing books on Lisp do not make allowances for their readers owning only simple Lisp systems, because the latter are such a recent development.

The basic "unit" of Lisp, as you'll see in Chapter 3, is called the "cons-cell". A cons-cell occupies four bytes of memory on the normal microcomputer, and Lisp programs create an awful lot of cons-cells. In compensation, any modern Lisp has what is called a "garbage collector", which continually collects up any cons-cells which are no longer in use and makes their memory-space available for re-use. Another point which may concern you is that in general the simpler the

Lisp the faster it is in execution. But usually, programs written in Artificial Intelligence languages are interesting and/or worthwhile for reasons other than mere speed. Conversely, it is also generally the case that the more sophisticated your Lisp the fewer idiosyncratic "bugs" (errors) it will inflict on you when you come to the point where you want to start writing your own programs from scratch. You may also need to know whether or not the Lisp you contemplate buying will allow you to include assembly-language sections in your Lisp programs. You might want to do that so as to be able to use, say, your computer's graphics capabilities from within Lisp. (This is really the same point as I was making earlier, about interfacing an external editor to Lisp.) And there is always, of course, the matter of sheer cost to be taken into account. Your best bet, as ever, is to discuss these matters with a reliable dealer.

There. That should help you to sort out the dealers from the salesmen! As a matter of fact, the majority of the microcomputer Lisps I have come across so far have been well thought-out pieces of software. But new ones are being produced all the time, so sooner or later a few rubbishy ones are bound to crop up.

Chapter 1
Getting started

1.1 The language

If your reason for picking up this book is that you would like to learn an Artificial Intelligence language and have decided to have a go at Lisp, you have made a very wise move. Given a working knowledge of a few basic facts and rules (and I promise you that there are only a few), Lisp is an astonishingly flexible language as it stands; and it is also indefinitely extensible, which means that if you don't like some of the facilities it provides, you simply write your own and incorporate them into your personal version of Lisp, with no necessary loss of efficiency or comprehensibility. Both the flexibility and the extensibility derive from the extraordinarily simple basic Lisp operations. The whole language operates in small, easily understood chunks, and the spaghetti-junction-like constructs familiar to users of languages such as BASIC or ALGOL are actually quite hard to duplicate in Lisp: instead, a good Lisp program would consist of a master routine with a number of associated subroutines, and probably none of them would be more than about twenty lines long, no matter how complex the overall effect.

Lisp has been around for a number of years now, and has undergone a considerable amount of development. This has taken two divergent paths: that of the Lisp Machines, computers which understand Lisp and Lisp alone and which offer the user a vast number of inbuilt system functions (a "function" is an instruction to the computer to DO something, often activated by typing a single word or "phrase", which always has the same effect); and the AI approach which is to explore ways of increasing yet further the extensibility of the language, so that it can be used for purposes its designers had never dreamed of. The former approach is the better if you want to sell a working Lisp system to – say – a business concern, for use with definable problems, but the latter approach wins if you're none too sure at this stage exactly what problems you will want Lisp to tackle. What I have to say in this book will concentrate on the latter type of Lisp.

Even so there are a number of dialects of the language, all with their own advantages and disadvantages. However, apart from a few very minor differences of syntax, all of them are similar enough for you to gain a fair degree of programming expertise in any one, and then to be able to use any other almost as easily. Only when you come to the stage of really advanced programming do the differences become more than trivial. In this book you'll be introduced to my own

1

dialect of Lisp – I call it Lithp becuase my intials are TH, but just remember that when I show you some code and say that this is Lisp, it is actually Lithp that I'm referring to. Lithp is based on a subset of MacLisp, with a very few and very minor syntactic changes. It is also syntactically very close to the Lisp produced by AcornSoft for the BBC and Electron microcomputers. The differences in the latter case are confined to the mapping functions, to APPLY and to PRINT.

At the end of this book you'll find an Appendix which will enable you or someone else easily to convert your own computer's Lisp dialect into Lithp. The reason for inventing Lithp at all is that otherwise I'd have to repeat every section of code in the book – once for each known Lisp dialect – and that would get very tedious both for you and for me.

As each new function is introduced in the text below, you'll see a note reminding you to check it in the Appendix. Please do so: the Appendix is important. In it, you'll usually find three things: (1) assistance in finding out whether or not your own computer's Lisp has the same or an equivalent function; (2) a simple test which you can carry out to make sure that the function in your Lisp behaves in the same way as its equivalent in Lithp (usually, there will be no difference at all); and (3) a simple definition of the function which will if all else fails enable you to add the function to your own Lisp. My assumption is that as you work through this book you will frequently refer to both your Lisp's own manual and the Appendix. That seems to me to be the best way of ensuring that the Lisp you have available is the same in all important respects as the one (Lithp) I'm talking about. Please also read the introduction to the Appendix.

I've written this book with the users of microcomputer Lisps very much in mind. However, what I have to say will also apply to larger, mainframe computer, Lisp systems. The only real difference between the two types of Lisp is that in the latter case there is more of it.

Despite the fact that Lisp is, uncompromisingly and simply, the best programming language yet devised, there are still some things it is notably bad at. In particular, most dialects aren't too hot on numbers – so if the arithmetical overtones of the word "programming" daunt you, read on with renewed enthusiasm. Most Lisp systems demand that any number they are asked to handle is first declared (or assumed, which can be even more confusing) to be of one of several types; and even quite large Lisp systems, such as you might find on a PDP11 computer, are quite incapable of coping with any number higher than about thirty thousand. Lisp isn't really the language for you if your imagination revels in the kind of problems FORTRAN was designed for. Lisp leaves such minor "book-keeping" jobs to the workhorses of the software world, and con-centrates on the really interesting stuff.

So, Lisp is not some kind of glorified pocket calculator. It is something several conceptual orders different – a manipulator of symbols. Of course, the human mind may also be thought of as a symbol-manipulator, but that is what is exciting about AI, not what is exciting about Lisp itself. Where Lisp scores over other symbolic languages is in its above mentioned simplicity of operation. This shows itself in two important ways. Firstly, it is (fairly) easy to visualise what is going on "inside" the language – that is, at one level above the electronic 0s and 1s which dash so frantically about; and secondly, its syntax is almost childishly simple to learn. For most everyday purposes, there are only six Lisp "punctuation marks" (and two of these are left-hand and right-hand brackets). Other advanced programming languages, such as POP11 or PASCAL, have not only a plethora of syntactic signs, but also syntactic words – which must be placed, for example, to mark the beginning and end of a block of program which to a human observer all too obviously begins and ends at those points. A well written Lisp expression very rarely contains anything whose purpose is not both obvious and crucial. In the course of this book you'll learn the significance of: the left-hand or opening bracket; the right-hand or closing bracket; the single-quote sign (which in ordinary English is the apostrophe); the full-stop or dot; the space; and the semicolon. All other "punctuation" is implicit, as you'll see.

You may have heard people who should know better say that Lisp is difficult to read and write because of "all those brackets". One might as well say that English is difficult to read and write because of all those letters. With the help of a halfway decent editor, and with a little practice, brackets are no problem at all. So, now it's time – I'm afraid – to get a few boring basics out of the way. In every case I shall do my best to tell you the truth, the whole truth, and nothing but the truth.

Lisp is an "interactive" language. That is, you type something in, and Lisp responds by printing something out: it replies to you, or interacts with you. The next few sections are intended to give you the beginnings of a feeling of how to interact sucessfully with Lisp. If at all possible, please have your computer or terminal in front of you, and have Lisp loaded. If you are using a microcomputer you'll have a manual which explains how to load a Lisp tape or disc into the machine; if you're using a mainframe computer and don't know how to summon Lisp, ask the operator. As you work through this book, I'd like you to DO the things I ask you to do. There isn't much point in reading a book about how to program if right from the outset you don't intend to do any.

1.2 Values in Lisp

The first essential fact to know about interacting with Lisp is that it ALWAYS "returns" a value. That is to say, you type something in at the terminal and Lisp replies. Usually the reply is different from whatever you typed, and what has happened is that Lisp has EVALUATED your entry and returned the result. This is easy to see if what you typed in was, say, an arithmetical expression: Lisp does the calculation for you and tells you the answer. But Lisp follows this procedure for every entry, of whatever sort. Therefore, anything you type in must have a value – although as you'll see it doesn't have to be a numerical value. If what you type has no value, you'll get an error message. To prove this point, type your own first name, followed by a carriage-return, like this:

```
.*- tony
```

(The "*-" is the "prompt": in the Lisp we are using, the machine prints it whenever it is waiting for you to do something. Your Lisp may use some other sign or word as its prompt, or may even have no prompt at all.)

Just type the name, but don't — ever — forget the carriage-return (some Lisps will accept a space in its place): provided that what you have just typed is correct Lisp, it tells the computer that you have finished what you wanted to say and are yourself waiting for a reply.

3

Lisp will reply in this case with an error message concerning an "unbound variable", and any error message means, in effect, "I don't know what you're talking about". The explanations of the terms 'unbound' and 'variable' will follow shortly; don't worry about them for the moment. The fact that an error message has been returned at all tells you that problems arose when Lisp tried to EVALU-ATE your entry. You can, if you like, regard the evaluator as an analogue of a mathematician, as above, or as an expert semanticist trying to fathom the 'meaning' of your words. It doesn't matter, provided you grasp the point that whatever you type must have some value or other, so that Lisp can return it.

Of course, this state of affairs is highly logical and also very inconvenient. There will obviously be times when you want Lisp to understand a symbolic shape (such as "tony") to be just that and nothing else. So, a neat trick has been devised to enable you to say to Lisp "I want the value of what I type next to be understood as: itself". Notice how, in English, when we want to indicate to the reader that some symbols are to be taken verbatim – as in the previous couple of sentences – we enclose them in quote-marks. Lisp has just the same convention, except that to save typing it uses a single quote sign. Try the above experiment again, but this time QUOTE the name:

```
*- 'tony
```

[Check QUOTE in the Appendix]

After the carriage-return, Lisp will reply:

```
TONY
```

The quote-mark has told it that the value of "tony" is TONY, and it has dutifully returned that value. Incidentally, don't worry if, as shown here, Lisp replies in upper-case letters even though you may have entered lower-case ones; very few Lisp systems reply in lower case unless you take special steps to ensure that they do so, and in microcomputer Lisps you're usually stuck with upper-case replies whatever you do! (Some Lisps also demand that your entries shall be in upper case. So it's safest to enter everything in upper case at this stage, even though I have used lower case to signify your entries and upper case to signify the machine's replies.) But notice that numerals (try typing one or two in) behave as though they were permanently quoted; in other words, the value of a number is always itself. This is reasonable, if you think about it: it is nonsensical to imagine that a number could have any other value. In such cases Lisp ignores any quote-mark.

Thus, when you make an entry at the terminal, Lisp goes through a standard cycle: it READS what you have typed, EVALUATES it, and PRINTS the result. Not surprisingly, this is universally referred to as the READ-EVAL-PRINT loop. It's not a bad idea to keep in mind the operation of this loop whenever you're using Lisp.

1.3 Atoms and variables

We may as well get these special terms explained and out of the way immediately.

They're not really confusing, although you may find that the (important) distinctions between them don't fully sink in until you've done a fair bit of Lisp programming.

Any English word can be used in Lisp, and all of them will be 'atoms'. That is, a single word all on its own with no extraneous characters is an atom. Additionally, Lisp allows you to use any other combination of the letters of the alphabet, and it will accept those as perfectly normal words, whose "meanings" are the values you give them (you'll see how to do this shortly). For all practical purposes, there is no limit to the number of characters in the "words" you may invent. In addition, numerals can be used within or at the end of legal atoms, as can most of the other odd signs on the keyboard. In general, though, the first character of a non-numeric atom must be a letter if Lisp is not to be confused: as we've seen already, the single quote in the first-character position completely alters the meaning (value) of the following atom, and some though not all of the non-alphabetic signs have similarly unexpected effects. Most dialects of Lisp will not accept a numeral as the FIRST character of an atom; unless (naturally!) the atom is a pure number such as 2256.

Most importantly a legal atom cannot include either a left or right parenthesis (this term may include all three of the bracket-shapes to be found on full-size keyboards). Parentheses are used in Lisp to separate and to disambiguate chunks of typed-in text, much as ordinary punctuation marks are used in written English. You'll learn more about this later.

The usual reason for creating or deciding upon a particular atom to be typed into Lisp is, as above, so that it can represent a value. The process of associating a value with a variable-name is known as BINDING, although the actual system functions you will use to effect the binding for you will have more mnemonic names such as SET. You can think of binding in algebraic or geometric terms: assuming "x" to have a certain value and then applying a mathematical formula to it to see what will happen is very analogous to binding "x" to a value and then applying a Lisp function to it. Alternatively, you can imagine that by giving "x" a value you are teaching the computer a (temporary!) fact, but that in order to retrieve this fact in the future it needs also to be told a name to call it by: in its little computer-like way, it "remembers" that x "is" whatever you have specified it to be – 3, a tabby cat, the first element of a certain list, the boy next door, etc.

The "x" – that atom which has the bound value – is known as a VARIABLE because it can have different bound values at different times, depending upon what you, the programmer, want it to represent. These variables are in fact the "symbols" which Lisp manipulates: they stand for, or represent, their bound values. Lisp manipulates the symbols by applying FUNCTIONS to them, as you'll see later in this chapter.

In passing, it is probably worth mentioning that the only thing the computer "knows" when you switch it on and load Lisp is a large handful of processes – system functions – which someone else has told it in advance and which are stored on your Lisp tape or disc. Beyond those, it knows nothing except what YOU tell it; and you are at liberty to tell it whatever you like: the computer is incapable of disbelief. Concomitantly, of course, if you tell it a load of nonsense it will reply with nonsense.

Type in the following, but where I have put "tony", put your own name.

(don't forget the quote-mark, though):

```
*- (set 'a 'tony)
```

[Check SET in the Appendix]

Follow that with a carriage-return, and Lisp will reply:

```
TONY
```

Do you see what you've done? You've told Lisp to associate a value, which can be expressed in print as your name, with the variable "a". As far as Lisp is concerned, "a" now means – is to be evaluated as – your name. And until you change things by assigning some new value to "a", every time you type that character by itself to Lisp it will reply with your name. Try it. And notice that Lisp replies with a value, which in this case is the same value that you assigned to "a".

What you have just achieved is the pattern for all successful interactions with Lisp. You have given it an instruction, which in this case consists of the request that it apply a function called SET to two things (i.e. "a" and "tony"). Lisp has obeyed your instruction, and has printed back the result. The two things on which SET operates are referred to as SET's "arguments". SET always needs two arguments, but what these arguments actually are is up to the programmer.

However, programmers are notoriously lazy (not to mention bad) typists, and so there is a simple convention to save you the gargantuan effort of typing the quote-mark before the variable-name whenever you use the SET instruction, and that is to use SETQ ("set-quote") instead:

```
*- (setq a 'concentration)
```

followed as ever by a carriage-return, will change the assignment of "a" in just the same way as would SET followed by the quoted variable-name. The reason why there is no similar dodge to save you the bother of typing the second quote-mark is that what goes in the "concentration" position will usually not be just another symbol, another name, but will be a Lisp S-EXPRESSION which requires the machine to do an arbitrarily complex amount of computing, and it is the returned VALUE of that computation – the result, if you like – which will be assigned to "a". In such cases, no quote will be necessary. Why? Because we're not saying to Lisp "associate this actual lexical shape with the variable a", but are asking it to compute some value and then to associate THAT with a.

Exercise 1.1

What is the value of each of the following instructions, taken in sequence?

```
(setq x 'pip)
(setq y 'squeak)
(setq z 'wilfred)
(setq y x)
(set y 'squeak)
(set 'z 'x)
```

6

1.4 Lists and S-expressions

The most important parentheses in Lisp are the (round ones). They have one significance each. The opening or left-hand round bracket tells Lisp to start doing whatever comes next, and the closing or right-hand one tells it to stop doing it. These meanings, START and STOP, are the values permanently attached to the round brackets by EVAL. What appears between the brackets will be the name of an action which you wish Lisp to perform, usually followed – still inside the brackets – by one or more "arguments"; that is, by a set of values upon which the action is to be performed. The action, which can get as complex as you like, is stored inside Lisp as an instruction or set of instructions which Lisp itself is capable of carrying out. The set of instructions is known as a FUNCTION. Here's an example of how to use a function:

```
*- (print 'tony)
TONY
T
```

prints the lexical shape "TONY". (Can I stop reminding you about the final carriage-return from now on, please?). Notice, however, that PRINT itself, which is a function already built into your Lisp, does its job (the printing) and then returns a value. Only in a few Lisps is this value the same as the thing printed. More usually it is T or NIL. Don't worry about what those symbols mean for now. Alternatively:

```
*- (print a)
CONCENTRATION
T
```

will print the VALUE of "a", which we assigned earlier: "a" gets evaluated before being printed because it isn't quoted. And PRINT itself still returns T or NIL.

SET and PRINT are models for the vast majority of Lisp functions. Their characteristic is that during execution they evaluate their arguments before doing anything else. That's why (print a) prints your name rather than the sign "a", and why arguments which ARE to be taken literally, such as those to SET, need to be quoted. The quote is in fact the name of a Lisp function in its own right, and its effect is to inhibit the above-mentioned evaluation.

There are a number of inbuilt "system" functions which are naturally used a great deal in programs, or as we shall see you can write your own functions.

Now we are going to combine the knowledge gained in the previous sections to produce something much more like "real" Lisp. Type in:

```
*- (setq animals '(cat mouse dog))
```

This is a list. It has three elements or members: the atom SETQ, the atom

ANIMALS, and another (quoted) list. In Lisp, every list is surrounded by its own pair of left-hand and right-hand parentheses (i.e. brackets). As well as being a list, the expression above is also an instruction to Lisp. Notice what it means. The first opening bracket tells Lisp that the next atom will be an instruction to do something: in this case to SETQ the second item to have the value of the third. OK, so "animals" doesn't need a quote, but will be taken as a literal symbol because of the Q of SETQ. The next opening bracket would normally have the same significance as the one before SETQ, i.e. "Do CAT to MOUSE and DOG". But, we've quoted that third item (which is actually SETQ's second argument), and as you saw just now the quote means "take the following as a sign rather than as a meaning". A concomitant of this is that Lisp must treat ANYTHING following a quote literally. So the whole of SETQ's second argument is treated as one complex symbol, whose value as above is itself. That's why Lisp replied:

```
(CAT MOUSE DOG)
```

and if you type in

```
*- animals
```

Lisp will reply again with the same thing. The entire list of three animals is now the value of "animals" — if you like, "animals" is the name of the list. (Isn't this fun?) Notice that Lisp didn't bother to type a quote in front of the list it returned. Only Lisp itself needs the quote to distinguish between a SHAPE and an item to be evaluated. When you, a much superior human being, see a shape you know it's a shape, and the quote wouldn't help you at all.

In fact, I may as well tell you straight away that EVERYTHING in Lisp is either an atom (which term includes numbers) or a list. As you'll see in Chapter 3, even functions are really lists. Here is a typical list:

```
(a b c)
```

It has three elements: the atoms A, B and C. Here's another:

```
((a b) c (d e))
```

This one also has three elements: the sublist (A B), the atom C, and the sublist (D E). I call two of them sublists only for the sake of this explanation; as far as Lisp is concerned a list and a sublist are the same kind of thing. Here is a third list:

```
((a (b c)))
```

This has only one element, the list (A (B C)). And this in turn has two elements: the atom A, and the list (B C). This "nesting" of lists can become as complex as you like.

For convenience (ours) Lisp defines the empty list "( )" and NIL to be the same thing. But please be clear on one point: if the value of an atom (or of anything else) is NIL, this is normally thought of in terms of "nothing", "no" or "false", depending on the context. But an atom bound to NIL definitely has a value: it is NIL. Conversely, an atom which has not been bound at all has no meaningful value to Lisp; it is "unbound", and will generate an error if you ask Lisp to return that meaningless value. To demonstrate the point, try this:

```
*- (setq a nil)

NIL
```

The variable "a" has now lost its previous binding and is bound to NIL. Lisp duly replies with that value, and you can prove that it IS the value of "a" like this:

```
*- a

NIL
```

OK – so "a" now has a value of NIL which Lisp handles quite happily. Now dream up a new variable-name, one which hasn't yet been heard of by your Lisp. Say, the variable "q". In the same way as above, ask Lisp what it understands by (what is the value of) "q":

```
*- q
```

And you get an error message. The difference between "a" and "q" is that between an atom which is known to have a value of NIL and an atom which is not known at all: one which is UNBOUND.

An expression like any of those in this section, that is to say a syntactically correct Lisp expression, is known as an S-expression. Winston (1977) says that the S stands for "symbolic".

Personally I prefer the term Lisp-expression, which is just as valid and a deal less confusing. But the former is so widely used that you'd better be introduced to it. Strictly speaking, ANY legal Lisp expression is an S-expression, including a simple atom, but most programmers tend to use "atom" and "S-expression" as though they referred to different categories, i.e. to words and to lists respectively. And, as you can see, the quote-mark remains "valid" for the whole of the S-expression which immediately follows it. As a rule of thumb, you can say that an S-expression is either a single atom, or a list of arbitrary complexity – but with strictly balanced opening and closing brackets:

SETQ, ANIMALS, CAT, DOG, MOUSE are all atomic S-expressions;
(CAT MOUSE DOG) or '(CAT MOUSE DOG) are S-expressions;
(SETQ ANIMALS '(CAT MOUSE DOG)) is an S-expression.

(Notice, in passing, that what looks like nonsense to us need not be nonsense to Lisp: if you were to write a function to add two numbers and call it CAT, Lisp would dutifully execute it, when asked, without the slightest reference to small

9

furry things which purr, mew, scratch and steal your supper. On the other hand, it is obviously good programming practice to avoid function names which can cause such semantic confusion amongst human readers.)

Whenever Lisp sees a non-atomic S-expression (i.e. a list) it always assumes that you want it to execute some function – as in (set 'a 'b) – unless either the S-expression is quoted or it is the final returned value of some computation or other, about to be printed back to you. An example of the latter occurred when you typed (setq animals '(cat mouse dog)). The returned value you saw was the list (cat mouse dog). Lisp DIDN'T try to take that as an instruction to execute a function called CAT.

Remember the READ-EVAL-PRINT loop? Well, Lisp reads what you type in only once (sensibly enough). Then it applies EVAL as many times as are necessary. EVAL starts from the left and at each stage (at each argument to the above SETQ, for example) it finds the value of the innermost set of brackets first. Then it uses that value in order to work out the value of the next innermost set of brackets, and so on. When it has dealt with all the brackets at any stage, it reads what remains from left to right. That way you can write something equivalent to, say, "Do so-and-so to the second sentence of paragraph three of subsection four of clause five of my memo":

```
(so-and-so (sentence 2 (para 3 (subs 4 (clause 5 memo)))))
```

and EVAL gets everything in the right order. The symbol immediately following each left-hand parenthesis is a function: something to be done, and each of them except the first has two arguments. CLAUSE, for example, retrieves that clause of the MEMO specified by its second argument – that is, CLAUSE 5. SUBS will then retrieve SUBSECTION 4 of that, and so on. When the various parts of your entry, including SO-AND-SO, have all been dealt with, EVAL stops and PRINT is called just once. (Of course, those functions don't actually exist at the moment, so there's no point in typing the line into Lisp.) If the end result of all that evaluation was a list, then a list is what you get — there is no attempt to evaluate it still further, unless you specifically order it, which you could do like this:

```
*- (eval (setq animals '(cat mouse dog)))
```

Try it if you like, but at this stage you'll only get an error message because SETQ returns the value it has assigned to ANIMALS – that is it returns the (now unquoted) list of CAT, MOUSE and DOG, and when you ask for that list to be EVALuated Lisp says that it has no function called CAT. So now, since error messages are what all programmers hate above all else, I'd better tell you how to write a simple function. (This is where the fun really begins.)

1.5 Function-definition

Programmers often refer to functions as "routines". A "program" is a set or suite of functions which together achieve some overall purpose. Running or executing a function once it has been defined (written) is known as "calling" the function or "making a call to" it.

10

Here's one you can have for free, just to get you started. And I guarantee absolutely that if you type it in carefully, and don't make any mistakes, it'll work first time (but do read the next two paragraphs first, and do check DEFUN in the Appendix):

```
*- (defun add-animals (new-animals)
      (setq animals (append animals new-animals)))
```

[Check DEFUN in the Appendix]

[Check APPEND in the Appendix]

This is actually all one Lisp S-expression. You can type it in exactly as I've shown it, or without the spaces at the start of the second line, or all on one line; Lisp will understand. But please be very careful that you get the right numbers of brackets in the right places.

When you've typed it in, Lisp will respond with a reassuring message which is simply the name of the function: ADD-ANIMALS. If you make a mistake, one that is too serious to put right with the ordinary keyboard DELETE or RUBOUT key, just type closing brackets until you get the prompt back, and then start all over again from the DEFUN. If you can't persuade the prompt to reappear, look in your manual to find out which is the "escape" character for your Lisp – the character which frees it from knots. Often, it's the character ESCAPE itself or BREAK. Your manual will also tell you how to print out the definition of ADD-ANIMALS which you've just written. In some Lisps you just type the name of the function (ADD-ANIMALS, of course); in others you have to give some other simple command. Let's have a good look at ADD-ANIMALS before you run it, so that you know what to expect.

First of all, and fairly self-evidently, the first instruction in what you have written – DEFUN – is shorthand for DEFINE-A-FUNCTION. I repeat: check in your manual to make sure that your Lisp doesn't use some other word for this purpose; if it does, you'll find advice on how to cope in the Appendix.

The opening bracket at the very beginning of the function warns Lisp that it is about to be told to DO something, and DEFine is what you want it to do: in other words, you want LISP to store whatever instructions follow the DEFUN, in such a way that it can execute them whenever you call the function by its name – in this case by the atom ADD-ANIMALS. And as you can see, the next item in your input was that very name. The third item is a list of the "formal parameters". When ADD-ANIMALS is called, each of these parameters, which are variable-names chosen by you, will be bound to one of the arguments given (by you) in the call. To put that another way, you have to write into the function-definition SOMETHING to represent the data on which the function itself will later operate. That SOMETHING is known as a formal parameter, and however many such SOMETHINGs you need (you're allowed any number including none) they must be grouped together in a list (or empty list if there are none) immediately following the function's name. The data is supplied when the function is called (as opposed to when it is defined), and automatically gets bound to the formal parameters. I'll have more to say about that later.

11

And following that is what is known as the "body" of the function: a set of instructions which together achieve the function's purpose. The order of these four items, by the way, is inviolable Lisp syntax. To get the order wrong is analogous to me asking you to "Own your function of write a now". You may have instantly sorted that out in your head, but Lisp isn't so tolerant, and will issue an error message complaining that this isn't the right sort of thing to say after DEFUN.

Something to notice (but to try not to get confused by) is that all of the items following DEFUN, including those not yet fully explained, are arguments to a Lisp system function called DEFUN. By writing the above, you have called DEFUN, which by now has done its job – which is to associate your set of instructions with the function-name you specified. DEFUN is now finished with, but your new function is callable, just as DEFUN was, by use of its name.

Right. So far we've understood a call to DEFUN, a function-name, and a list of arguments for that function. Now we come to the actual instructions themselves:

```
(setq animals (append animals new-animals))
```

[Check APPEND in the Appendix]

Pretend for a moment that you're EVAL, having to cope with a call to ADD-ANIMALS. You know that when you see a set of nested brackets you've got to start with the innermost, and that subsequently you work from left to right. So, the first thing you must look at is the (unquoted) list

```
(append animals new-animals)
```

and again the list's opening bracket means (to Lisp) "do the following".

APPEND is a system function, and does just what one would expect it to do: it joins two lists together in the order in which they are given. ANIMALS is known to be a list (we set it so, up above, in case you've forgotten), but what of NEW-ANIMALS? Well, NEW-ANIMALS is the single argument which must be used whenever a call is made to ADD-ANIMALS, so you (EVAL) can find out what that is too. Let's say for the sake of example that a call to ADD-ANIMALS is:

```
(add-animals '(bear rabbit))
```

You, as EVAL, can see that '(bear rabbit) – which you don't have to evaluate because of the quote – is a list and that it occupies the argument-slot of ADD-ANIMALS. So, to evaluate the three elements of the innermost list

```
(append animals new-animals)
```

you have to call APPEND, you have to replace ANIMALS with '(cat mouse dog), and you have to replace NEW-ANIMALS with '(bear rabbit). APPEND then gets two lists as its arguments, which is what it expects, and the result of APPEND is the result of joining those two lists together. So somewhere inside Lisp the

12

entire set of instructions now looks like:

```
(setq animals '(cat mouse dog bear rabbit))
```

Now, the innermost list here is quoted, and is therefore to be taken verbatim, so EVAL can't do anything more with it. Reading what remains from left to right produces a call to SETQ, with the arguments ANIMALS (effectively quoted by the Q) and a list which is different from the list which was formerly the value of ANIMALS. Having done that (i.e. having called SETQ to operate on those two arguments), a value must be returned to the terminal, and the rule is that the value returned by a function is the value of the last instruction contained within it. In this case, clearly, the value (= result) of SETQing ANIMALS to the new list is that new list itself. The old value of ANIMALS gets completely forgotten.

To demonstrate this to yourself (back as yourself and no longer playing at being EVAL), type:

```
*- (add-animals '(bear rabbit))
```

and you'll see what I mean.

One thing which must be made clear at this stage is that APPEND requires two LISTS as its arguments, and won't accept anything else. (add-animals 'bat) will produce an error message because "bat" isn't a list. But if you want to add a single item to the ANIMALS list, all you have to do is use a single quote, and then manually make "bat" into a list: (add-animals '(bat)). Once you've typed a quote, you can put whatever you like after it, and so long as it is a legal Lisp expression, Lisp will accept it and treat it just as you would expect.

And another point which is probably worth stressing is that the "this is a list" interpretation of a pair of brackets is not some kind of default meaning. Lisp always assumes that you mean "Do this" — and will issue an error message if it has no corresponding function — unless, as described above, you use a quote or the list is the final result of some computation.

Let's go into the latter point a bit further. Type:

```
*- (setq extra-animals '(platypus octopus dinosaur))
```

and Lisp will dutifully reply with the value of EXTRA-ANIMALS:

```
(PLATYPUS OCTOPUS DINOSAUR)
```

(Alright, so an octopus isn't an animal but a fish. This is AI, not biology.)
Now type:

```
*- (add-animals extra-animals)
```

and the reply, which as I hope is clear is the value both of the current call to the function ADD-ANIMALS and of the latest version of the list ANIMALS, is:

```
(CAT MOUSE DOG BEAR RABBIT PLATYPUS OCTOPUS DINOSAUR)
```

See how clever EVAL is? In the long-winded description above, there came a point where the argument to ADD-ANIMALS couldn't be evaluated because it was quoted. But this time around is isn't quoted (it is "extra-animals") and so EVAL promptly replaces it with its current value, which gets appended to the current value of ANIMALS just as before. The point to grasp here is that as EVAL chews its way through your (perhaps very complex) list of instructions, it relies on its simple rules of starting from the right and taking each item in turn, of which it tackles the most deeply nested set of brackets first and within that works from left to right; but every time it finds that it can't "dig into" your list any further, it has a go at evaluating what it finds there. You don't have to try to remember the order in which EVAL tackles things, because that is specifically designed so that programmers can forget about it, but it is most important to keep in mind the fact that if something can be evaluated, EVAL will do it. I guarantee that a depressingly large number of your early bugs (programmers' slang for elusive errors) will derive from forgetfulness of this fact, and that it won't be long before you'll want to put your foot through the screen every time you see the words "UNBOUND VARIABLE".

1.6 Simple pattern matching

I'll return to the questions of function definition and of list manipulation later: the above was just to give you the flavour, so that what I say later on won't be a total mystery to you. But first you should know about a couple of other very useful and very basic things Lisp can do. Type:

    *- (equal animals animals)

        [Check EQUAL in the Appendix]

and Lisp replies

    T

that is to say, Yes (or TRUE). As you might have expected. EVAL produced the same list for each occurrence of the atom "animals", and of course the two lists were EQUAL. But OCTOPUS was a bone of contention, so let's create a better ANIMALS list without it. Let's use the Lisp function DELETE to produce a new animals list which is as we want it to be:

    *- (setq real-animals (delete 'octopus animals))

        [Check DELETE in the Appendix]

    (CAT MOUSE DOG BEAR RABBIT PLATYPUS DINOSAUR)

14

Now try EQUAL again:

```
*- (equal animals real-animals)
```

And Lisp says No (i.e. FALSE) because the lists ANIMALS and REAL-ANI-MALS are different:

```
NIL
```

Notice that the inbuilt Lisp function EQUAL is much more general than the usual (arithmetical) use of the word: it is not merely matching two numeric quantities, but a pair of very complex patterns involving a large number of distinct symbols. EQUAL takes two arguments, each of which may be of arbitrary complexity. It is even possible to say something like:

```
*- (equal (foo animals) (blah real-animals))
```

in which case EVAL works out the result of applying the function BLAH to the list REAL-ANIMALS, and then the result of applying the function FOO to the list ANIMALS, before applying EQUAL to the pair of results. Of course, you can't actually try this because FOO and BLAH haven't been defined yet. So let's put that omission right, in such a way that the above call to EQUAL will work – i.e. will return the result T.

The simplest way of all would be to make BLAH do nothing to its argument (that is, to REAL-ANIMALS), whilst making FOO do just what we did to ANIMALS in order to create REAL-ANIMALS: we DELETEd from it the symbol OCTOPUS. So (type this in):

```
*- (defun blah (L) L)
```

BLAH is now defined as taking a single argument, which I have called L simply to remind you that in this case we expect it to be a list, and the body of BLAH (the set of instructions which achieve its overall effect) is simply L again. So when BLAH is called and is subsequently evaluated, the value it returns is the value of L, unchanged. The value of BLAH is therefore whatever you put in the position of L when you call BLAH. To put that another way, BLAH has no effect whatever.

```
*- (defun foo (L)
      (delete 'octopus L))
```

Again, you can type it as I have, or all on one line.

FOO is now defined as taking a single argument, also a list and also called L; but the value which FOO returns is L minus the element OCTOPUS. Notice that Lisp is clever enough not to be confused by the two versions of L – if you think they might confuse you, re-define one of the functions using LL, or L1, or something. Now:

```
*- (equal (foo animals) (blah real-animals))
```

15

will return, as we hoped,

T

because the effect of BLAH on REAL-ANIMALS is to return it unaffected:

(CAT MOUSE DOG BEAR RABBIT PLATYPUS DINOSAUR)

and the effect of FOO on ANIMALS is to DELETE the atom OCTOPUS from it, returning the result:

(CAT MOUSE DOG BEAR RABBIT PLATYPUS DINOSAUR)

and, as you can see, these two lists are the same. So EQUAL returns the Lisp equivalent of "Yes", which is T.

BUT, notice that if you ask Lisp for the current values of ANIMALS and REAL-ANIMALS (which you do, remember, simply by typing in one or other of those words), they are still exactly as they were. In particular, FOO did not delete OCTOPUS from the list ANIMALS itself, but merely returned what would have been the result of doing so. That is to say that, unless you take specific measures to the contrary, the arguments to functions are unchanged by the operations of the functions; no matter how complicated FOO or BLAH may become, Lisp "remembers" the original values of the arguments as entered, and restores them once FOO and BLAH are finished with. Obviously it wouldn't be much help if you had some huge and complex set of data to run your Lisp functions on, only to find at the end that all of the data had been altered by the operations of the functions themselves. So Lisp functions are designed to leave data strictly alone, and instead to RETURN values which are the "answers" to whatever operations were carried out. As you've seen already, it is easy to use these returned values (as with that of APPEND) as stages in some continuing computation.

Now glance back at ADD-ANIMALS and notice that it has a SETQ inside it, put there purposely so that it WOULD permanently affect the value of ANI-MALS. SET and SETQ, and a couple of functions which you'll read about in Chapter 3, are exceptions to the above general rule.

1.7 List manipulation

Lisp is, above all, a language designed for LISt Processing. As you will have gathered by now, Lisp would not work at all if it were not expert at creating and modifying lists. So I should give you an idea of how to make use of those abilities.

There are two basic inbuilt functions which manipulate lists, and the names of both of them are hopelessly unmnemonic. The CAR of a list is its head, or first element ; and the CDR of a list is its tail, or what remains of it after the head has been removed. A list in Lisp is like a worm: long, slippery and liable to wriggle out of your grasp if you're not careful. But the main similarity between a list and a worm is that if you chop off the head, you are left with the tail. There is nothing in between. Type:

*- (car animals)

16

and Lisp will reply:

    CAT

Type:

    *- (cdr animals)

and Lisp will reply:

    (MOUSE DOG BEAR RABBIT PLATYPUS OCTOPUS DINOSAUR)

Notice that the CAR of a list is an atom, not a list of one element; whilst the CDR remains a list. Suppose that you wanted to pick out the second element of the list, as an atom, rather than the first? What you want in this case is actually the CAR of the CDR of the original list:

    *- (car (cdr animals))

    MOUSE

but Lisp allows you to simplify such commands. It will take the C and the R as applying to every A or D that comes between them, thus:

    *- (cadr animals)

    MOUSE

Most Lisps let you put up to three As and Ds, in any combination, between the C and the R, which is usually enough if you ever expect anyone else to understand your programs. I'll return to the problem of what to do if it isn't enough, in a moment.

So: CAR and CDR will pick bits out of a list for you; APPEND will add two lists together to make one list, and DELETE will get rid of any unwanted items. There is one more very useful function, CONS. You can look on it as a sort of mini-APPEND: it adds an S-expression (an atom or a list) to the head of any existing list:

    *- (cons 'octopus (delete 'octopus animals))

will effectively "move" the element OCTOPUS from its position well down the list of ANIMALS to its head:

    (OCTOPUS CAT MOUSE DOG BEAR RABBIT PLATYPUS DINOSAUR)

and obviously this is the same thing as CONSing OCTOPUS onto the front of REAL-ANIMALS (do it). Notice, again, that manipulating lists with these functions does not alter the lists themselves, but merely returns the result AS IF

17

the lists had been altered. This is because CAR, CDR and the rest are functions very like FOO and BLAH, so that when they have finished their jobs they restore the original values of their input arguments. And if you want to change a list permanently using CONS or any of the others, what you must of course do is embed the whole thing in a SETQ, e.g.

```
(setq animals (cons ...whatever...whatever...))
```

Exercise 1.2

Evaluate these S-expressions (i.e. what would be returned if you typed them into Lisp?)

```
(cons 'tony (cddr animals))
```

```
(caddr animals)
```

```
(delete 'tony (cons 'tony '(a b)))
```

Before leaving the subjects of values, of lists and of function definitions, there are a few other points I want to mention. The first is a simple one: you may have wondered whether or not it is permissible to use the SAME atom as both the name of a function and the name of a variable. The answer, I'm afraid, is either yes or no. Some Lisps will let you do that, some will not. Some Lisps will let you write weird things like:

```
(list 'list list)
```

> [Check LIST in the Appendix]

in order to have Lisp return the result of calling the function named LIST (which creates a list out of its arguments) to operate on two arguments, the first of which is the quoted atom 'LIST and the second of which is another atom – also named LIST – which has some value or other. (For those who really like brain-twisters, you could even SETQ the last argument to have the value 'LIST, whereupon the above S-expression would return "(LIST LIST)"!) But, as you can probably imagine, to squeeze a sophisticated language like Lisp into the memory-space of a microcomputer is no mean feat in itself, so it wouldn't be surprising if yours had some of these more abstruse features missing. Many microcomputer Lisps store function definitions as the VALUES of the functions' names, so that if you DEFUN an atom to do something or other you automatically destroy any value you had previously given it with SETQ, and vice versa. It is a trivial restriction, and will almost never matter.

1.8 FEXPRs

Now to a quite different point. There are several types of function in Lisp. The ones you've seen so far are by far the commonest type, and are known as EXPRs.

The characteristic of EXPRs is that they evaluate their arguments and save those values away to be restored when the EXPR itself has been executed. Try this as a demonstration:

```
*- (setq x '(the fire has gone out))

(THE FIRE HAS GONE OUT)
```

This gives the atom X a value. Now we need a simple function whose formal parameter is also X:

```
*- (defun foo (x)
     (print x))

FOO
```

Now call FOO, during whose execution X will be bound to something else, as is proved by the fact that the something else gets printed:

```
*- (foo 'good)

GOOD
T
```

Now check that X's previous value has been restored:

```
*- X

(THE FIRE HAS GONE OUT)
```

A less common type of function is called a FEXPR, and its arguments are NOT evaluated: the function is applied to them verbatim, just as they are given (by you) in the function call. For example, both of these function calls print the atom TONY:

```
(baz 'tony)        (gort tony)
```

but GORT is a FEXPR, so its argument doesn't need to be quoted.

What is more, when defining a FEXPR you give it just one formal parameter. During evaluation of the FEXPR, this gets bound to a LIST of whatever arguments the FEXPR was given in the call. GORT would therefore need to be defined like this:

```
(defun gort x
   (print (car x)))
```

[Check FEXPR in the Appendix]

19

As GORT is executed, the X inside it gets temporarily bound to a LIST of its argument; that is, to (TONY).

Notice that the formal parameter after the function-name has no brackets around it. This is crucial: it is the signal to Lisp that you are defining a FEXPR and not an EXPR. (But remember that in your Lisp, FEXPRs may be created differently from the way they are created in Lithp). An everyday example of a FEXPR is the function QUOTE. If you ignore the usual quote-mark abbreviation for it, and type it out in full:

```
(quote tony)   instead of   'tony
```

you can see that it doesn't evaluate its argument; if it did, that would destroy the whole purpose of using QUOTE at all. So QUOTE takes its argument verbatim. I shall be using a FEXPR in a later chapter to write a fascinating function-definition. There is a third type of function available in some Lisps, called the MACRO. I shall talk about macros at the end of Chapter 5.

In the course of this book you will come across several examples of FEXPRs. Please make sure, as you type their definitions into your computer, that you have made allowances for: (1) any different word and syntax which your Lisp uses instead of DEFUN; and (2) any differences in the way your Lisp denotes that the function being defined IS a FEXPR and not an EXPR. In general, and throughout the literature on Lisp, a function is an EXPR unless it is explicitly stated to be otherwise.

1.9 Summary

In this chapter you have been introduced to the following Lisp terminology:

PROMPT	a sign or word printed by Lisp to tell you that no computation is currently in progress, and that the system is waiting for some input from you.
VARIABLE	an item like "x" in an algebraic equation (or like a pigeon-hole), which can have a different value (have a different thing in it) at different times.
BOUND VALUE	the "meaning" of a variable: its significance to Lisp. Controlled by SETQ or SET.
ATOM	any sequence of keyboard characters not beginning with a number, and not including either a bracket, or a space, or a carriage-return.
LIST	any sequence of atoms surrounded by a pair of left-hand and right-hand brackets, or any sequence of lists surrounded by a pair of left-hand or right-hand brackets.
S-EXPRESSION	any legal Lisp expression. Either an atom, or a list

α - character Block

	of arbitrary complexity whose left-hand and right-hand brackets balance.
FUNCTION	a special form of list which Lisp sees as a series of instructions to be executed.
ARGUMENT	an atom or list supplied as data for a function to work on.
RETURNED VALUE	the "result" of executing a function or of evaluating a bound variable.
EXPR	a function which automatically evaluates its arguments before the function itself is executed.
FEXPR	a function which does not evaluate its arguments before the function itself is executed.
NIL	a value of nothing. Directly equivalent in Lisp to the empty list "( )". A variable which is not bound at all will not have a value of NIL.
T	a value (unspecified) of other than NIL. Often returned by system functions.

You have also been introduced to the following Lisp system functions:

QUOTE	in most Lisps, the shorthand apostrophe or single-quote is available; in others, the word QUOTE is used as a normal function. In either case, it prevents evaluation of the S-expression which immediately follows it.
SET	the basic value-assigning function. Both arguments must be quoted.
SETQ	identical to SET except that its first argument should not be quoted.
PRINT	prints its argument's value. What it then returns depends on the Lisp dialect concerned.
EVAL	Lisp's basic evaluating function.
DEFUN	the function with which to define your own functions.
APPEND	concatenates the values of its two arguments, which must be lists.

EQUAL	returns T if the values of its two arguments are the same, otherwise it returns NIL.
DELETE	removes its first argument from its second. The second must be a list.
CAR	returns the first element of its argument – which must be a list.
CDR	returns its argument – which must be a list – minus its first element.
C—R	permissible combinations of CAR and CDR.
CONS	"includes" its first argument at the head of its second argument, the latter being a list.
LIST	creates a list out of any number of arguments.

Now you know the least interesting part of the basics of Lisp. The next chapter will introduce you to some programming techniques which will add something of a "how to" dimension to your knowledge.

1.10 Answers to Exercises

Exercise 1.1

The first three exressions successively bind the value PIP to the atom X, the value SQUEAK to the atom Y, and the value WILFRED to the atom Z.

The fourth expression binds a new value to Y, discarding the old value, and that new value is itself the value of X – i.e. the value of Y is now PIP.

The fifth expression uses SET (not SETQ). SET evaluates both of its arguments. The value of its first argument is PIP, owing to the effect of expression 4; and the value of its second argument is SQUEAK because the latter is quoted. So the atom PIP acquires the value SQUEAK.

The last expression simply binds the atom X as the value of the atom Z.

Exercise 1.2

The first expression adds the atom TONY onto the front of the CDDR of the list ANIMALS – that is, to ANIMALS minus its first two elements:

    (TONY CAT MOUSE DOG BEAR RABBIT PLATYPUS DINOSAUR)

The second expression returns the CAR of the CDDR of ANIMALS, which is the atom DOG.

The third expression DELETEs TONY from the result of CONSing TONY onto the list (A B) – in other words, it has no net effect at all.

Chapter 2
Some programming techniques

2.1 Recursion

Supposing that you want to do something to your list, such as returning the seventh member of it – something which the three available As and Ds of CAR and CDR combinations can't cope with. Obviously, you could write the thing out in full rather than abbreviating it:

```
(car (cdr (cdr (cdr (cdr (cdr (cdr animals)))))))
```

but that looks terrible, not to mention the chances of its containing a mistake. And in any case, it may be that you want the seventh element today but will want the fifth tomorrow. What you really would like is a simple little function to take two arguments – the list and the number of the element you want – and which will sort out all the rest for itself. Some Lisps have such a function, usually called NTH. But many haven't, so we're going to write it now.

In common with most high-level programming languages, Lisp has an extraordinarily useful facility called RECURSION. Lisp makes more use of recursion than other languages do: in fact the technique is so frequently encountered that one could almost say that it is a part of the meaning of the word "Lisp". Recursion is a term borrowed from mathematics, so if you happen to understand it in that context you'll understand it in a programming context as well. But for some reason, although once it has been grasped the recursive process is almost painfully obvious, very many learners find it brain-twistingly complex, so please bear with an extended explanation. Recursion resembles the effect you get by standing between two parallel mirrors; or one of those paintings in which a figure is holding a copy of the painting itself, within which can be seen a copy of the same figure holding another copy of the painting, within which...

The first thing to understand is the idea of "levels". So far, you have only used Lisp at "top" level; that is to say, you called inbuilt system functions such as DELETE or CAR, or you called simple routines of your own which worked without calling anything OTHER than inbuilt system functions. That is what top level is: the simplest possible use of Lisp.

However, it won't be long before the functions you write become more complex, and when they do you'll find it convenient often to make them call other functions also written by you. When the function called at top level contains an instruction which calls a second function, we say that the second function operates at one level "down from" top level, or at the second level. If the second function in turn calls a third, we say that the latter operates at two levels "down", or at the third level, and so on.

The important thing to realise is that a second-level function is necessarily called from WITHIN a top-level function. That is to say, computation of the top-level function is suspended whilst the second-level function does its stuff, and cannot be completed until the second-level function is completely finished with. Extending this idea:

```
Top level calls
   Level 2, which calls
      Level 3, which calls
         Level 4, which calls
         .....................
            Level N, which terminates. Then,
         .....................
         Finish off the Level 4 function
      Finish off the Level 3 function
   Finish off the Level 2 function
Return the final value to Top level
```

Only when the function at Level N, which is the "deepest" level of the recursion, has been completed can "control" – the actual activity of the computer – return to level N-1; and computation ceases altogether, returning to top-level, only when the functions at all levels have been successively finished with.

Now then. Remember that a normal function "stores" the values of its formal parameters, and restores them afterwards? Well, that happens at every level during recursion. So, suppose you could have a function which said something like:

```
(defun shorten (L)
   (print L)
   (stop if the list L is empty)

      [of course, this isn't real Lisp code]
   (shorten (cdr L))
   (print L))
```

and supposing you applied this function to the good old list of ANIMALS. The top-level call of SHORTEN would print the full list of animals, and then it would set up an entirely new call to SHORTEN, supplying as its argument the CDR of ANIMALS. Not until this new call to SHORTEN was completed could the top-level call be proceeded with. So the second-level call to SHORTEN would print the ANIMALS list minus its first element. Then it too would be "suspended" whilst a third call to SHORTEN was set up and executed. And so on until the list was exhausted. At this latter point the current call to SHORTEN wouldn't get past the "stop if" proviso, and so there would be no further calls to keep the

24

recursion going. And unless something specifically keeps it going, recursion will immediately start to "unwind" back towards top level. That is a part of its nature.

During the recursion, the lowest and last call to SHORTEN will have as its argument an empty list of ANIMALS. And it will duly print NIL – and then stop, as I've said. Unwinding of the recursion involves now completing all the so-far unexecuted bits of the various calls to SHORTEN until top level is reached again and the prompt can be restored. So once the lowest and last call has come to a halt because of the empty list, the remainder of the PREVIOUS call has to be dealt with. And what remains of it is of course the Lisp code subsequent to the line

```
(shorten (cdr L)).
```

This code, as you can see above, merely asks it to print the list again, and then it is done with. And what is the value of the list at this point? Why, exactly (and reassuringly) the same as it was on the way down, because the innermost call to SHORTEN didn't affect it – the value, as I've said, was safely stored and then restored as the innermost call began and ended. So this last-but-one call to SHORTEN prints ANIMALS as a list having only one element. And at the next level up, the same thing happens again so that this time ANIMALS is printed as two elements long. And so on, right back to top level where ANIMALS has its original full value. To save my typing finger, imagine that the original ANIMALS was only three elements long: this is what the call to SHORTEN would do:

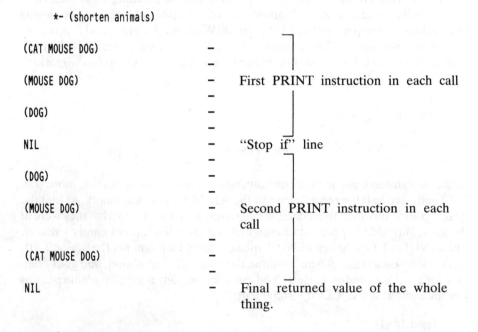

The return of the prompt shows that Lisp is back at top level, ready for your next instruction. In order to demonstrate this to you with a practical example, it's necessary to make a slight diversion and describe yet another of Lisp's extraordinarily simple and yet extraordinarily useful facilities.

2.2 Conditional statements

The second line of the above program is not written in normal Lisp. As I said right at the beginning, it is possible to re-write the top-level syntax of Lisp to conform to any standards you happen to fancy, and there is nothing inherently wrong with that line as it stands; it is just that the standard unmodified Lisp doesn't understand the phrase "stop if", because no-one has yet told it what it should do when it comes across it. However, without going into the complexities of re-writing the language, there is a simple and very commonly-used Lisp function which will enable you to write the equivalent of such phrases as "if this is true, do that" and so on. It is called the Conditional Statement. Please read what follows carefully, because it is crucially useful in almost every function ever written. A Lisp function which does not contain a COND or some equivalent is a rarity and in all probability also a triviality.

The syntax of COND in its simplest form is:

```
(cond (a b))
```

It tells Lisp that IF condition A applies, THEN action B should be performed. In Lisp's own terms, if the condition A EVALUATES to anything other than NIL, the action B should be executed; otherwise not. The two opening and two closing brackets above are parts of the COND itself. What goes in the A and B positions will be S-expressions (often function calls with their own normal bracketing). Usually, condition A is a test. For example, using NULL, a Lisp function which returns T only if a list is empty:

```
(cond ((null L) nil))
```

[Check NULL in the Appendix]

would be a suitable line in the above function to tell Lisp to do nothing more (i.e. NIL) and so to halt the recursion when the ANIMALS list was empty, so that the system could "unwind" the recursion and so restore all values to what they were at the start. But what happens at intermediate levels when L is not empty – that is, when (NULL L) evaluates to NIL? In such cases Lisp ignores the action (NIL means don't do anything) which follows the unsatisfied condition, and goes on to look for a further conditional test. You can write as many condition-action pairs as you like in a single COND statement:

```
(cond (a a1)
      (b b1)
      (c c1)
       .
       .
      (z z1))
```

26

Lisp will faithfully go through them all in order, until it finds a condition which is satisfied. When it finds such a condition, it performs the associated action and then ignores the rest of the COND statement.

However, if NONE of the conditions can be satisfied, Lisp merely drops off the end of the statement and goes on to the rest of the function in which the COND appears. So it is useful to have an "otherwise" or "if all else fails" condition. This is achieved simply by writing T (which can never be NIL) as the condition part of the final clause:

```
(cond (a a1)
      (b b1)
        .
        .
      (t (something suitable) ) )
```

If there is no T clause, and if none of the previous conditions were satisfied at all, the whole COND returns NIL.

Notice that all the brackets balance. Also, I hope it's clear that in a real COND statement the a, b, a1 etc. might well all be separate Lisp S-expressions in their own rights. Hence the characteristic (though not inviolable) double opening bracket after the word COND, as in the example above. You're also allowed to have several actions to be performed when any condition is satisfied, as in the T line here:

```
(cond ((null L) nil)
      (t (shorten (cdr L))
         (print L)))
```

Each of these multiple actions returns its own value, and so of course the overall value returned by that "clause" of the COND, and hence of the whole COND, is the value of the last of them. If there were no T clause, and if none of the conditions were satified, so that none of the actions were executed, the COND would return NIL. And incidentally, if a condition is satisfied but has no corresponding action at all (not even NIL), the value of the condition itself is returned. Here's an experiment you can try. Its only purpose is to demonstrate how COND works:

```
*- (defun trycond (L)
      (cond ((null L) (print 'empty))
            ((eq (cadr L) 'a) (print L))
            (t (print 'yes))))

TRYCOND

*- (setq thislist '(a b c))

(A B C)

*- (trycond thislist)
```

The final expression will cause TRYCOND to be evaluated with its formal parameter L bound to (A B C). The first two clauses of the COND therefore fail. The third must succeed because it is a T clause, so the word "YES" is printed and Lisp returns the value returned by the PRINT instruction, which is T:

```
YES
T
```

Now:

```
*- (setq thislist '(b a c))

(B A C)

*- (trycond thislist)
```

This time, L gets bound to (B A C). So the first clause of the COND fails but the second succeeds. So the value of L is printed and T is returned by the PRINT instruction, and hence by the whole COND:

```
(B A C)
T
```

Finally:

```
*- (setq thislist nil)

NIL

*- (trycond thislist)
```

Since the value of L is now NIL, the first clause of the COND succeeds. The word "EMPTY" is printed and T is returned:

```
EMPTY
T
```

2.3 NTH

OK, so let's have a go at writing the real version of the NTH function:

```
*- (defun nth (n L)
      (cond ((null L) nil)
            ((eq n 1) (car L))
            (t (nth (difference n 1) (cdr L)))))
```

[Check DIFFERENCE in the Appendix]

If you haven't made any mistakes, Lisp will say:

NTH

Do you see how this function works? It is recursive. It takes a number N, and a list
L. And this is what happens:

The second clause works straight away if you've asked for the first element of
the list, and it dutifully returns the CAR. In all other cases, NTH calls itself
recursively, reducing N by one and taking the CDR of the list. So suppose you had
originally wanted the second element of the list. During the first call to NTH, N is
equal to 2; so the first two clauses of the COND fail, and the third clause of the
COND calls NTH again recursively, this time with N reset to 1 and L reset to its
own CDR. During this recursive call N would be 1 as before, and the CAR of the
current list would therefore be returned – but it is the CAR of the CDR of the
original list, which of course is its second element. For the third, fourth etc.
elements recursion just continues until N has been reduced to 1, and then unwinds
to return the CAR of whatever then remains of the list.

The first clause of the COND is simply to guard against people who ask for
the fourth element of a list which is only three elements long – there is no Nth
element where the list contains less than N elements, so the correct answer in such
cases is NIL, which the COND returns as the value of the "action" slot in its first
clause. (I haven't tried to protect the function against really clever dicks who ask
for the 0th, or -Nth, member of the list. They'll get an error message from Lisp,
and that's their own fault).

Here's how NTH would be used:

    *- (nth 3 '(1 2 3 4 5))

    3

Or, alternatively:

    *- (setq L '(1 2 3 4 5))

    (1 2 3 4 5)

    *- (nth 4 L)

    4

Now that you've (I hope) successfully written your first Lisp function, turn to
the Appendix and see what it has to say about saving the function so that you don't
have to rewrite it every time you switch your computer off and on again. As you
glance through the Appendix, notice that almost all of the function definitions
given there use recursion. Recursion is a very powerful programming technique,
and well worth mastering.

Here's another example of a recursive function: one which measures the length of a list L (that is, of a list which is the VALUE of the variable L. It is temptingly easy, and relatively harmless, to slip into the habit of referring to variable-names when you're really talking about their values). I've called the function LENGTH1 because there is a high probability that your Lisp already supplies LENGTH as a system function. If your Lisp has no LENGTH, name this function LENGTH rather than LENGTH1 (don't forget to change line 3 of the definition as well!).

```
(defun length1 (l)
  (cond ((null l) 0)
        (t (plus 1 (length1 (cdr l))))))
```

[Check PLUS in the Appendix]

LENGTH1 recursively calls itself on successive CDRs of L until L is empty (i.e. NIL). But notice the point at which recursion occurs: it is on the second argument to PLUS. Therefore the recursive call itself, being more deeply nested, was evaluated BEFORE the PLUS; and so as recursion unwinds all these PLUSes remain to be evaluated. The final recursive call returned 0, because of L being empty, as the second argument to PLUS in the PREVIOUS call. (PLUS 1 0) of course returns 1, and this becomes the returned value of a complete call to LENGTH1 – which value again appears as the second argument to the next-previous PLUS. And so on. So all the PLUSes get done, all the way back up to top level. And the final result is, of course, the same as the number of elements in the original list L:

*- (setq q '(a b c d e f g))

(A B C D E F G)

*- (length1 q)

7

Here is another recursive function:

```
(defun reverse1 (L)
  (cond ((null l) nil)
        (t (append (reverse1 (cdr l)) (list (car l))))))
```

This function returns its input list with the original elements of L, be they atoms or sublists, in reverse order. Again, your Lisp may well have an identical function called REVERSE. The APPENDs pile up, just as the PLUSes did, waiting to be evaluated when recursion unwinds. The last call to REVERSE1, at the bottom of the recursion, returns NIL because of the first clause of the COND. The APPEND in the previous call does something like (APPEND '(Z) NIL) – which, as you'll see if you type in that same S-expression, returns a list of 'Z: i.e.

(Z). So the next-previous APPEND does something like (APPEND '(Z) '(Y)), returning (Z Y), and so on.

I've given you several examples of recursive functions in order to make a general point. Notice how similar the three above definitions are: a COND; a recursion-halting first clause; an optional second clause which handles special cases and which (may) also halt the recursion; and a final T clause which includes the recursive call. If you glance at the Appendix you'll see many more recursive functions of a similar shape. Of course it's not an inviolable rule that a recursive function should be that shape. It can be any shape the programmer chooses, as long as it works. But when I was going through my own struggles to master recursion, I found this a very useful starting-point.

It is always the last clause of the COND which is the hard one to write. And that is because the expression which contains the recursive call also decides the format of the final result. Trying to work out exactly what a function will do as recursion unwinds is like trying to think backwards. But I maintain that it is possible to tell just by inspecting a recursive call what the final result will look like, without thinking through the recursion as closely as I have in the examples above. For example, I know that CONSing one atom onto an empty list is going to make a list of that atom, and that thereafter CONSing another atom on is going to make a list of the two atoms. So I know that lots of CONSes in a row are going to produce a great long list. Similarly, adding two numbers together will produce their sum, so doing that repeatedly is going to produce a total. That's a bit vague, but provided that the COND has a sensible halting clause and provided that it copes with special cases, it's accurate enough for most occasions. And I found that I was able to make that kind of educated guess about the form recursive functions should have long before I could honestly say that I fully understood what was going on. So I hope it helps you. Now, on to something different.

Exercise 2.1

Write NTHCDR, which takes two arguments like those of NTH but returns the Nth CDR of the list.

Write NTHCAR, which returns the first N elements of the list.

2.4 Iteration

Recursion is one way of making the machine keep on having another try at the problem you set it, until it reaches an answer. Another technique which achieves a similar effect but in a different way is use of the loop function. Remember how recursion repeatedly set up an entirely new call to (that is, an entirely new copy of) the same function until it got where it wanted to get to? That was what made it difficult to understand. Well, the loop is very much easier: it simply cycles ("iterates", as in "reiterates") round and round the same piece of Lisp code, within a single copy of one function, until some exit condition is satisfied, whereupon it stops and returns the result of the last iteration.

This is what a programming loop has to do, expressed in English:

1. Set up some variable-value bindings to be used within the loop; these bindings to be undone when the loop has halted. Go to 2.

2. Test the variables' values to see if the loop should halt. If so, halt. If not, go to 3.
3. Do the repetitive part of the loop – its "body". It is assumed that this will affect the values of the variables. Go to 2.

The code in steps 2 and 3 is re-executed each time around the loop. And when step 2 says looping should stop, it merely stops. There is no notion of "unwinding" or of having to execute any leftover bits and pieces.

The above kind of English-language description of what a program or a piece of code does is called an ALGORITHM. That is a beautiful word and means not merely a plan of action, but a plan in which each step could be carried out by a computer and which, if all of its steps ARE carried out, inevitably leads to the desired end-result.

Most microcomputer Lisps provide a looping function which fulfils only steps 2 and 3. The prior assignment of variables has to be done (by you) explicitly and separately from the loop. The reasons why this may matter will be dealt with in Chapter 3; you needn't worry about them now. Looping functions are almost invariably what are known as "constructs". COND and DEFUN are also constructs: they provide you with "slots" into which only certain types of data can be put if the function is to work; and – this is especially obvious with COND – there is a certain logic to the surface syntax or shape of the function. The ideal looping construct would therefore resemble in shape the above sequence of three steps. For example (this isn't a real Lisp function, as you can tell from the scraps of English enclosed in angle brackets):

```
(loop (<variables and bindings>)
      (<exit-test>)
      <body>)
```

A typical microcomputer loop construct is like this:

```
(loop (until <exit-test>)
      <body>)
```

For example:

```
*- (setq x 0)

0

*- (loop (until (equal x 10))
         (print x)
         (setq x (plus 1 x)))
```

will print the numerals from 0 to 9 and then stop. (The "body" in this case comprises the two instructions – S-expressions – to PRINT X and to PLUS 1 onto X). The LOOP construct in your Lisp may allow you to specify what value is returned when the loop halts, and may have other niceties. It may also be called something other than LOOP. (Check in the Appendix). It will almost certainly allow at least one different kind of exit-test, such as:

```
(loop (while L)              (while L
      (print (car L))              (print (car L))
      (setq L (cdr L)))            (setq L (cdr L)))
```

Either, of course, halts when the list L is empty. However, loop constructs are not complicated things, as you can see, and I feel sure that now you've understood both DEFUN and COND in action you won't have any trouble in understanding what your manual has to say about them. Read your manual, is the best advice I can give you at the moment, although I shall show you how to create a general-purpose looping function in Chapter 3.

2.5 Making use of the returned values

From time to time I have stressed the fact that Lisp functions ALWAYS return some value or other: either to you sitting at the terminal or to another function. For example, during execution of this expression:

```
(setq animals (append animals new-animals))
```

APPEND returns a value which is the result of concatenating the two lists ANIMALS and NEW-ANIMALS, and it returns it TO the SETQ. The SETQ changes the value of ANIMALS to this new value, and then it returns the same thing – which you see printed out on your terminal. (I've said all that before, but as I've just been explaining, repetition never did anyone any harm.) You can make use of the fact of returned values to keep your code concise and elegant. An instance of how not to do it concerns a one-time student of mine, who somehow acquired the habit of writing things like

```
(cond ((equal (null L) 't) <do domething...>) ...
```

in other words, if the test (null L) returns T to signify that L is an empty list, go on to do something. That would work, but is very long-winded. As you've seen already,

```
(cond ((null L) <do something>...) ...
```

is all that is necessary. NULL will return T if L is an empty list, and the EQUAL test to see if it has done so will return T as well. So the COND sees the same thing whether or not the EQUAL is there.

Conversely, you can with care introduce a kind of shorthand into your functions. Suppose you needed to do something like this:

```
(cond ((not (null <the result some complicated calculation>))
       (print <the result of the same complicated calculation>)))
```

33

which means: if my complicated calculation returns anything other than NIL, I want that result printed out, please. But, obviously, as things stand the poor computer has to do the same complicated calculation twice in a row: once for the NULL and once for the PRINT. A neat way around this (to save typing time and to make your function run faster) is to use a temporary variable which is set to the result of the complicated calculation:

```
(cond ((not (null (setq temp <complicated calculation>)))
       (print temp)))
```

The complicated calculation returns its result, which SETQ promptly binds to the new variable TEMP, after which it RETURNS the same value to the NULL – the same value as NULL would have seen without the SETQ. Then PRINT can print the value of TEMP without doing the complicated calculation again. You can also take things one stage further: in Lisp as in everyday English, that double negative (NOT (NULL . . .)) is a sure sign of more words than are necessary. If the result of the complicated calculation, and hence of the SETQ, were NIL, that is what the SETQ would return. Otherwise, the SETQ would return something which was not NIL – i.e. NOT NULL. So all we really need in order to achieve the above effect is:

```
(cond ((setq temp <complicated calculation>)
       (print temp)))
```

That may look weird the first time you see it, but it is also awfully elegant. So remember: if in the course of this book or in your manual you come across some Lisp code which looks like nonsense, try working out exactly what is returned by each function in the code: usually that resolves any mysteries. Remember, also, that an atom within a piece of code will always be evaluated, just like any other S-expression. You're probably quite happy with

```
(cond ((null L) nil)
   ... )
```

by now, but this:

```
(cond ((null L) variable-name)
   ... )
```

works in exactly the same way, returning the value of VARIABLE-NAME rather than NIL.

Exercise 2.1

Although the following expression is perfectly legal Lisp, there are two things about it which make it bad programming practice. Can you say what those two things are?

```
(cond (foo) (t nil))
```

Assume FOO to be bound.

2.6 Reading other people's code

This is a notoriously difficult exercise, as you may have discovered already. No two programmers program in exactly the same way, and what seems to be the very acme of concise elegance to one may resemble near-gibberish to another. In order to help with this problem, Lisp code is normally written or printed using a system of indenting, as you've seen above. Indenting is intended to work rather like the indenting of paragraphs in a novel, but on a smaller scale: its purpose is visually to separate chunks of code which to us seem to do separate things. For example, in the following COND expression the indenting starts each clause on a new line, one clause under another; and if a single clause is too long for a line it puts the <condition> part on one line and the <action> part on the next, moving the <action> one space to the right so that you can see at a glance what has happened.

```
(cond ((setq temp (append animals new-animals))
       (print temp))
      ((null new-animals) (print 'end))
      (t nil))
```

(Don't worry about what the COND may be intended to do!) Without indenting, the COND would look like this:

```
(cond ((setq temp (append animals new-animals)) (print temp)) ((null new-anima
ls) (print 'end)) (t nil))
```

which I'm sure you'll agree is harder to read. But remember that indenting is only for our (human) convenience. Lisp itself completely ignores all the extra spaces and lines involved. So on occasion you may come across a piece of code which looks something like this:

```
(list a
      b
      c)
```

and that is exactly the same thing as:

```
(list a b c)
```

There is one slight drawback to all this. And that is that a "pretty printer" (a printing function which automatically prints function definitions and lists with the proper indenting) is very complicated to write. In order to save memory space, your Lisp may have no pretty printer at all, or a very simple one. Have a look at some of the function-definitions printed in your manual: they'll almost certainly be indented in the way that your Lisp indents things. It may not be the same as the indenting in this book. But don't worry – as I say, Lisp ignores the indents anyway.

2.7 Writing Lisp code

As you may have noticed by now, Lisp is pretty tolerant of odd-looking entries, such as:

```
*- (  setq x  (append  list1  list2
)
)
```

It tends to wait, not accepting your entry until (a) the left-hand and right-hand brackets balance, and (b) you have typed a final carriage-return. Then it proceeds to remove from your entry all extraneous spaces, together with any carriage-returns which may have been typed BEFORE the point at which the brackets balanced. Its rules for removing the spaces are: there should be no space immediately following a left-hand bracket; there should be no space immediately preceding a right-hand bracket; there should be no space immediately after a quote-sign; and otherwise there should be just one space between any two S-expressions. These rules enable Lisp to reduce quite startling pieces of garbage to decent-looking Lisp code – the exception, of course, being if you omit a space between two atoms. In that case Lisp can't tell whether it is looking at the concatenation of what should be two atoms, or at merely one long atom. Of course, Lisp uses the same rules to enable it to ignore any indenting which you may type in as parts of your function-definitions. So it's not a bad idea to get used to the format with which your Lisp prints things, and to acquire the habit (as I have!) of typing your own Lisp code in the same way.

2.8 Debugging

Your Lisp will have some system of showing you what has gone wrong when one of your functions fails because of an error within the function: one which Lisp cannot evaluate. The available systems vary enormously, from very simple ones which merely print something like

```
ERROR 42
```

and expect you to look that up in your manual (and to make sense of what you find there!) to quite sophisticated "debuggers" which can show you the actual S-expression in which the error arose and what Lisp tried to make of it.

When Lisp functions are called from within each other, as they usually are, what happens is exactly what I described when discussing recursion: the uncompleted parts of the various functions are suspended until the inner functions have been completed. These so-far uncompleted bits are stored on a "stack" – which of course is actually yet another list. Exactly what is stored there and exactly how it is stored are details we needn't worry about, but the effect is that at any moment (such as when an error occurs) the stack holds a record of everything that has happened since the computer was last at top level. Sophisticated debuggers will let you explore the stack, finding out what happened to your variable-bindings etc. at any stage in the computation.

Your Lisp may have a special function called TRACE, which is switched on like this:

```
*- (trace <function-name>)
```

and switched off again like this:

```
*- (untrace)
```

If you have it, TRACE sits on the sidelines when a program is being executed and prints you a message every time control passes from one function to another. Some tracers will also print other information, such as the values of the new function's formal parameters and the value returned by the outer, calling function. And of course, the last entry-point that is noted by TRACE is the start of the function in which the error occurred. You'll see how to write a simple tracer in Chapter 4.

Failing either of those, you're still not completely lost. The function PRINT is one of the most useful debugging tools there is. Do you remember that silly function SHORTEN?

```
(defun shorten (L)
  (print L)
  (stop if the list L is empty)
  (shorten (cdr L))
  (print L))
```

It has two PRINT statements in it, whose only purpose was to show you what happened as recursion wound and then unwound. So a neat debugging trick is to insert temporary PRINT statements at strategic points in your program, to print out the values of crucial variables, or to announce that such and such a function has just been entered, and so on. I frequently find myself inserting instructions to (print 'a), (print 'b) etc. into the separate clauses of complex COND statements, so that as the program runs I can see at a glance which clauses succeed, and when.

Two errors which plague Lisp novices are as follows. Both are due to the micro-Lisp itself rather than to any serious misunderstanding on the part of the user.

2.8.1 CAR or CDR of NIL

In larger Lisps, both the CAR and the CDR of NIL are defined also to be NIL, which makes intuitive sense: if a list is empty, the CDR of it should also be empty (not UNBOUND or UNDEFINED). And similarly with the CAR of such a list. Once you've read the first part of Chapter 3 you'll have a better idea why defining the CAR and CDR of NIL to be NIL is a sensible idea. But, supposing that you had written a function which worked its way down a list, performing some test at each stage and stopping if the test succeeded. And suppose that the test was simply that the element should be EQ to C. You might have used a loop, or a recursive function which said something like:

37

```
(defun nil-test (L)
  (cond ((eq (car L) 'c)
         (print 'ok))
        (t (nil-test (cdr L)))))
```

That would be fine except in cases where the test NEVER found an element which was EQ to C and so progressively (and in its T clause) reduced L to NIL. At the next level of recursion, the first clause of the COND would try to apply CAR to NIL – and unless this were defined by Lisp so that its CAR was also NIL the result would be an error message. You can use the above function to test your own Lisp in this respect; give it a list which has no C in it, like this:

```
*- (setq L '(a b d e f))
```

Unfortunately, there's not much you can do about it if your Lisp fails the test. You will probably be obliged merely to remember that little foible, and to include pre-emptive traps for empty lists:

```
(defun new-nil-test (L)
  (cond ((null L) nil)
        ((eq (car L) 'c)
         (print 'ok))
        (t (new-nil-test (cdr L)))))
```

In Chapter 4, you'll learn about the function AND which will simplify matters by allowing you to combine the first two COND clauses in functions like NEW-NIL-TEST.

2.8.2 Auxiliary functions

This section may not make much sense to you until you have read a bit more of the book. There are certain inbuilt Lisp functions whose purpose is to allow you to take some argument or set of arguments and apply some OTHER function to it. Examples of such functions are APPLY, MAPC, MAPCAR and SORT. Usually, the "other" or "auxiliary" function is the first argument to the APPLY or whatever:

```
(apply 'plus '(1 2))
```

would cause PLUS to operate on the numbers listed as APPLY's second argument and therefore would return the value of 3.

That's perfectly clear and straightforward. But problems arise because some Lisps do, and some Lisps do not, require the auxiliary function's name to be quoted, as I have just done in my example. If you do the wrong thing, you'll get an error message about "function in function position is not a function" or something similar. In other words your auxiliary function has been quoted when it shouldn't have been, or vice versa. You should be able to find out from your Lisp manual which is correct for your Lisp. In Chapter 3 you'll see how the auxiliary function's name can be replaced with its equivalent LAMBDA expression. In such cases, and in all Lisps that I have ever seen, the LAMBDA expression MUST be quoted.

2.9 Comments

This seems as good a time as any to mention one more thing: the semicolon. If your manual says nothing about either the semicolon being a special character, or about COMMENTS, you can if you like ignore this section and treat the semicolon as though it were just another alphabetic character on your keyboard.

COMMENTS are English phrases and sentences intended to remind YOU of what a particular function is for and of how it works, and they are actually written into the function definition itself so that you can read them whenever you get Lisp to print out the definition. The secret is in the COMMENT CHARACTER – the semicolon. If a semicolon appears anywhere on a line of the definition, EVAL completely ignores the rest of that line, and the semicolon itself. So, after the semicolon and on the same line, you can put whatever you like. It will never be evaluated:

```
(defun length1 (L)
   ; Finds the LENGTH of a List
  (cond ((null L) nil)
        (t (plus 1 (length1 (cdr L))))))
```

If your Lisp allows comments, I can't recommend them highly enough. One can spend far too much of one's life puzzling over how a function works, three weeks after one has written the thing.

2.10 Summary

In Chapter 2 you have been introduced to the following Lisp terminology:

RECURSION	the programming technique whereby a function repeatedly re-calls itself (with suitably adjusted arguments) until the desired result is achieved.
LEVELS	a way of describing each of the above calls with reference to "top level".
UNWINDING	the gradual return of the computer, level by level, from the end or bottom of the recursive process to top level.
CONSTRUCT	a Lisp function (such as DEFUN or COND) which provides "slots" for the programmer to fill.
CONDITIONAL STATEMENT	a programming technique (in our case using the Lisp construct COND) which allows you to write the equivalent of the English form "IF... THEN... ELSE".

ITERATION	a programming technique whereby the SAME piece of Lisp code is repeated over and over again until some desired result is achieved.
ALGORITHM	a plan of action via which the computer can reach some goal.
BODY	that part of a function comprising the Lisp instructions which together achieve the function's purpose. In most cases, this is the whole of the function-definition except its name and its list of formal parameters.
INDENTING	a system of added spaces and carriage-returns, ignored by EVAL, which makes printed or written Lisp code easier for human beings to read.
DEBUGGING	the painful process of finding the mistakes in your programs.
COMMENTS	remarks added to a function-definition by the programmer but ignored by EVAL because they are prefaced by the comment character: in our case, the semicolon.

And you have been introduced to the following Lisp system functions:

APPLY	calls some other function, supplying it with the S-expressions which appear LISTED as APPLY's second argument.
COND	a Lisp CONSTRUCT which allows you to write CONDITIONAL STATEMENTS.
NULL	takes a single argument and returns T if the argument evaluates to NIL. Otherwise, it returns NIL.
DIFFERENCE	takes two numeric arguments and returns the difference between the first and the second.
PLUS	takes two numeric arguments and returns the sum of the first and the second.
LENGTH	takes a single argument which is a LIST, and returns the number of top-level elements the list has.

40

LOOP (UNTIL, WHILE)	a function which permits iteration.
SEMICOLON	the comment character in almost all Lisps.

You now have a pretty good idea of what Lisp is all about: it represents both data and function-definitions as S-expressions — usually as lists — and then manipulates the one with the other. Chapter 3, I'm afraid, is a toughie: mainly because I'm going to do two things at once. I'm going to clarify the notion of what a list is and of how Lisp manipulates it, and at the same time I'm going to show you how to use that knowledge to give your microcomputer Lisp a facility which, as it stands, it almost certainly hasn't got. Even if it has got the function, the exercise will do you good. (You didn't expect all of this to be EASY, did you?)

2.11 Answers to Exercises

Exercise 2.1

It is a horrible expression. Whoever wrote it (who, mc?) intended it EITHER to return the value of FOO if that value was non-nil; OR to return NIL. At a casual glance the word FOO, all by itself except for a pair of brackets, looks like a call to a function named FOO. But it isn't: the two brackets belong to the COND form. This isn't illegal, and there are even times when you might want to do it. But not in this particular expression because of course the atom FOO alone, when it was evaluated, would also return EITHER its bound value OR NIL. The COND is completely redundant.

Exercise 2.2

```
(defun nthcdr (n L
  (cond ((null L) nil)
        ((eq n 0) L)
        (t (nthcdr (difference n 1) (cdr L)))))

(defun nthcar (n L)
  (cond ((null L) nil)
        ((eq n 0) nil)
        (t (cons (car L) (nthcar (difference n 1) (cdr L))))))
```

Chapter 3
Inside Lisp

3.1 Cons-cells

It's time to tell you a bit more about what "really" goes on inside Lisp as it creates bindings, lists and function-definitions at your command.

A CONS-CELL is a structure which Lisp creates inside your computer's memory. It is the simplest possible LIST, and can be represented graphically as a box divided into two halves:

Fig 3.1

Each half may contain a "pointer" to some location in memory (a pointer is usually the actual memory-address of that location), or to NIL. The list (A) is represented thus:

Fig 3.2

And is created by the simple instruction

```
*- (cons 'a nil)
```

```
(A)
```

Of course, you can't actually SEE the resulting cons-cell. You have to infer its existence from the normal Lisp printout : (A).

The arrow signifies a pointer to the memory-location where the atom "A" is

42

held, and the diagonal line in the other half of the cell signifies a pointer to NIL. The left-hand half of the cell is the CAR of the original list (A), and the right-hand half is its CDR – which is NIL, of course.

But the right-hand half may alternatively contain a pointer to another cell:

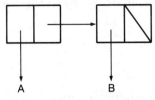

Fig 3.3

This represents the list (A B), and is created by:

    *- (cons 'a (cons 'b nil))

or

    *- (cons 'a '(b))

    (A B)

Similarly, the list ((a b) (c d)) looks like this in cons-cell notation:

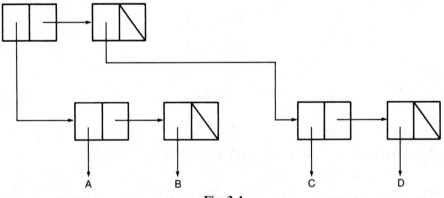

Fig 3.4

For convenience, that can be simplified to:

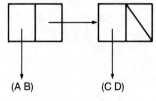

Fig 3.5

As programmers, we understand that the first cell doesn't really point to the list

43

(A B), but to a group of cons-cells like those in Fig 3.3. But it is this simplified form which is usually most useful for thinking about what your programs actually do inside Lisp – as you'll see shortly.

You are allowed to put a pointer to an atom or to a list into each half of a single cons-cell. You would do so by typing, for example:

```
*- (cons 'a 'b)

(A . B)
```

Such cells are printed in Lisp notation with a dot showing the division between the two halves of the cell:

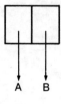

Fig 3.6

is printed by Lisp as (A . B), and

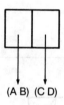

Fig 3.7

is printed by Lisp as ((A B) . (C D)).

This is also a dotted pair, but the term is usually reserved for cons-cells with pointers to atoms, as in the previous example. Naturally, you can type something with dotted notation directly into Lisp if you want to, e.g.:

```
*- (setq y '(a . b))

(A . B)
```

but the spaces on either side of the dots are essential if Lisp is to understand what you mean. Most Lisps freak out if they see a dot without at least one space before it and at least one space after it (for example, if you absent-mindedly type a full-

44

stop at the end of a Lisp "sentence"!).

The list (A . (B C)) is shown in cons-cell notation like this:

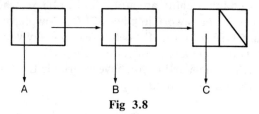

A   B   C

Fig 3.8

which is indistinguishable from the cons-cell representation of (A B C). Lisp will always choose to print the latter, simpler form.

Now, supposing that you set Q to some list, and then do

```
(setq x q)
```

Pretty obviously, since the Q isn't quoted, the value of X is now the value of Q, i.e. the SAME list. But supposing that, for whatever reason, you happened to want X's value to contain the same things as Q's (to be lexically the same shape) but actually to be a different list, with its elements stored in different memory-locations from those of Q? That way you could mess around with the Q-list to your heart's desire, but still retain a copy of its original form as the value of X.

Well, APPEND will do that. Remember that APPEND takes two lists as its arguments and returns the result of concatenating them – but without altering either of the original lists. Clearly it must somehow create a copy of one of them in the process, and what it returns is the result of joining that copy onto the other (uncopied) list. APPEND actually copies the list which appears as its first argument, and leaves that of its last argument alone. So by the simple trick of making the second of two input lists empty (i.e. NIL), we can get APPEND to copy the first one:

```
*- (defun copy (L)
     (append L nil))
```

If your Lisp has EQ as well as EQUAL, you'll find that if X is some list and Q is a COPY of that list, the two lists are EQUAL but not EQ. In other words, they are the same lexical shape, but composed of elements stored in different memory-locations – they aren't the SAME list:

```
*- (setq x '(a b c))

(A B C)

*- (setq q (copy x))

(A B C)

*- (equal x q)

T

*- (eq x q)

NIL
```

45

So now the mysterious difference between EQ and EQUAL is explained. As a general rule of thumb, for efficiency's sake one would use EQ when the arguments to be tested for equality are atoms and EQUAL when they are lists. EQUAL will, however, always work in place of EQ. Now, having introduced the idea of an identical COPY of a list, I'd better tell you why you might need such a thing. There are two Lisp system functions called RPLACA and RPLACD. And what they do is this: imagine that you have a variable L whose value is the list (A B C). And suppose you could write

    (set (car L) 'x)

so as to alter the value of L to (X B C). Of course you can't, because SET demands an atom, and not a list, as its first argument. But RPLACA will do it:

    (rplaca L 'x)

has exactly that effect. Moreover, the change is "surgical": RPLACA actually changes the pointer in the first cons-cell of the list L so that instead of leading to A it leads to X. That means two things: first, you shouldn't try to use a SETQ with RPLACA: unlike most other Lisp functions you've met so far, RPLACA DOES affect the value of its (first) argument. And second, any other variable (other than L) which happens to have the SAME list as its value (as with Q and X, above) will inevitably also acquire the new value. To prove that, try this sequence of instructions:

    *- (setq L '(a b c))

    (A B C)

    *- (setq S L)

    (A B C)

    *- (rplaca L 'x)

    X

    *- L

    (X B C)

    *- S

    (X B C)

Notice that although you didn't explicitly tell Lisp to touch S at all, its value has changed to correspond with that of L. It has to, because S and L are bound to the SAME list. Incidentally, most RPLACAs do return their second arguments, as I've shown. The RPLACA in your Lisp may possibly return something else, but in this example we don't really care what it returns. Now try a similar sequence using SETQ instead of RPLACA:

```
*- (setq L '(A B C))

(A B C)

*- (setq S L)

(A B C)

*- (setq L '(X B C))

(X B C)

*- L

(X B C)

*- S

(A B C)
```

In this case, L and S are not the same afterwards. SETQ has given them values which are DIFFERENT lists. Clearly, RPLACA is a very powerful and a very dangerous function: its surgical alteration of list structure means that the original form of the list is gone for good. So, if ever you want to use RPLACA, you may also have a use for COPY so that the original list is still around afterwards (as the value of some other variable, of course):

```
*- (setq L '(A B C))

(A B C)

*- (setq S (copy L))

(A B C)

*- (rplaca L 'x)

X

*- L

(X B C)

*- S

(A B C)
```

You may be thinking why use RPLACA at all if it's such a hassle, when SETQ seems to do more or less the same thing quite safely. You'll see what magic RPLACA and RPLACD can achieve as this chapter wears on and on.

RPLACD does a very similar thing to RPLACA, except that instead of replacing the CAR of a list it replaces the CDR. And in this case the CDR of L, if L has the value '(A B C), is '(B C). Remember the cons-cell structure:

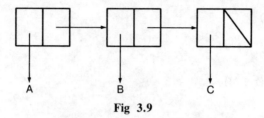

Fig 3.9

Like RPLACA, RPLACD alters the pointer from the first cell, so that instead of pointing to what was the rest of the list it points to something else. If you do this:

    *- (setq L '(a b c))

    (A B C)

    *- (rplacd L 'x)

you'll end up with a cons-cell which looks like this:

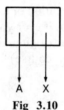

Fig 3.10

which is more or less the same as Fig 3.6 and which Lisp prints as

    (A . X)

Once again, if you were going to need the original form of L later, you would need to have kept a COPY of it before using RPLACD. Now before we go on to the promised magic function, here is a bit more about a different aspect of the "innards" of Lisp.

3.2 LAMBDA expressions

A Lambda expression is a list. Its first element is the atom LAMBDA, its second element is a list of variable-names, and the remainder of it is a series of arbitrary S-expressions:

    (lambda (x y z) <series of S-expressions>)

(remember, the angle brackets mean "this bit is in English rather than Lisp").

48

This is the form in which Lisp stores any function you may write, and your own Lisp will keep the LAMBDA expression either as the VALUE of the atomic name of the function, or on that same atom's PROPERTY-LIST (you'll learn about property-lists in Chapter 4 – for the moment just accept that the property-list is another place to keep information about an atom). In such cases the series of S-expressions in the LAMBDA list is the same series that forms the body of the function – i.e. the set of Lisp instructions that make the function "do" whatever it does do. For example:

```
(defun foo (x)
  (print x)
  (print 'done))
```

is stored in the form:

```
(lambda (x) (print x) (print 'done))
```

Notice a very important point: the formal parameters given to FOO in its definition also appear, exactly the same, as the variables in the LAMBDA list. Notice also that FOO is a normal EXPR. FEXPRs too turn into LAMBDA expressions but with slight variations in their form. What follows refers to EXPR-type expressions.

Now then. When you call FOO, like this:

```
(foo 'tony)
```

what happens is that EVAL sees from the opening bracket that Lisp is expected to DO something, so it goes off and looks for the "meaning" of the atom FOO: either as its Functional Value if your Lisp stores function-definitions as normal values; or as its Functional Property if it keeps them separately on the property-list. At any rate, what EVAL retrieves is the LAMBDA expression shown above, and you can think of it as inserting that expression in place of the atom FOO:

```
((lambda (x) (print x) (print 'done)) 'tony)
```

If you were to type this into your Lisp (notice the double opening brackets) it would have exactly the same effect as the above call to FOO itself: you would merely be saving EVAL the bother of hunting for the LAMBDA expression. And that's the significance of the atom LAMBDA, of course: it tells EVAL not to bother to go hunting because the expression it needs is right here.

What EVAL does with such an expression, whether EVAL found it for itself or you typed it in, is first of all to save away somewhere (it doesn't matter where) any previous value of the LAMBDA-variable X, and then to bind X to the value given at the end of the LAMBDA expression: in this case, 'TONY. Then it executes the remaining S-expressions with this binding in force – i.e. it is TONY, and not any previous value of X, which gets printed by the first S-expression. When the last S-expression has been executed by EVAL, any saved value of X is restored. The effect of this is, of course, that FOO also saves and restores the value of X, just as you would expect.

49

A LAMBDA expression can have NIL, or the empty list ( ) which is the same thing to Lisp, in its variables-slot. In which case there would also be no value to bind the variable to at the end of the expression. However many variables the LAMBDA is given (= however many variables the function has, whose LAMBDA list this is), there MUST be the same number of initial values to bind them to:

```
((lambda (x y z) <S-expressions>) nil nil nil)
```

ensures that, regardless of any previous values they may have had, X, Y and Z all start off at NIL before the first of the S-expressions is executed. Incidentally, X is bound to the first of these NILs, Y to the second, and Z to the third.

So, a Lambda expression gives you a way of writing what is in effect a function-definition, without specifying a corresponding function NAME. It is as though you had used DEFUN in the normal way but had somehow managed to trick DEFUN into accepting an empty name-slot. That may seem a bizarre thing to want to do, but you'll see it's usefulness shortly.

3.3 PROG

Now then. This is going to get very exciting. We're going to bring together the stuff about cons-cells, the stuff about RPLACD, your knowledge of recursion, and a LAMBDA expression to write our own looping function. It will in fact be Lisp's basic looping function, which is supplied in very few microcomputer Lisps but which all large Lisp systems have available. When we've written it, I'll tell you why some programmers say that you shouldn't use it if there is any possible alternative.

There is one point I should make very strongly first. Your Lisp will almost certainly have its own inbuilt looping functions, and these will be inherently and substantially faster in execution than any loop you could write for yourself – unless your system is sophisticated enough to allow you to "compile" your programs. Writing a loop from scratch, as below, will teach you a lot about how Lisp works; and throughout the rest of this book I have used it as though no other loop were available. This is simply because there is so much variation from Lisp to Lisp in the precise syntax and effects of looping constructs. You will soon be expert enough to see more or less at a glance how to alter my programs so as to incorporate your own Lisp's loop rather than my function PROG; and in almost every case this will be well worth doing for the sake of speed.

First of all, imagine that you had a function called MAPC, which would go through a list from its first element to its last, doing the same thing to each element as it went. For example, MAPC would be used like this:

```
*- (setq L '(a b c))

(A B C)

*- (mapc 'print L)

A B C

NIL
```

The NIL is what the MAPC returns after it has done all the PRINTing. MAPC will work with any EXPR function, as well as with PRINT. In general, you use it like this, where FN is any EXPR:

```
(mapc fn L)
```

A companion function to MAPC is MAPCAR, which does exactly the same things as MAPC except that it returns, not NIL, but a list of the results of each application of whatever function you specify in the FN position:

```
*- (setq l '((a b) (c d)))

((A B) (C D))

*- (mapcar 'car l)

(A C)
```

Your Lisp will probably already have these or similarly-named functions which do the same things. It is very important for what follows that you check both carefully in the Appendix.

However, these MAPPING functions, as they are called, are even more useful than you might think because, instead of merely putting in the FN slot the name of a Lisp system function or the name of one of your own functions, you can instead put a LAMBDA expression. (As before, this simply saves EVAL the bother of looking up the LAMBDA expression). So, if you want MAPC to perform some quite complicated operation on each element of the list, you don't have to first define a function to do it to one element and then call that function via the MAPC to do it to each of the elements in turn – that's terribly long winded. All you do is write the appropriate LAMBDA expression directly into the MAPC. You'll see an example soon, but for the moment imagine what would happen if L were some arbitrary sequence of S-expressions, and that what you asked MAPC to do was EVALuate each:

```
(mapc 'eval l)
```

This will do exactly what you would expect – i.e. evaluate each S-expression in turn until the end of the sequence is reached.

3.4 A preliminary definition of PROG

First, please check PROG in the Appendix.
Now look at this:

```
(defun prog $args$
    (eval (list (list 'lambda (car $args$)
                      '(mapc 'eval (cdr $args$)))
                nil
                nil
                nil)))
```

Real hard-core Lisp, eh? But simple enough to understand on the basis of what you know already. PROG is a FEXPR, and the two crucial facts about a FEXPR are that it DOESN'T evaluate its arguments and that it forms those arguments, however many there may be, into a list which becomes the value of its single atomic formal parameter – $ARGS$, in this case. Don't worry about that odd-looking name for the variable. The idea is to avoid any possible conflict between it and any variable-names of your own later on. The only thing to make sure of is that the dollar-sign isn't a special character in your Lisp: see Chapter 4, section 4.5. If it is, use some other symbol in its place.

Now, PROG is normally used INSIDE another function (as COND is). Something like this:

```
(defun foo (a)
  (prog (x y z)
    <a sequence of S-expressions involving A, X, Y and Z>))
```

Like any other Lisp function, PROG saves away and later restores any previous values of its formal parameters X, Y and Z. Unlike other functions, PROG also presets these formal parameters to NIL before proceeding to execute the sequence of S-expressions. Does that sound familiar? It's exactly what I said about the LAMBDA expression we were discussing earlier. And sure enough that hairy-looking code in the above definition of PROG is going to turn into a fairly simple LAMBDA expression. But first notice that if PROG is used as in FOO then the variable $ARGS$ is going to get bound to a LIST whose CAR is the list of formal parameters (X Y Z) and whose CDR is the sequence of S-expressions.

Have a good look at the definition of PROG above and imagine what that call to EVAL will make of its argument. I hope you can see easily that what it turns into is:

```
((lambda (x y z) (mapc 'eval (cdr $args$))) nil nil nil)
```

In fact, EVAL has done nothing more nor less than what it is told to do: it is told to create a list (that's what the function LIST does!) of four elements, the first being complicated and the remaining three being NIL, NIL and NIL:

```
(<complicated stuff involving another LIST and LAMBDA> nil nil nil)
```

The complicated bit is to be itself a list: a list of the quoted atom LAMBDA, the unquoted (and therefore to be evaluated) CAR of $ARGS$, and a quoted MAPC expression. And of course the CAR of $ARGS$ is the list of PROG variables (X Y Z). So, after the call to EVAL and a respectable bit of indenting, we can say that somewhere inside Lisp the definition of PROG temporarily looks like this:

```
((lambda (x y z)
   (mapc 'eval (cdr $args$)))
 nil
 nil
 nil)
```

And, as you've certainly guessed already, that is a perfectly normal LAMBDA expression. However, you may be wondering why there has to be that extra call to

52

EVAL inside PROG's definition: why wouldn't this do?:

```
(defun prog $args$
  ((lambda (car $args$)
     (mapc 'eval (cdr $args$)))
   nil
   nil
   nil))
```

and the reason is that LAMBDA is not, despite appearances, a function-name. That (car $args$), just because it is inside a LAMBDA expression, wouldn't get evaluated. Instead, it would be treated as though it belonged to some function whose two formal parameters were CAR and $ARGS$! Glance back at the examples of LAMBDA expressions at the start of this section. As I said there, the variables which appear in a list immediately following the LAMBDA itself are precisely the formal parameters of the corresponding function-definition. LAMBDA is in fact that rarity in Lisp: a KEYWORD. And its only purpose is to tell EVAL that what follows is a certain kind of list – i.e. a LAMBDA expression.

So at this point we cheat, by using EVAL itself to create the LAMBDA list we actually want. When FOO is called, the call to PROG inside it has to be evaluated in the normal way. But since Lisp habitually works out the value of the most deeply-nested S-expressions first, the explicit call to EVAL in PROG's definition happens PRIOR to the normal evaluation. The normal evaluation gets the LAMBDA expression, rather than the definition of PROG, to work on.

This is the first of several versions of PROG I shall show you. But it is already a useful function, and to explain that I need to digress a bit.

3.5 Scope of variables

Now and again in this book I've asked you to type into your Lisp an instruction involving SETQ, which as you know binds some VALUE to a VARIABLE. But what happened to that binding as you turned the page, and forgot about it? Well, I'm afraid it just sort of hung around, unnecessarily blocking up a part of your computer's memory, until such time as you switched the machine off. And clearly that isn't a very satisfactory state of affairs. In contrast, look at this simple program:

```
(defun foo (x)
  (print x)
  (blah x))

(defun blah (y)
  (print (plus 1 y)))
```

Assume for the moment that the variables X and Y have no values at all: you've just powered your computer up, and have done nothing but type in the definitions of FOO and BLAH. So now suppose that you type (foo 3). The previous value of X (nothing) is saved away by FOO, and X gets bound to 3. And it will remain bound to 3 until FOO has finished – in other words throughout not only FOO itself but also throughout the execution of FOO's subroutine BLAH. FOO prints the 3 and then calls BLAH with X bound to that same value. BLAH in its turn saves away the (nothing) value of Y and then binds Y, also, to 3. And then BLAH dutifully prints 4.

At that point BLAH ends, and so the value of Y is restored to what it was before (nothing). And immediately afterwards FOO also ends, restoring the old value of X as well. So, if X and Y were as we assumed unbound at the start, they are now unbound again. The point is that "passing" values as formal parameters from one routine to another is one way of ensuring that no bindings get left around to clutter up your computer's memory. In the case of our example, we say that the "scope" of Y's binding to 3 lasts throughout BLAH, and that the scope of X's binding to 3 lasts throughout FOO and hence throughout BLAH as well. A variable whose binding is restricted to one routine, or to one routine and its subroutines, is called a LOCAL variable. The converse, which our primitive operations with SETQ created earlier, is a GLOBAL binding: it is never saved away or restored, and is always in force until you specifically alter it with another SETQ. Or until you switch off.

Clearly, it is better to have local variables wherever possible. But unfortunately it isn't always convenient to pass values through from one function to another as formal parameters. So it'd be nice to have some way of saying to Lisp "this is a local variable: please save and restore its value as normal". And that is precisely the usefulness of our current version of PROG, because as I've pointed out already the LAMBDA expression it turns into saves away the variables X, Y and Z – and also presets them all to NIL so that you know where you stand. So:

```
(defun foo (a)
  (prog (x y z)
    <S-expressions, and perhaps subroutine calls>))
```

treats PROG as an insulator for its three formal parameters: they can be SETQ'd as much as you like by the S-expressions and/or the subroutines, but will remain firmly local to FOO and so will lose all such internal bindings when FOO ends.

3.6 A second version of PROG

That was the hard part. Now the fun really begins. I'm going to show you how to make our current PROG into a construct which many programmers, with considerable justification, abhor. I'm going to show it to you for several reasons: (1) if used with the restraint and common sense which I'm sure is second nature to you, it can be very useful indeed – especially if like many novice programmers you can understand loops easily enough but find recursion a bit of a mystery; (2) many would-be Lisp programmers have been brought up on simpler languages such as BASIC, and it seems contradictory of me to tell you that Lisp is the best programming language in the world and then to say that it has no direct equivalent of BASIC's GOTO instruction; and (3) PROG enables you to write your own "LOOP UNTIL" etc. functions if your Lisp doesn't have them or if you don't like the syntax of the ones it has. So here we go.

Do you recall RPLACD's dangerous ability surgically to alter the structure of a list? Well, suppose we had a MAPC with an EVAL, faithfully chuntering through some list of S-expressions as in our current definition of PROG, and suppose that one of those S-expressions contained a RPLACD which caused a copy of the full list of S-expressions to be tacked onto the end of the list currently being worked on by the MAPC. Then, when the MAPC reached what would have been the end of the list, it would find that it effectively had to start all over again with the first S-expression in the list – then the second, and so on. And since it would of course eventually get to the RPLACD again, this evaluation of the list of S-expressions would continue indefinitely. This is, approximately, how we're going to create our looping PROG; and here's the latest version of it:

```
(defun prog $args$
  (eval (list (list 'lambda (cons '$body$ (car $args$))
                    '(mapc 'eval $body$))
              (list 'quote (copy (cdr $args$)))
              nil
              nil
              nil)))
```

EVAL makes it into this, prior to the normal round of evaluation:

```
((lambda ($body$ x y z)
   (mapc 'eval $body$))
 <COPY of S-expressions>
 nil
 nil
 nil)
```

What this does that the last version didn't do is allow the MAPC to work on a COPY of the CDR of $ARGS$ – i.e. of the list of S-expressions. This is desirable because otherwise the RPLACD which we're shortly going to add, besides surgically altering the list of S-expressions which the MAPC was working on in the previous definition of PROG, would also affect the (same) list of S-expressions which appears as the CDR of the $ARGS$ in PROG's definition as its formal parameter. We need to give MAPC a COPY of the list to work on, so that we can keep $ARGS$ as the unmodified original version. The tricky bit comes in passing this copy into the MAPC. And once again the LAMBDA comes to our rescue. We simply CONS a new variable – $BODY$ – onto its list of formal parameters, and supply a suitable value for it at the end of the LAMBDA list. In supplying this value, we want COPY to do its stuff first, and then to have its returned value – that actual lexical shape – appear in the LAMBDA list. What we certainly don't want is the function-call

```
(copy (cdr $args$))
```

appearing in our final LAMBDA expression at the point where there should be a value for $BODY$! That is why we get that outer EVAL to make yet another LIST, this time of the atom QUOTE (which naturally enough will later behave in exactly the same way as the single-quote sign preceding the MAPC instruction) and of the returned value of the COPY instruction. Notice that in this latest version MAPC now works on $BODY$ – that copy – rather than on the original CDR of $ARGS$.

Right. The next question is how and where to add the RPLACD. Remember, whatever list we tack onto the end of $BODY$ will be faithfully evaluated by

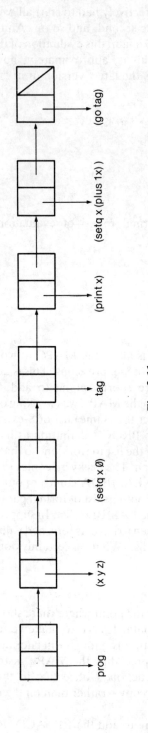

Fig 3.11

Fig 3.12

the MAPC, element by element. Should we simply give it a complete new copy of the whole list of S-expressions – that is, a new copy of the CDR of $ARGS$? We could, but there's a more useful solution. Look at a simple but typical use of PROG:

```
(defun foo ()
  (prog (x y z)
    (setq x 0)
    tag
    (print x)
    (setq x (plus 1 x))
    (go tag)))
```

As you might expect, this sets the value of X from NIL to 0 before entering a looping section. Within the loop, which extends from TAG to (GO TAG), the current value of X is printed and then augmented by 1. So, each time around the loop a higher value of X is printed. Each time the function GO is encountered, evaluation starts again at the TAG specified as GO's single argument. In our terms, GO effects a RPLACD, adding onto the end of $BODY$ a copy of that portion of the CDR of $ARGS$ whose CAR is "TAG". Visualise it as shown in Figs. 3.11 and 3.12.

Now, letting $BODY$ get longer and longer like this (which it will do because MAPC, although it works its way down the list, doesn't alter the list itself) is very wasteful of your computer's memory. And of course at any given moment that part of $BODY$ which has already been dealt with by MAPC will never be needed again. So let's put another of those useful LAMBDA expressions inside the MAPC, so that we can chop the redundant head off $BODY$ each time the MAPC has finished with it:

```
(defun prog $args$
  (eval (list (list 'lambda (cons '$body$ (car $args$))
                    '(mapc '(lambda (element)          <--
                              (eval element)            <--
                              (setq $body$ (cdr $body$)))) <--
                          $body$))
              (list 'quote (copy (cdr $args$)))
              nil
              nil
              nil)))
```

Here, the effect of the MAPC is to supply, as a value for its own internal LAMBDA expression's single formal parameter, each element of the list $BODY$ in turn. So far so good. But, what happens when the MAPC reaches the element "TAG"? The EVAL inside the MAPC will generate an error message about "TAG" being an unbound variable, for certain. So we'd better put a stop to that possibility. And now that we have a LAMBDA expression inside the MAPC it's a trivial matter to include also a COND which will bypass the call to EVAL if one of the members of $BODY$ turns out to be a simple atom:

```
(defun prog $args$
  (eval (list (list 'lambda (cons '$body$ (car $args$))
                    '(mapc '(lambda (element)
                              (cond ((atom element) nil)   <--
                                    (t (eval element)))))  <--
                           (setq $body$ (cdr $body$)))
                    $body$))
              (list 'quote (copy (cdr $args$))))
         nil
         nil
         nil)))
```

[Check ATOM in the Appendix]

And that is the final version of PROG. Notice that the new COND implies a specification for the use of our PROG: that any TAG must always be an atom and must occur at the "top level" of the list $BODY$ – in other words, it must itself be a member of $BODY$ rather than nested within a member of $BODY$. PROG itself effectively ignores TAG, which is used only by GO. And here's GO, which is also a FEXPR to save you the bother of quoting its argument:

```
(defun go key
  (rplacd $body$ (copy (memq (car key) (cdr $args$)))))
```

MEMQ finds that portion of the CDR of $ARGS$ which begins with KEY — i.e. with "TAG" (in some Lisps, MEMQ will return not that portion but its CDR. But that doesn't matter here since MAPC is going to ignore the CAR ("TAG") anyway). COPY makes a copy of that portion so that the CDR of $ARGS$ is safely isolated, and then RPLACD tacks it onto the end of the current version of $BODY$.

Now, you may have been thinking that this is all very smart, but how do we ever stop the thing? As it stands, it will happily loop for ever. The answer is simple: another function called RETURN which acts just like GO except that what it tacks onto the end of $BODY$ is: NIL. When this happens MAPC finds that the next element of $BODY$ it has to work on is NIL. So it at last stops. Here's a preliminary definition of RETURN:

```
(defun return ()
  (rplacd $body$ nil))
```

Notice that neither GO nor RETURN need to be top-level members of $BODY$. So you can nest either or both deep inside a COND if you want to. EVAL will find them and execute them just as it would any other function:

```
(defun foo ()
  (prog (x y z)
    (setq x 0)
    tag
    (cond ((eq x 10) (return))
          (t (print x)))
    (setq x (plus 1 x))
    (go tag)))
```

58

This will print the numerals from 0 to 9 and then stop. Two final points. Our PROG is designed always to take three formal parameters: X, Y and Z. Of course you can give them any alternative names you like when you're writing a PROG into one of your functions, but there must be three of them. If you need less, just treat the remainder as dummies: write them into the list following PROG, but otherwise ignore them. When you've done the exercises at the end of this chapter, such restrictions will not apply.

Finally, the promised reasons why you shouldn't use PROG without careful thought. Mainly, because it is offensive in a Lisp context: it is what is called "unstructured". Whereas well-written Lisp programs usually have a master routine which calls a series of subroutines, each of which performs one straightforward thing, PROG allows you to use multiple TAGs and GOs (the TAGs being different atoms, of course) which can soon make the flow of control as tortuous as the "spaghetti junctions" familiar to users of BASIC. Besides which, it can tempt you into writing very long function-definitions.

On the other hand, if you use PROG without TAGs or GOs, simply to keep the scope of your variables tidy, that is perfectly acceptable programming practice. And since all Lisp dialects offer at least one looping construct, I don't see why you shouldn't be allowed to use PROG as above, with just one TAG and one GO: it amounts to the same thing. Personally I always find a simple use of PROG far easier to understand than one of the very many variations of LOOP etc. offered by the various Lisp dialects. So: avoid using PROG as though you were writing your program in BASIC, and you shouldn't go far wrong. If you glance back to Chapter 2, section 3, you'll see how closely a simple PROG as used in FOO conforms to what I suggested as the ideal looping construct. One major dialect of Lisp — MacLisp – has a better one called DO which is emulated in some micro Lisps. But for most Lisps and for most purposes, PROG is as good as you can get when you need a loop.

3.7 Summary

In Chapter 3 you've been introduced to the following Lisp terminology:

CONS-CELL	the basic LIST, as stored inside Lisp.
DOTTED PAIR	a cons-cell represented in normal Lisp notation.
LAMBDA	a keyword understood by EVAL to be the first element in a LAMBDA expression.
LAMBDA EXPRESSION	a function-definition as it is stored by Lisp, rather than as it is written by you using DEFUN.
MAPPING FUNCTION	a function which applies some other function to each member of a list in turn, starting with its CAR.
SUBROUTINE	a function ("routine") which is normally only called from within some other function.

59

SCOPE OF VARIABLES	the "range" over which a given variable remains bound to a given value. The "range" may be thought of in terms of area, in a file of functions; or in terms of time during the execution of functions.
LOCAL VARIABLE	a variable whose binding (to a given value) remains valid only throughout a single function and that function's subroutines if any.
GLOBAL VARIABLE	a variable whose binding (to a given value) remains valid for all functions and subroutines.

You have also been introduced to the following Lisp system functions:

RPLACA	"surgically" alters a list by replacing the pointer from its CAR.
RPLACD	"surgically" alters a list by replacing the pointer from its CDR.
MAPC	a mapping function which returns NIL.
MAPCAR	a mapping function which returns a LIST of its results.
MEMQ	if its first argument is a top-level member of its second (the latter being a list) it returns that portion of the list which begins with the same first argument. Otherwise, it returns NIL.

That was, I expect, the hardest chapter in this book. If you've got your PROG to work and have understood it, you're in excellent shape for understanding not only the rest of what I have to say, but also what other people have to say on the subject of Lisp. From now on, provided that your definition of PROG is loaded whenever Lisp itself is loaded (see the section in the Appendix on INIT files), you don't of course have to remember all the details of Chapter 3 every time you use it: it becomes a new "system" function, like DEFUN or COND. You only need to remember how to use it and what it does!

As already mentioned, PROG is used a great deal in this book, for two purposes:
1. to create local variables, local to the function in which the PROG appears; and
2. to allow iteration via tags and GO.

If you can't get it to work at this stage, don't despair. Your Lisp will certainly have its own way of creating local variables, perhaps via a LET instruction, or perhaps via special syntax in the second argument to DEFUN. And it will certainly have some kind of loop structure. The two together will be precisely equivalent to PROG in all circumstances; so a little study of your Lisp manual should enable you to cope with a non-working PROG for the time being!

To make up for the strains of Chapter 3, Chapter 4 will be something of a relaxation.

Exercise 3.1 (easy)

It would be nice if RETURN would cause the PROG, which currently always returns NIL because MAPC always returns NIL, to return any specified value or the result of any specified computation, e.g. if we could put

```
(return (plus 25 x))
```

into FOO and have the appropriate value (35) returned by the PROG. Give PROG's LAMBDA expression yet another formal parameter, preset to NIL, and rewrite RETURN so that before doing its RPLACD it sets the value of this variable to be whatever is the result of the specified computation. Then make sure that the PROG's LAMBDA expression returns the value of this variable.

Exercise 3.2 (harder)

Currently our PROG takes exactly three formal parameters. Rewrite its definition so that it will take any number of variables, all of which will be saved, preset to NIL, and restored. Hint:

```
(mapcar '(lambda (v) nil) (car $args$))
```

will, if your MAPCAR works the way it should (check in Appendix 1), return a list of as many NILs as there are elements in (car $args$). You can then splice this list into the values-slot of the PROG's LAMBDA list using APPEND, so that the series of NILs is no longer listed separately from the other values there.

Exercise 3.3 (completely different)

FEXPRs are often used to create new "system" functions. Write a FEXPR called IF which takes two or more arguments and which has the following syntax. If the first argument, which is a test, evaluates to anything other than NIL, IF evaluates its second argument and returns the result. Otherwise, the second argument is ignored and IF evaluates the remainder of its arguments (if any), returning NIL. This kind of syntax is known as "IF-THEN-ELSE" syntax, by analogy with everyday English.

3.8 Answers to Exercises

Exercise 3.1

```
(defun prog $args$
  (eval (list (list 'lambda (cons '$body$ (cons '$temp$ (car $args$)))
                      '(mapc '(lambda (element)
                               (cond ((atom element) nil)
                                     (t (eval element))))
                             (setq $body$ (cdr $body$)))
                      $body$)
                    '$temp$)
             (list 'quote (copy (cdr $args$)))
             nil
             nil
             nil
             nil)))

(defun return $result$
  (setq $temp$ (eval (car $result$)))
  (rplacd $body$ nil))
```

Exercise 3.2

```
(defun prog $args$
  (eval (append (list (list 'lambda
                            (cons '$body$ (cons '$temp$ (car $args$))
                            '(mapc '(lambda (element)
                                     (cond ((atom element) nil)
                                           (t (eval element))))
                                   (setq $body$ (cdr $body$)))
                            $body$)
                          '$temp$))
                (list (list 'quote (copy (cdr $args$))))
                '(nil)
                (mapcar '(lambda (v) nil) (car $args$))))))
```

APPEND's first, second and third arguments are exactly as they were before, except that each is LISTed so that APPEND can join them all together to give the same result as previously. It can also now join on the final MAPCAR's result, which is of course already a list.

Exercise 3.3

```
(defun if expressions
  (cond ((eval (car expressions)) (eval (cadr expressions)))
        ((cddr expressions) (mapc 'eval (cddr expressions)))))
```

EXPRESSIONS is bound to the list of IF's arguments, e.g. to the second and subsequent S-expressions in the call:

```
(if (eq x 5) (print x)
    (setq x (plus 1 x)))
```

and it doesn't matter how many such S-expressions there are (this would not, of course, be the case if IF were defined as an EXPR). The COND checks to see if the first S-expression evaluates to non-NIL, and if so it evaluates the second, returning automatically the value of that operation. If the first S-expression returns NIL (if the test fails), the second clause of the COND is evaluated. This checks to see that SEXPR has a CDDR – i.e. that the call to IF had more than two arguments – before going on to evaluate them in turn. Since MAPC returns NIL, the second clause of the COND will return NIL. And since there are no further possible contingencies to allow for, the COND does not need a T clause.

Chapter 4
Your Lisp toolbag

In this chapter is a series of short sections, each covering a group of functions. These groups represent the various "tools" which Lisp provides for various programming purposes. It is merely a convenient classification: there is nothing special about the way any of these functions are used, and they exist to be included in your own function-definitions in the same way as any of the system functions you have met so far.

4.1 Boolean functions

Don't be put off by that word if you've never seen it before. Boolean functions behave analogously to the English words AND, OR and NOT, and most Lisps provide them. As always, consult the Appendix.

AND and OR take any number of arguments. NOT (or NULL, which is precisely the same function with a different name) takes only one.

AND evaluates its arguments in order, and continues to do so provided that each one evaluates to non-NIL. If it runs out of arguments in the process, AND returns T. Otherwise – that is, if one of the arguments evaluates to NIL, AND returns NIL immediately and doesn't bother to evaluate any remaining arguments. Take this English sentence:

"If it is Thursday, and it is raining, and he is not there, I shall shoot myself."

And then look at this Lispified equivalent:

```
(AND (isthursday day) (israining weather) (isabsent him) (shoot self))
```

One interpretation of the first sentence is that if it is Thursday, and if it is raining, but if he turns up, I won't have to die. The Lisp AND works in a similar way to that particular interpretation: all of the first three arguments in the second form of the sentence must evaluate to true (T) if the last is to be evaluated at all.

64

Here's a demonstration you can try:

```
*- (setq x 0)

0
  *- (and (eq x 0) T)

T
```

The first argument, (eq x 0), returns T. So AND continues and evaluates its second and last argument. This, being T, can of course never be anything but T. And T is what is returned by the whole expression.

```
*- (setq x 2)

2

*- (and (eq x 0) T)

NIL
```

In this case, (eq x 0) returns NIL. So the T is never reached and the whole AND returns NIL.

OR does just the opposite: it evaluates its arguments in turn and returns NIL only if it gets through them all without any one evaluating to T. If any one does evaluate to T, the OR returns T and ignores the rest:

```
*- (or (eq x 0) (eq x 5))

NIL
```

Neither argument evaluates to T, so OR returns NIL.

```
*- (setq x 0)

0

*- (or (eq x 0) (eq x 5))

T
```

The argument (eq x 0) evaluates to T, so the OR stops at once and returns T.

NOT takes one argument, which must obviously evaluate either to NIL or to something non-NIL. In the former case, NOT returns T, and in the latter case it returns NIL. That is, NOT returns the opposite logical state from the one supplied as its argument:

```
*- (not nil)

T

*- (not t)

NIL

*- (not x)

NIL

*- (not (eq x 20))

T
```

NULL has exactly the same effect as NOT under all circumstances. It is just another name for the same function. Most Lisps provide both for the sake of readability of your code:

```
(null L)
```

seems more appropriate than (not L) if L is a list, but

```
(null (eq x 20))
```

looks a bit peculiar. So, feel free to use either NOT or NULL (provided of course that your Lisp has both) as the mood takes you.

Boolean Algebra – which was invented by the mathematician Boole, hence its name – is a way of describing the internal operations of closed systems, such as computers, within which there are only two possible basic "states": ON or OFF, T or NIL, 1 or 0. The algebra, as you may imagine, has a great many more "logical operators" than merely AND, OR and NOT. But most Lisps provide only the three equivalent functions because it is usually a trivial matter to write any others if you need them. For example, Boolean Algebra has NAND, which can be defined in Lisp as (not (and <arguments>)); and NOR, which can be defined in Lisp as (not (or <arguments>)). In fact, you can if you prefer forget the whole Boolean analogy, and just use AND, OR and NOT as common sense dictates.

AND and OR can on occasion save you a great deal of typing, because as you may have noticed they behave rather like mini-versions of COND. If you recall the little COND at the heart of our famous definition of PROG:

```
(cond ((atom element) nil)
      (t (eval element)))
```

the whole statement could have been written as:

```
(and (not (atom element)) (eval element))
```

66

which you may now think far easier to read. Many of the function-definitions in the Appendix could be rewritten using Boolean functions. Here's a version of PROG's COND using OR:

```
(or (atom element) (eval element))
```

which is even simpler-looking. However, please beware of writing huge AND/OR/NOT complexes: if the equivalent COND would have more than two clauses, it's probably safer (for the sake of being able to understand it three weeks later) to use the COND form.

Exercise 4.1

Say what the following S-expressions will return under all possible conditions:

```
(and (not (or a b)) t)

(not (or a b))

(or a b (not (or c d)))

(or (and a b) (not (and c d)))
```

4.2 Predicates

Predicates are functions which take a single argument, perform a test on it, and return T if the test succeeds or NIL if it fails. Very often, though not always, the NAME of the predicate has the letter P tacked onto the end of it. Have a glance through your Lisp manual. You will find at least some of these common predicates:

ATOM	GREATERP	ZEROP
LISTP	LESSP	ONEP
NULL	EQUAL	NUMBERP

Predicates are most often used in COND clauses. You've seen NULL used that way quite often, and ATOM occurs in the definition of PROG. ATOM returns T if its argument is an atom (i.e. not a list). Conversely, LISTP returns T only if its argument is a list and not an atom. So LISTP, for example, is very easy to write if you have ATOM and NUMBERP:

```
(defun listp (x)
   (and (not (atom x)) (not (numberp x))))
```

(Incidentally, NIL is classed as an atom in almost all Lisps.)
You're quite free to invent new predicates for yourself if you find it convenient to do so. Your own predicates will be just as validly predicates as any on the

67

above list! For example, to check whether or not the current head of a given list is an atom:

```
(defun atom-first (L)
  (atom (car L)))
```

Exercise 4.2

If your Lisp lacks any of the following predicates:
  Define LESSP in terms of GREATERP and EQUAL.
  Define ZEROP in terms of EQUAL.
  Define ONEP so that it behaves like this:

```
*- (onep 0)

NIL

*- (onep 1)

T

*- (onep 2)

NIL
```

4.3 Functions for arithmetic

Even the most inveterate number-hater, if he or she is also a programmer, will occasionally need simple arithmetic. You've already seen how in a function using PROG you might want to augment a counter each time around the loop, and to stop after so many iterations:

```
(defun foo ()
  (prog (x y z)
    (setq x 0)
    tag
    (cond ((eq x 10) (return))
          (t (print x)))
    (setq x (plus 1 x))
    (go tag)))
```

We've also written LENGTH1 or LENGTH, to tell us the length of a list. So presumably we might one day want to know if the length of list L1 is greater than the length of list L2. And so on. Even the smallest Lisps usually have one or two basic number-crunching functions. Here are the commonest; all of them take only numeric arguments:

GREATERP takes two arguments and returns T only if the first argument is numerically greater than the second. It returns NIL if the arguments are equal:

```
*- (greaterp 4 3)

T

*- (greaterp 3 4)

NIL

*- (greaterp 3 3)

NIL
```

LESSP does the opposite, returning T only if its first argument is less than its second.

```
*- (lessp 4 3)

NIL
   *- (lessp 3 4)

T

*- (lessp 4 4)

NIL
```

PLUS returns the sum of its two arguments.

```
*- (plus 3 4)

7
```

DIFFERENCE returns the result of subtracting its second argument from its first.

```
*- (difference 4 3)

1

*- (difference 3 4)
```

returns −1 if your Lisp will handle negative numbers, otherwise it returns an error message.

TIMES returns the result of multiplying its two arguments together.

```
*- (times 3 4)

12
```

TIMES can be defined like this:

```
(defun times (x y)
  (cond ((eq x 1) y)
        (t (plus y (times (difference x 1) y)))))
```

but notice that it recurses to X levels; if your Lisp has a limited stack size (see Foreword) this definition would not work where X exceeded that limit. A solution to that problem would be to use the same idea as above to define TIMES as a looping function.

QUOTIENT returns the result of dividing its first argument by its second, the result being rounded down to the nearest lower whole number if it is not already a whole number.

```
*- (quotient 10 5)

2

*- (quotient 10 3)

3
```

With the same proviso as for TIMES, QUOTIENT can be recursively defined, including a trap for attempts to divide by zero:

```
(defun quotient (x y)
  (cond ((eq y 0)
         (print (list 'quotient: 'zero 'error)))
        ((lessp x y) 0)
        (t (plus 1 (quotient (difference x y) y)))))
```

REMAINDER applies QUOTIENT to its two arguments and returns as a whole number any remainder of the division;

```
*- (remainder 5 3)

2

*- (remainder 5 5)

0
```

REMAINDER, too, can be defined as a recursive function:

```
(defun remainder (x y)
  (cond ((eq y 0)
         (print (list 'remainder: 'zero 'error)))
        ((lessp x y) x)
        (t (remainder (difference x y) y))))
```

70

If (difference 3 4) worked, it's worth trying negative numbers out on your Lisp's TIMES, QUOTIENT and REMAINDER. Also (for the sake of avoiding future bugs) see what your Lisp makes of an attempt to divide by zero:

    *- (quotient 1 0)

It may well have struck you that there is something odd about these functions. For example, to add 3 to 4 you would type

    *- (plus 3 4)

there would be an implicit "=" whilst EVAL did its stuff, and then back would come the answer:

    7

It is as though you had written out the sum like this:

    + 3 4 = 7   instead of   3 + 4 = 7

But, if you think about it, the order of those five items (or, at any rate, of the first four) doesn't matter a bit provided that both you and the machine are using the SAME order. Some electronic calculators require you to use the third possibility:

    3 4 + = 7   (again, the "=" is usually implicit)

The "+" is known as the OPERATOR, and in mathematics an operator behaves very analogously to what we programmers refer to as a FUNCTION. The "normal" way of writing the sum:

    3 + 4 = 7

is known as INFIX notation because the position of the operator is FIXed IN-between the things it has to operate upon. Or, in Lisp terminology, the function comes between its two arguments. Clearly, that's inconvenient for us because in Lisp the function ALWAYS precedes its arguments. Our way of writing the sum is known as PREFIX notation. And of course it is just as valid as any other arrangement, so long as we remember to use it consistently. The normal infix notation:

    (3 plus 7)

will always make Lisp complain that it has no defined function named 3!
    But, once it is accepted that we must use prefix notation for arithmetic because that is the format Lisp requires, it is of course quite correct to treat

71

arithmetical functions just like any other Lisp functions:

```
*- (setq L '(1 2 3))

(1 2 3)

*- (quotient (times (cadr L) (caddr L))
             (plus (car L) (cadr L)))

3
```

The above S-expression can be translated into English as: "multiply 2 by 3 and divide the result by the sum of 1 and 2".

```
*- (mapcar '(lambda (n)
              (plus n 1))
            L)

(2 3 4)
```

Which means "add 1 to each member of L and return a list of the results".

Small Lisps will usually only let you do arithmetic on whole numbers. They won't understand either decimal points or fractions – even if you figure out a way of typing them in. This means that if you type, say:

```
(quotient 3 4)
```

the answer to which is of course either 0.75 or 3/4, the computer will "round off" this result to the nearest whole number: usually to the nearest whole number downwards – to 0, in this case.

Naturally, this imposes some quite severe restrictions on the types of calculation you can do: there's not much point in writing a function to perform some complex calculation if its answers are ALWAYS going to lie between the same two whole numbers – say between 0 and 1 – because it will ALWAYS return 0. But sometimes it is possible to make use of the restriction to do useful things. The following procedure tests to see if the number X is an exact multiple of the number Y:

```
(defun multip (x y)
  (eq x (times y (quotient x y))))
```

It first divides X by Y, knowing that if X is NOT an exact multiple of Y the result will be rounded down. Now, if no rounding occurred (if X was an exact multiple of Y), multiplying the result by Y again should produce X. In all other cases the EQ test fails.

Exercise 4.3

Express the following in Lisp:
   "3 added to the product of 4 and 7"
   "four times the sum of 3 and 7"
   "divide 100 by the result of adding 8 to the product of 5 and 2"

4.4 Sorting

This example will use the predicate LESSP. If your Lisp hasn't got it, (or the predicate GREATERP – see Exercise 4.2) it will still be worth your while to read this section and to try to understand it without your computer's help. It discusses a more complex recursive-looping program than any you have yet seen.

Some Lisps provide you with a handy function for sorting lists into some kind of order – say, to sort (2 4 3 1 5 7 0 6) into the correct numerical order (0 1 2 3 4 5 6 7). Microcomputer Lisps usually don't provide one, but now that we have PROG we can write one. We shall in fact need two functions for SORT: the master routine of that name which you call whenever you need it, and a subroutine which it calls for itself. First of all, let's bind a convenient variable to the list to be sorted:

```
*- (setq q '(2 4 3 1 5 7 0 6))
```

```
(2 4 3 1 5 7 0 6)
```

One way to sort such a list can be written out as follows:

(1) See if the first member of the list is smaller than the second. If so, go to (2). If not, go to (3).

(2) Remember the first element and repeat (1) on the CDR of the list.

(3) Remember the second element and repeat (1) on a list comprising the first element and the CDDR of the list.

This will turn into a recursive function which chunters through the list until the list is exhausted, applying the three rules as it goes. For those parts of the list which are already in order, only rules (1) and (2) will be needed. But whenever the function encounters a list element which is succeeded by a number smaller than itself, rule (3) effectively reverses those two elements.

Since we shall be using a recursive function, the elements which have to be "remembered" will be stored up in the recursion as CONSes waiting to be executed, and at the end of the recursion all those CONSes will create a list of all the remembered bits. A single application of the above rules to the list Q would generate this new version:

```
(2 3 1 4 5 0 6 7)
```

Clearly that's not good enough yet. But (here comes the LOOP) we could easily now do it again and again until we got the result we wanted. Here are the results of successive applications of the rules:

```
(2 1 3 4 0 5 6 7)
(1 2 3 0 4 5 6 7)
(1 2 0 3 4 5 6 7)
(1 0 2 3 4 5 6 7)
(0 1 2 3 4 5 6 7)
```

So, what I propose is a master routine which contains a PROG loop (the

PROG of Exercise 3.1, because I want the final sorted form of the list to be returned – the LOOP function in your Lisp may not allow you to specify what is returned). Within the loop will be a call to the recursive function described above. And each time around the loop, the form of the list which it is asked to sort will be the one it itself returned on the previous iteration. Which is a long-winded way of saying that the recursive function will be asked to work on the successive forms of the list as shown above. Here's a first try:

```
(defun numsort (L)
  (prog ()
    loop
    (setq L (subsort L))
    (go loop)))
```

SUBSORT is the recursive function which hasn't been defined yet. But notice the SETQ which sets L (initially bound to the original list, of course) to its new value each time around the loop.

The next stage is to think of a way of stopping the thing when it has done its job. The easiest way is to have a FLAG. The flag will be a logical variable – it will only ever have the values T or NIL – which will start off at NIL and which will stop the loop if it is ever set to T:

```
(defun numsort (L)
  (prog (flag)                    <--
    loop
    (setq flag nil)               <--
    (setq L (subsort L))
    (cond (flag (go loop))        <--
          (t (return L))))))       <--
```

FLAG is, of course, preset to NIL by the PROG. Subsequently, SUBSORT will set it to T every time rule (3) operates – that is, every time SUBSORT finds that the list still has a couple of elements out of order. The COND then checks the logical state of the flag. If it is T, another iteration is needed. That is why FLAG has to be set back to NIL each time around the loop. Eventually, SUBSORT will find that all the elements of the list are in their correct order, and so will not reset FLAG to T. And on that cycle the COND will cause the latest value of L to be RETURNed. Notice the absence of the characteristic double opening bracket in the first clause of the COND. We are not asking it to execute some function, but merely to inspect the value of FLAG.

Right. That looks OK. Now SUBSORT:

```
(defun subsort (L)
  (cond ((eq (length L) 1) L)
        ((apply 'lessp (list (car L) (cadr L)))
         (cons (car L) (subsort (cdr L))))
        (t (setq flag t)
           (cons (cadr L) (subsort (cons (car L) (cddr L)))))))
```

74

This isn't as bad as it looks. Take the second COND clause first. It represents rule (1), and applies LESSP to the first two members of the list L. (I'll explain the APPLY in a moment.) LESSP returns T if the first member is numerically less than the second. In which case rule (2) operates, i.e. to remember the first element and to apply SUBSORT again to the CDR of L.

Now, there isn't much point in calling LESSP, which wants two numbers, at the point where recursion has reduced the list to only one number. So the first clause of the COND checks for that condition, and is as usual the recursion-halting clause. However, all those CONSes are going to be stacked up waiting to be executed, and also we don't want to lose the final member of the list. So the first clause returns the current value of L, which is a list of one element (the last element) and which is therefore suitable for the CONSes to unwind into.

Now the third clause. It is the Lisp equivalent of rule (3). The first thing it does is set FLAG to T, because it is the section of SUBSORT which handles out-of-sequence numbers in the list. Otherwise, it does almost exactly the same thing as the second clause, except that it remembers the second element and in effect takes that element out of the list, calling SUBSORT again on the remainder.

Overall, each of the CONSes waiting to be executed when recursion unwinds will always add into SUBSORT's final list the smaller of any two numbers given to LESSP.

There's just one more thing. What happens if the list contains two EQUAL numbers? Sooner or later they will be placed next to each other by SUBSORT. And when LESSP is asked to say if the first is smaller than the second it will return NIL. So rule (3) operates. On the next iteration exactly the same thing happens again. And again, and again. What we really want to happen is the same thing as on clause two of the COND, even though the LESSP test has failed. So let's put in an extra test just for that special case:

```
(defun subsort (L)
  (cond ((eq (length L) 1) L)
        ((or (eq (car L) (cadr L))                    <--
             (apply pred (list (car L) (cadr L))))
         (cons (car L) (subsort (cdr L))))
        (t (setq flag t)
           (cons (cadr L) (subsort (cons (car L) (cddr L)))))))
```

And that's almost that. There is just one refinement you might like to add. You may not of course always be wanting to sort mere lists of numbers. It would be nice to be able to use essentially the same function to sort any list, according to a criterion (predicate) chosen by you. Perhaps, even, a predicate written by you. So let's replace LESSP in the definition by the atom PRED, and let's make this a new argument which is fed in through SORT itself whenever you call it. And at the same time let's rename NUMSORT:

```
(defun sort (L pred)                                  <--
  (prog (flag)
    loop
    (setq flag nil)
```

```
            (setq L (subsort L pred))              <--
            (cond (flag (go loop))
                  (t (return L)))))
     (defun subsort (L pred)                       <--
        (cond ((eq (length L) 1) L)
              ((or (eq (car L) (cadr L))
                   (apply pred (list (car L) (cadr L))))
               (cons (car L) (subsort (cdr L) pred)))  <--
              (t (setq flag t)
                 (cons (cadr L)
                       (subsort (cons (car L) (cddr L)) pred)))))  <--
```

The function which goes in the PRED slot must, of course, be a two-argument
function like LESSP, and it must also be an EXPR. Apart from that, it can be
anything you choose which is suitable for comparing the first and second elements
of a list in order to sort them. Notice that although in the first attempt at
SUBSORT we could have said

```
    ((lessp (car L) (cadr L)) ...
```

we can't now say

```
    ((pred (car L) (cadr L) ...
```

because Lisp would try to evaluate PRED as a function-name. Hence the APPLY.
APPLY itself is quite simple to use, but as you can see it requires the arguments to
the applied function (LESSP or the value of PRED in this case) to be formed into
a LIST. But do check APPLY in the Appendix.

For more information on sorting methods see Knuth (1973).

4.5 Input/Output in Lisp

In this section I'm not talking about the business of saving and reloading your
programs via tape or disc; but about how the things you type at the keyboard get
transferred into Lisp, and about how the values returned by Lisp are typed back to
you. In other words, about how to use Lisp's READ and PRINT functions as
parts of your own programs, just as you have already used EVAL. Under normal
circumstances, the functions which follow would be used within a loop, so that
they could be called over and over again to deal with your successive keyboard
entries. Like this:

```
....
loop
(setq input (READ))
<do clever things with the input — i.e. EVALuate it in some way>
(PRINT <result>)
(go loop)
```

(a) READ and its siblings.

READ is the standard function for accepting your typed input into Lisp. Its most important characteristic is that it waits for more input from you until what you have typed overall is a legal S-expression – atom or list. Most Lisps recognise the carriage-return as the terminator; that is, your S-expression has to be completed by a carriage-return before READ will read it. In some Lisps you have the option of resetting some global system variable so that the S-expression is read as soon as the final balancing bracket (or space, if the S-expression is an atom) is typed. READ does not supply any prompt, but is usually clever enough to recognise and to handle the normal keyboard RUBOUT or DELETE key so that you can correct your entries as you make them.

```
*- (read)
```

> [Lisp waits for an S-expression to be typed, and will not act upon any carriage-return until this happens]

```
foo
```

> [Followed by a carriage-return]

```
FOO
```

> [READ has accepted the S-expression and has read it into Lisp. The value of a call to READ is the expression it has read: no evaluation is involved]

READ is the function to choose when you want to read into a running program things which actually are S-expressions, as in the noughts-and-crosses game in Chapter 6.

READCH may have a different name in your Lisp, but most Lisps have one. It simply reads in from the keyboard the next character to be typed, and returns it:

```
*- (readch)a
```

```
A
```

What READCH does if a carriage-return is typed in place of the "a" varies from Lisp to Lisp.

One thing to be careful of: some READCHs return not the character itself but its ASCII (American Standard Code for Information Interchange) code number. The ASCII code is simply a set of numbers from 1 upwards, each representing a different character. For example, the ASCII code for the lower-case "a" is 97, and for the SPACE it is 32. If your READCH does this, there will certainly be a companion function in your Lisp which converts the ASCII number back into a character.

LINEREAD is less commonly available, but can be very useful if you want your program to interact with non-Lisp-users (see Micro-Eliza, Chapter 7). It takes in everything you type up until a carriage-return and makes a list out of it:

```
*- (lineread)it never rains in southern Milton Keynes <carriage-return>

(IT NEVER RAINS IN SOUTHERN MILTON KEYNES)
```

Beware of READLINE. which exists in some Lisps and works similarly to LINEREAD except that it makes some kind of "atom" out of the result – including the spaces between words in the above example! This could perhaps be useful for printing canned messages such as "Please enter your move", but since the exact behaviour of READLINE can vary drastically from Lisp to Lisp, I don't use it in this book.

(b) Special characters.

The special characters in most microcomputer Lisps are limited to:
    left-hand bracket
    right-hand bracket
    single-quote
    semicolon
    full-stop or dot
    space
    carriage-return
    linefeed

Of the last two, CARRIAGE-RETURN causes the cursor to move back to the start of the line it is on, and LINEFEED causes it to move vertically down to the next line. The carriage-return KEY on the keyboard sends both of these characters to the computer (which then echoes them back to your terminal): first CARRIAGE-RETURN and then LINEFEED.

Most Lisps have a way of printing these characters on their own, should you need to (see below). In a typical Lisp there are "character atoms" which when printed produce the desired thing, for example:

```
*- (print LHB)

(
```

The returned values vary from Lisp to Lisp, as may the names of the actual "character atoms". Larger Lisps permit double-quoted strings of atoms to be printed verbatim, so that the same effect can be achieved.

(c) TERPRI and SPACE.

TERPRI is a function having the same effect on the terminal as a typed carriage-return; that is, the cursor moves from wherever it is to the start of the next line. In some Lisps there is no TERPRI, but instead there is a "character atom" called CR (or something equally obvious!) which can be printed normally. This enables you to "PRINT" a carriage-return in just the same way as you would print an alphabetic character – which is a perfectly sensible alternative to TERPRI itself. Exactly the same remarks apply to the function SPACE, except of course that it prints a space. Both normally return NIL, so beware of using them in AND clauses – if you must, change the AND to a COND.

(d) PRINT and its siblings.

The basic printing function in Lisp is usually called PRIN, although it may alternatively be called PRIN0 or PRIN1. PRIN usually takes just one argument – atom or list – and prints it; but in some Lisps PRIN can be given as many arguments as you like. In the latter case you should expect that PRIN will not insert spaces between its arguments as it prints them, even though you may have done so when you typed them in:

```
*- (prin a b c)

ABC
```

and if you want the spaces you have to use SPACE or your Lisp's equivalent interleaved with the arguments themselves, e.g.:

```
*- (prin a blank b blank c)

A B C
```

In this case BLANK is a "character atom" which is printed as a space.
    Whatever PRIN does, PRINT normally does the same except that it does a carriage-return after printing. Again, it is normally the case that PRINT takes only one argument. Here is the definition of a version which takes multiple arguments and inserts a space after each as it is printed:

```
(defun print args
    (mapc '(lambda (x)
            (prin x)
            (space))
        args)
    (terpri))
```

This is a FEXPR, and returns NIL because TERPRI returns NIL.
    PRINT will often do odd things if asked to print special characters (see above). You can get around this using PRINC, which will accept them as arguments and print them normally. PRINC will also print ordinary characters and S-expressions, and is therefore handy when you want to print several things on the same line. Usually, each call to PRINC is allowed only one argument.

(e) EXPLODE and IMPLODE.

These are used to turn an atom into a list of its separate characters, and back again:

```
*- (setq q (explode 'var))

(V A R)

*- (implode (append q '(1)))

VAR1
```

IMPLODE may alternatively be called READLIST or (rarely) MAKNAM. IMPLODE is a good name for the function if you think of it as the converse of EXPLODE. However, the name READLIST reminds you that it expects its input list to turn into an S-expression, such as might be returned by READ.

Exercise 4.4

Define LINES and SPACES. Each of them takes a single numeric argument, and prints that many carriage-returns or spaces before returning T. (Since these functions are likely to be useful to you in the future, do use your own Lisp's equivalents of TERPRI and SPACE.) LINES and SPACES both return T.

Exercise 4.5

It isn't usually a good idea to redefine the printing functions in any Lisp, since of course it uses them in its normal READ-EVAL-PRINT loop, and you could get some very unexpected effects! However, it is usually safe to define any (such as TERPRI) which may be missing. I'm afraid I can't give you a specific solution to this Exercise since the printing functions in any Lisp tend to be slightly idiosyncratic. But for the purposes of this book you'll need a TERPRI and a PRINT; the latter doing a PRIN followed by a TERPRI – hence its name. (TERPRI, by the way, was used in early Lisps as a signal to the system that it should PRInt the contents of its output buffer to the TERminal.) You should by now be confident enough to write TERPRI and PRINT, or equivalents of them, with the aid of your Lisp manual.

You may also need a PRIN occasionally. For example, in Chapter 5 you'll need to be able to print either an exclamation-mark or a vertical bar; if one of them is available on your keyboard and is not a special character in your Lisp, you're OK. But otherwise you'll need a PRINC. Again, you should by now be able to figure out how to write one.

4.6 Property-lists

Every atom used in Lisp can have associated with it a property-list. The property-list gives you an entirely different way of associating values with the atom. Some Lisps store function definitions on the property-lists of the atomic names of the functions; some store ordinary SETQ bindings on the property-lists of the atoms concerned. Nonetheless, the property-list is used quite differently from DEFUN or SETQ, and can conveniently be thought of as a separate thing – a thing (a list) which is somehow "carried about" with the atom it belongs to, wherever that atom might go.

Essentially, the property-list is a list of associated pairs of things. The first thing in each pair is like an address or heading; the second is a piece of data (an atom, a list, or even a function definition) which you feel should be classified under that heading. So you can alternatively think of the property-list as a table:

	mother	father	brother	sister	
tony					

The atom TONY in the left-hand column has a property-list whose "headings" are the various relationships along the top of the table. The pieces of data stored under each heading are (presumably) the names of TONY's mother, father, etc. Notice that this is a two-dimensional structure of data – whereas the faithful old SETQ can only manage one dimension. Lisp dialects vary in the way they actually store the property-list. Here are two common alternatives:

    (MOTHER <her name> FATHER <his name> BROTHER <his name> SISTER <her name>)

    ((MOTHER . <name>) (FATHER . <name>) (BROTHER . <name>) (SISTER . <name>))

But, exactly how it is stored doesn't matter: there are standard Lisp functions for manipulating property-lists which will work no matter how your particular Lisp does the actual storage.

There are, naturally, correct names for the various parts of the list. The atom whose property-list it is (TONY in the example), is referred to as the IDENTIFIER. The "heading" (MOTHER, FATHER etc.) is called the PROPERTY. And the piece of data stored there (the name of the MOTHER, FATHER etc.) is, confusingly, known as the VALUE. The standard way to put something on a property-list is:

    (put <identifier> <property> <value>)

    [Check PUT in the Appendix]

For example:

    (put 'tony 'sister 'maggie)

This inserts into the above table the name MAGGIE in the row beginning with TONY and in the column headed by SISTER. It doesn't matter whether or not the heading SISTER already exists on TONY's property-list. If it doesn't, PUT will put it there; and if it does, PUT will overwrite with the new datum (MAGGIE) anything which is already stored under that heading. Later on, when you want to find out what value is stored on TONY's property-list under the property SISTER, you do:

    (get 'tony 'sister)

So you can store arbitrary amounts of information on the property-lists of atoms (remember, the data don't have to be simple atoms as in this example), and afterwards you can retrieve any desired bit of it. PUT and GET work very fast: much faster than, say, hunting down an alist with ASSOC, which you will hear about in Chapter 6.

There is also a function REMPROP which will delete any desired property-value pair from the list:

    (remprop 'tony 'sister)

(Whether this deletes the property-name from the list as well as the value, or leaves the property-name and merely sets the value to NIL, varies from Lisp to Lisp and is of minimal importance). If your Lisp has PUT and GET, or equivalent functions, but no REMPROP, define the latter like this:

    *- (defun remprop (id prop)
          (put id prop nil))

This sets any existing value under PROP to NIL, and does not remove the PROP heading itself from the property-list.

The way to inspect a property-list is thus:

    (plist 'tony)
                [Check PLIST in the Appendix]

In some Lisps, as the Appendix will tell you, you use CDR (of a quoted atom!) instead of PLIST. Again, this is because of unimportant differences in the way property-lists are stored.

In the next and subsequent chapters you will see many examples of the usefulness of property-lists.

4.7 Macros

Besides the EXPR and the FEXPR, there is another type of Lisp function called the MACRO. Macros aren't usually permitted in microcomputer Lisps, but they exist in many other programming languages as well as in larger Lisp systems, so it's only fair to give you an idea of what they are.

Essentially, a macro is a function which, when evaluated, yields an S-expression rather than a value. The very fact of it being a macro also ensures that during execution it goes through two rounds of evaluation rather than the normal one: the first round produces the S-expression, and the second (normal) round evaluates that as though IT had been the definition of the macro. In effect, a macro is a function which during execution replaces itself with something else.

What on earth for? Well, you've already seen an example of a macro simulated via a FEXPR in the definition of PROG. There, we used an extra and explicit call to EVAL in order to build precisely the LAMBDA expression we wanted. And this took place BEFORE the normal round of evaluation. In a Lisp which allowed macros, it would be instinctive on the programmer's part to use a macro rather than our FEXPR version, and the effect would be the same. But the code would be easier both to write and to read!

Macros can also be used in the context of home-made data structures (see Chapter 5), and have other advantages where the Lisp has a "compiler" to translate Lisp code into the much faster form known as "machine code".

4.8 A simple tracer

If your Lisp has no TRACE facility, you may by now have felt the need for something which will help you to see exactly what is happening as Lisp works its way through a substantial program. TRACE can help a great deal – at the very least it can tell you precisely in which subroutine an error occurred. So here as an additional project is a simple tracer for you to build. This little utility will trace only your own EXPR definitions – not system functions or FEXPRs. It occupies a little over 2K bytes of memory, which I think you'll agree is well worth it.

The principle behind tracing in Lisp is that a function called TRACE will take the definition of any other function and rewrite it so that it contains extra PRINT statements. The latter will then be printed in the normal way when the function is executed. A companion to TRACE, called UNTRACE, restores the modified function definition to normal, so that the extra PRINT statements no longer appear. Tracers print the name of the function as control enters it during execution, plus the values of its formal parameters. As control exits from the function, they print its returned value and a suitable ending message. The one I'm about to show you will print "Enter" and "Exit" when appropriate, plus the relevant values. Tracers can be very much more elaborate than this.

So the first thing we need is a way of storing the original version of a function definition. Then TRACE can do what it likes to the definition, and "restoring" it will simply be a matter of replacing the TRACE-modified version with the stored original.

Your Lisp will itself store function definitions either as the bound VALUES of their atomic function-names, or as the EXPR (or FEXPR) properties of the same atoms. You can find out which by looking in your manual, or by the following test. If you type the function name with no brackets, as though it were the name of a variable, the function definition will be returned if your Lisp stores definitions as bound values. Otherwise, if it stores them on property-lists, the definition will be returned if you call PLIST with the function-name as its argument. So let's write a retriever which will return the function's definition. For Lisps which store definitions as bound values:

```
(defun get-def (fn)
  (and (listp (eval fn))
       (eq (car (eval fn)) 'lambda))
```

```
                (or (null (second (eval fn)))
                    (listp (second (eval fn))))
                (eval fn)))
```

This checks that the function-name's bound value is a LIST, whose first element is the atom LAMBDA. Then it checks that the second element of the list (the LAMBDA expression's variables-slot) is either NIL or a list. If it were a non-nil atom, this would signify that the function was a FEXPR. If all is well, GET-DEF returns the LAMBDA expression. For Lisps which store definitions on property-lists:

```
    (defun get-def (fn)
      (get fn 'expr))
```

Right. Now we need to save that definition away somewhere so that UNTRACE can restore it later. As good a place as any is the property-list of the atom TRACE itself:

```
    (put 'trace fn (get-def fn))
```

So, if you decide to have several routines within your program traced at once, the definition of each will be put onto TRACE's property-list under its own name.

Let's call the traced function FOO (as you may have gathered, words such as FOO, BAZ and GORT are universally used by programmers to denote functions of no specific purpose, used as examples!). The tracer will create a temporary version of FOO, which in fact will not look anything like the original version at all. When you run the program of which FOO is a part, the traced version of FOO will be evaluated by EVAL in the normal course of events. What EVAL will find inside FOO is a series of instructions to PRINT this and that, and an instruction to APPLY the original version of FOO – retrieved at this point from TRACE's property-list – to its normal arguments. The clever touch lies in the fact that the traced version of FOO is a LAMBDA expression having the same formal parameters as the original FOO, so that in the course of evaluation these get bound in the normal way to the arguments which FOO gets as the program runs. It (the traced version) also takes care to return the result of APPLY, so that its net effect on the program itself is exactly the same as that of the original version.

The only difficult thing about TRACE is that it works like a macro: it has to contain instructions which actually WRITE a new definition of FOO. That makes the code of FOO itself hard for humans to read. The idea is that the code of TRACE is evaluated when you call TRACE, and the result of that evaluation is a LAMBDA expression. When FOO is called – by itself or from within a larger program – the LAMBDA expression is evaluated in its place, so generating the "Enter" and "Exit" messages. My advice is that, as when trying to understand PROG in Chapter 3, you pretend to be EVAL and see what you make of it. Here's a line from TRACE:

```
    (list 'print (list 'list ''enter fn))
```

That says: make a list of two elements, the first being a quoted atom whose value is

84

PRINT; for the second element, make another list, this time of three elements, the first being the atom LIST. The second element of the second list is the double-quoted atom ENTER, which evaluates (reasonably enough) to a single-quoted ENTER. And the final element is FN, which in this case evaluates to FOO. So EVAL will turn that into

```
(print (list 'enter foo))
```

which, as you can see, is a normal Lisp instruction. TRACE will create the traced version of FOO out of a series of such lines, and when the program containing FOO runs they will be evaluted in the normal way to print, in this case,

```
(ENTER FOO)
```

Now let's consider what we would like the traced version of FOO to look like. This is the new form of FOO's definition which will be passed to EVAL in the normal way when FOO is called from within your program. It has to be a LAMBDA expression as all function definitions are, and to take the same formal parameters as does FOO itself. Let's say for the moment that FOO's parameters are X and Y. Beyond that, we want the LAMBDA expression to print "Enter" and "Exit" as it is evaluated:

```
(lambda (x y)
   (printc 'enter 'foo)
   (printc 'exit 'foo))
```

This, if typed directly into Lisp, would generate "ENTER FOO" and "EXIT FOO", each on a new line as required. The function PRINTC is like PRINC, except that it does a carriage-return first, prints as many arguments as you like, and prints a space after each. It is a FEXPR:

```
(defun printc L
   (terpri)
   (map '(lambda (e)
           (princ e) (spaces 1))
        L))
```

The next stage is to get the LAMBDA expression to print the values of X and Y after "Enter", and to apply the ORIGINAL definition of FOO to a list of X and Y:

```
(lambda (x y)
   (printc 'enter 'foo)
   (princ <values of X and Y>)                              <--
   (apply '<original definition of FOO> (<values of X and Y>)) <--
   (printc 'exit 'foo))
```

Notice the PRINC on the third line – I want the values of X and Y to be printed

85

alongside the "Enter FOO" announcement, rather than on a new line. APPLY is going to be given the original defintion of FOO directly – i.e. it will also be a LAMBDA expression – and therefore the latter will need to be quoted.

The next thing is to arrange for the result of that APPLY to be held in a temporary variable, so that it can be printed alongside the "Exit FOO" announcement. More importantly, we want the trace version of FOO to return that result, just as the normal FOO would. Otherwise, the traced FOO would not work properly inside your program:

```
(lambda (x y)
  (prog (trace)                                        <--
    (printc 'enter 'foo)
    (princ <values of X and Y>)
    (setq trace (apply '<original definition of FOO>   <--
                    (<values of X and Y>)))            <--
    (printc 'exit 'foo trace)                          <--
    trace))                                            <--
```

I've called the temporary variable TRACE, just to keep things tidy: everything connected with a traced function will be associated in some way with the atom TRACE — as the original definition of FOO will be. It has to be a local variable, whose value is saved on entry to the LAMBDA expression and restored on exit, because if you were to trace several functions at once, or if a traced function were recursive, its value would be reset repeatedly. So a simple global variable won't do.

There is just one more thing to arrange: the traced output will be very much more readable if it is indented according to the number of recursive levels deep at which FOO is executed. Imagining for a moment that FOO itself is a recursive function, we would hope for a printout something like this:

```
Enter FOO 4 (A B C D E)
 Enter FOO 3 (B C D E)
  Enter FOO 2 (C D E)
   Enter FOO 1 (D E)
   Exit FOO D
  Exit FOO D
 Exit FOO D
Exit FOO D
```

(In this case, FOO is NTH, of course.) The indenting is easy to arrange, because this time we CAN use a global variable to hold the current level of indenting. In fact it is convenient not to use a variable in the normal sense at all, but to PUT the current value onto TRACE's property-list:

```
(lambda (x y)
  (prog (trace)
    (spaces (get 'trace 'stack))                       <--
    (printc 'enter 'foo)
    (princ <values of X and Y>)
```

86

```
(put 'trace 'stack (plus (get 'trace 'stack) 1))        <--
(setq trace (apply '<original definition of FOO>
(<values of X and Y>)))
(put 'trace 'stack (difference (get 'trace 'stack) 1))  <--
(spaces (get 'trace 'stack))                            <--
(printc 'exit 'foo trace)
trace))
```

Right. Now comes the difficulty of defining TRACE2, which is a subroutine to the top-level TRACE function and which actually writes the above LAMBDA expression. It isn't really hard in principle, but can get very confusing! Having created the LAMBDA expression, it will put it in place of FOO's original definition, a copy of which is by now safely stored on the property-list of TRACE. That complication is disposed of by PUT-DEF, which is the inverse of GET-DEF. Again there have to be two alternative versions. For Lisps which store function-definitions as bound values:

```
(defun put-def (fn lambda-exp)
  (set fn lambda-exp))
```

And for Lisps which store them as properties:

```
(defun put-def (fn lambda-exp)
  (put fn 'expr lambda-exp))
```

A LAMBDA expression, as you know, is a three-element list consisting of the atom LAMBDA, a sublist of variables, and a series of S-expressions forming the body of the function. So:

```
(defun trace2 (fn)
  (put-def fn (list 'lambda (second (get 'trace fn))
                    <body>)))
```

This would evaluate to

```
(put-def 'foo '(lambda (x y) <body>))
```

which is exactly right, as far as it goes. FOO's formal parameters X and Y are retrieved from the original version of FOO and appear in their correct place in the LAMBDA expression.

The BODY of the expression begins with a PROG and its list of variables, followed by a series of S-expressions:

```
(defun trace2 (fn)
  (put-def fn (list 'lambda (cadr (get 'trace fn))
                    (list 'prog '(trace)
                          <S-expressions>))))
```

which would evaluate to:

```
(put-def 'foo '(lambda (x y)
            (prog (trace)
              <S-expressions>)))
```

Now to the S-expressions themselves. Remember, the LAMBDA expression is created by EVALUATION of TRACE2, so the latter has to contain code such as will evaluate to the instructions we want. Here's the first:

```
(defun trace2 (fn)
   (put-def fn (list 'lambda (cadr (get 'trace fn))
              (list 'prog '(trace)
                    (list 'spaces (list 'get ''trace ''stack))   <--
                    <remaining S-expressions>))))
```

It says: make a two-element list out of the atom SPACES and a sublist of three elements, the first being the atom GET, the second being the QUOTED atom TRACE, and the third being the quoted atom STACK:

```
(spaces (get 'trace 'stack))
```

So this line will print spaces corresponding to the current value of TRACE's STACK property every time the traced version of FOO is executed. The next S-expression is easy:

```
(defun trace2 (fn)
   (put-def fn (list 'lambda (cadr (get 'trace fn))
              (list 'prog '(trace)
                    (list 'spaces (list 'get ''trace ''stack))
                    (list 'printc ''Enter (list 'quote fn))   <--
                    <remaining S-expressions>))))
```

This will become (PRINTC 'Enter 'FOO) if FOO is the traced function, (PRINTC 'Enter 'BAZ) if BAZ is the traced function, and so on. Incidentally, if your PRINC works the way mine does, it will print "Enter" and "Exit" in partial lower case, which looks much nicer than all upper case. Notice the trick of writing (LIST 'QUOTE FN). Under normal circumstances, if you type a quoted atom into Lisp, the quote-sign acts as a function in its own right:

```
'tony  becomes  (quote tony)
```

Here, we are telling Lisp to make a list of the (quoted) atom QUOTE and the value of FN. Hence, it returns "(QUOTE FOO)" which is the same thing as 'FOO.

Now we need a list of the actual VALUES of FOO's arguments. The traced version of FOO is a perfectly normal function-definition, so its variables will as usual be bound during evaluation to the arguments with which it was called. Inside

your program the call is (FOO <arg1> <arg2>), and so the variables of the
LAMBDA expression, which we have taken care are identical to those of the
untraced version of FOO, get bound to ARG1 and ARG2. Within the LAMBDA
expression, the variables can simply be evaluated whenever their values are
wanted:

```
(defun trace2 (fn)
  (put-def fn
           (list 'lambda (cadr (get 'trace fn))
                 (list 'prog '(trace)
                       (list 'spaces (list 'get ''trace ''stack))
                       (list 'printc ''Enter (list 'quote fn))
              -->       (list 'princ
              -->          (list 'mapcar ''eval
              -->             (list 'cadr (list 'get ''trace
              -->                               (list 'quote fn)))))
                       <remaining S-expressions>))))
```

Notice the double-quoted EVAL. This latest line evaluates to:

```
(princ (mapcar 'eval (second (get 'trace 'foo))))
```

The next line is easy again:

```
(defun trace2 (fn)
  (put-def
    fn
    (list 'lambda (cadr (get 'trace fn))
          (list 'prog '(trace)
                (list 'spaces (list 'get ''trace ''stack))
                (list 'printc ''Enter (list 'quote fn))
                (list 'princ
                   (list 'mapcar ''eval
                      (list 'cadr (list 'get ''trace
                                        (list 'quote fn)))))
                (list 'put ''trace ''stack                        <--
                   (list 'plus (list 'get  ''trace ''stack) 1))   <--
                <remaining S-expressions>))))
```

and becomes:

```
(put 'trace 'stack (plus (get 'trace 'stack) 1))
```

Now comes the nub of it: the APPLY instruction which makes the
LAMBDA expression behave exactly like the real FOO, as far as your program is
concerned:

89

```
        (defun trace2 (fn)
          (put-def
              fn
              (list 'lambda (cadr (get 'trace fn))
                    (list 'prog '(trace)
                          (list 'spaces (list 'get ''trace ''stack))
                          (list 'printc ''Enter (list 'quote fn))
                          (list 'princ
                                (list 'mapcar ''eval
                                      (list 'cadr (list 'get ''trace
                                                        (list 'quote fn)))))
                          (list 'put ''trace ''stack
                                (list 'plus (list 'get  ''trace ''stack) 1))
        -->               (list 'setq 'trace
        -->                     (list 'apply (list 'quote
        -->                                        (list 'get ''trace
        -->                                              (list 'quote fn)))
        -->                            (list 'mapcar ''eval
        -->                                  (list 'cadr
        -->                                        (list 'get ''trace
        -->                                              (list 'quote fn))))))
                          <remaining S-expressions>))))
```

which turns into:

```
        (setq trace (apply (list 'quote (get 'trace 'foo))
                           (mapcar 'eval (cadr
                                          (get 'trace 'foo)))))
```

and when it is later evaluated as FOO itself runs:

```
        (setq trace (apply '<definition of FOO> (<values of X and Y>)))
```

And the rest is pretty much a repeat of what you've seen already:

```
        (defun trace2 (fn)
          (put-def
              fn
              (list 'lambda (cadr (get 'trace fn))
                    (list 'prog '(trace)
                          (list 'spaces (list 'get ''trace ''stack))
                          (list 'printc ''Enter (list 'quote fn))
                          (list 'princ
                                (list 'mapcar ''eval
                                      (list 'cadr (list 'get ''trace
                                                        (list 'quote fn)))))
                          (list 'put ''trace ''stack
                                (list 'plus (list 'get  ''trace ''stack) 1))
                          (list 'setq 'trace
                                (list 'apply (list 'quote
                                                   (list 'get ''trace
```

```
                                                        (list 'quote fn)))
                                    (list 'mapcar ''eval
                                                (list 'cadr
                                                      (list 'get ''trace
                                                            (list 'quote fn))))))
                        (list 'put ''trace ''stack
                              (list 'difference (list 'get ''trace ''stack) 1))
                        (list 'spaces (list 'get ''trace ''stack))
                        (list 'printc ''Exit (list 'quote fn) 'trace)
                        'trace)))
```

OK so far? Don't worry: if you've understood all that, the rest of the tracer will be trivial by comparison. Here's the top-level function TRACE:

```
(defun trace fns
   (put 'trace 0 'stack)
   (map '(lambda (fn)
           (cond ((and (get-def fn)
                       (not (memq fn (get 'trace 'tracedfns))))
                  (put 'trace 'fn (get-def fn))
                  (trace2 fn)
                  (addprop 'trace 'tracedfns fn)))
                 (t (print (list fn 'not 'traceable)))))
        fns)
   (get 'trace 'tracedfns))
```

TRACE is a FEXPR, so that you can give it as many functions to trace as you like when you call it from top level. It contains a mapping function which does the same thing to each member of FNS. The mapping function contains a COND, which essentially is there to check that any function to be traced is suitable for tracing – in our terms this means that it must be an EXPR only. So the COND calls GET-DEF to make the necessary tests on FN. Then, provided the FN isn't traced already (which can be found out from yet another list kept on TRACE's property-list) it saves away the original version of FN's definition and calls TRACE2 to create the traced version.

TRACE returns the list of traced functions. Since you will almost invariably be using TRACE from top level, this returned value will be printed for you to see. And if at any time you forget exactly which functions ARE traced, you can find out very easily by calling TRACE with no arguments.

Now UNTRACE:

```
(defun untrace fns
   (cond ((null fns) (setq fns (untrace2)))
         (t (mapc '(lambda (fn)
                      (and (memq fn (get 'trace 'tracedfns))
                           (put-def fn (get 'trace 'fn))
                           (put 'trace 'tracedfns
                                (delete fn (get 'trace 'tracedfns)))
                           (remprop 'trace fn)))
                   fns)))
   (put 'trace 'stack 0)
   fns)                          91
```

Considering the second COND clause first, UNTRACE checks that the FN to be untraced is in fact traced, and if so restores to it its original definition as stored on TRACE's property-list, and removes that property-list entry. Hence the need to check that FN is traced first: if it weren't, the PUT-DEF instruction would PUT NIL, cleverly destroying FN's definition altogether. At the same time it DELETEs FN from the list of traced functions.

UNTRACE returns the list of untraced functions. However, to save you unnecessary typing, it will be possible to call UNTRACE with no arguments, whereupon it will understand that it is to untrace everything which currently is traced. And that is the purpose of UNTRACE2 in the first COND clause. It retrieves from TRACE's property-list the full list of traced functions and applies UNTRACE to each. Then it returns the list of untraced functions:

```
(defun untrace2 ()
  (setq fns (get 'trace 'tracedfns))
  (mapc '(lambda (fn)
           (eval (list 'untrace fn)))
        fns)
  fns)
```

UNTRACE itself also resets the STACK counter to zero. The assumption is that, if FOO runs correctly, the counter will normally be returned to zero anyway. But if an error in FOO causes evaluation to stop prematurely this may not be the case. It is likely that then you would want to edit FOO, to put right the error. But the existing "definition" of FOO is the traced version – not the original one which you want to edit. So you need to modify your EDIT function. Or, more precisely, you need to write a new edit function which calls your old one, but does an UNTRACE before and a TRACE afterwards. That way, traced functions can be edited normally, but will still be traced (in their edited form) when the edit is finished. If your EDIT function is an EXPR (if you have to quote the function to be edited) do this:

```
(defun edit2 (fn)
  (eval (list 'untrace fn))
  (edit fn)
  (eval (list 'trace fn)))
```

If, as is more likely, it is a FEXPR, do this:

```
(defun edit2 fn
  (setq fn (car fn))
  (eval (list 'untrace fn))
  (eval (list 'edit fn))
  (eval (list 'trace fn)))
```

The point of the (LIST 'UNTRACE...) is that UNTRACE is a FEXPR, so to write

```
(untrace fn)
```

would result in UNTRACE trying to untrace a function called FN, rather than a function whose name was the VALUE of FN. The same applies to the other (LIST '... ...) lines.

Now you can try your tracer out on, say, NTH. You should get a printout similar to the above, and the original version of NTH should be safely stored away on TRACE's property-list. If you have problems, you can of course also inspect the traced version of NTH, to see where it differs from the desired LAMBDA list. This will help you to find any errors in TRACE2.

Finally, you may have minor problems with differences between my Lisp's printing functions and yours. Remember, it is always possible to write tailor-made printing functions like PRINTC to produce the effects you want using more basic system functions.

4.9 Summary

In this chapter you have been introduced to the following Lisp terminology:

BOOLEAN function	AND, OR, NOT and NULL.
PREDICATE	a function whose purpose is to perform a test, and (usually) to return either T or NIL.
PREFIX NOTATION	a different way of ordering the items in an arithmetical expression, so that the order corresponds to that of a Lisp S-expression.
SORTING	has in Lisp exactly the same connotations as it has in English.
MACRO	an advanced type of function which rewrites itself in use. Rarely available in small Lisps.
SPECIAL CHARACTER	a character such as LINEFEED, which is not treated as a normal alphanumeric character by READ.

and you have been introduced to the following Lisp system functions:

AND	returns T if all of its arguments return T; otherwise it returns NIL.
OR	returns NIL if all of its arguments return NIL; otherwise it returns T.
NOT	returns T if its single argument returns NIL, and vice versa.
NULL	same as NOT.

GREATERP	returns T if its first argument is numerically greater than its second argument.
LESSP	returns T if its first argument is numerically less than its second argument.
PLUS	returns the arithmetical sum of its two arguments.
DIFFERENCE	returns the result of subtracting its second argument from its first argument, both of them being numbers.
TIMES	returns the product of its two numerical arguments.
QUOTIENT	returns the result of dividing its first argument by its second argument, both of them being numbers.
REMAINDER	returns the remainder of dividing its first argument by its second, both of them being numbers.
READ	takes in one S-expression (an atom or a list) from the keyboard. If READ is called explicitly in a program, the S-expression — READ's "argument" — is not evaluated, but is returned verbatim by READ.
READCH	similar to READ except that it reads just one character.
READLINE	similar to READ except that it takes in everything typed up as far as a carriage-return and returns a LIST of it.
TERPRI	is a function of no arguments which has the same effect on the screen as a typed carriage-return.
SPACE	is a function of no arguments which prints one space.
PRIN	takes one argument, and prints it with no spaces or TERPRIs.
PRINT	takes a single argument. It PRINs the argument, then does a carriage-return.
EXPLODE	takes one S-expression as its argument and returns a list of the single characters which make up that argument.

94

IMPLODE	takes a list of single characters and forms them into an S-expression.
PUT	places a VALUE on the property-list of an IDENTIFIER, as one of that identifier's PROPERTIES.
GET	retrieves a value from an identifier's property-list.
REMPROP	deletes a value from an identifier's property-list.

4.10 Answers to Exercises

Exercise 4.1

```
(and (not (or a b)))
```

returns T if both A and B evaluate to NIL. Returns NIL in all other cases.

```
(not (or a b))
```

returns T if neither A nor B evaluates to T. Otherwise it returns NIL.

```
(or a b (not (or c d)))
```

If both A and B evaluate to NIL, and if either C or D evaluates to T, this returns NIL. If either A or B evaluates to T, or if both C and D evaluate to NIL, it returns T

```
(or (and a b) (not (and c d)))
```

If both A and B evaluate to T, or if either C or D evaluates to NIL, this returns T. Otherwise, it returns NIL.

Maybe now you see why I suggested avoiding large Boolean constructions!

Exercise 4.2

```
(defun lessp (a b)
  (and (not (greaterp a b))
       (not (eq a b))))

(defun zerop (n)
  (eq n 0))

(defun onep (n)
  (eq n 1))
```

Exercise 4.3

```
(plus 3 (times 4 7))
(times 4 (plus 3 7))

(quotient 100 (plus (times 5 2) 8))
```

Exercise 4.4

```
(defun lines (n)
  (cond ((zerop n) t)
        (t (terpri)
           (lines (difference n 1)))))

(defun spaces (n)
  (cond ((zerop n) t)
        (t (space)
           (spaces (difference n 1)))))
```

Chapter 5
Project – noughts and crosses

This project is a program to play noughts and crosses (in America it's called tic-tac-toe). It will illustrate most of the programming principles mentioned above, besides being – I hope – fun. But its main purpose is to take you step by step through the actual process of constructing a Lisp program – program specification, data representation, procedure algorithm and coding. Please don't (this means you) simply type the code into your computer and then assume that you've "done" this chapter. I want you to understand how each piece of code was chosen, why it is there, and why the code as given is or is not sufficient. In my experience, the actual writing of the code is the easiest, the most trivial, part of the whole business of programming. Right: homily over, now read on.

5.1 Program specification

Noughts and crosses is a structured game. That is to say, from any given board position there is a definite sequence of moves which will lead inevitably to a win – or at least to a draw. To see what this means, consider the winning line:

X X X

This line, in any direction in which it will fit on the board, represents a win for the player playing X. Now consider what must have been X's previous position:

X X -   or   X - X

(—X X is the same as the first of these cases, turned through 180 degrees.) Under such circumstances, O is forced to play on the vacant square, or lose. The previous situation in the sequence is the situation which must produce this same "forcing" pattern, i.e.:

```
X X -     X - X     X X -
X - -     - - -     - - -
- - -     X - -     X - -
```

A triple threat is also possible:

```
X - X
- X -
- - -
```

And that's about as far back as you can follow the sequence in noughts and crosses. There are other games (in particular a Japanese one called Go-Moku, where the board is 19 squares by 19 and the object is to achieve a line of five Xs or Os) in which this kind of "route to a win" structure can be greatly extended. But the point is that the structure defines each player's OBJECTIVES during the course of the game: to make moves such that a step in the structure becomes a part of his/her overall board position, and at the same time to obstruct the opponent's efforts to achieve the same thing. Once any step in the structure has been actualised on the board, the player it belongs to knows that he/she will win. If you think for a moment about your own tactics when playing noughts and crosses, I think you'll agree that that is a fair description of what goes on in your mind, even though you may never have heard it expressed in just that way before.

Since the game is structured, and so is a game of skill rather than a game of chance, we can state our program's first specification:

S1) it must be able to respond to any board position in such a way as to maximise its own chances of winning.

This automatically implies the second specification:

S2) it must be able to judge the "worth" of any board position or potential board position.

And this in turn leads to specification number three:

S3) it must be able to represent (= describe) any board position.

Besides these goals, our program will also have to take care of a number of relatively boring book-keeping details. First, at any moment it will need to know what squares remain available for its or its opponent's next move. One easy way to keep track of this is to have a running list of what squares are NOT available (because they have been moved upon already) and to "subtract" this from an inbuilt representation of the empty board. This section of any board game playing program is known as the Plausible-Moves Generator. We shall only need a very simple one, but in more complicated games it is often worthwhile in terms of processing time to restrict the list of empty squares according to some suitable criterion of "plausibility".

So:

S4) Plausible-moves generation.

Next, our program needs to be able to interact with its opponent: to accept a typed-in version of his/her moves and to translate it, if necessary, so that it will fit into the machine's own internal representation of the state of play. Much of what goes on here is duplicated by the functions which generate the machine's own move:

S5)   Mymove/Yourmove sequences.

There is then the question of generating a screen (or teletype) "picture" of the current state of play – that is, of the board including all moves made so far – and of updating it as each successive move is made by either player:

S6)   Display function.

And finally, we need an overall master routine to tie all of this together so that things happen in the right order and stop when a win occurs:

S7)   Master routine.

5.2 The main loop

The above is known in computer jargon as a "top-down" analysis of the problem: starting with its most complex aspect and gradually decomposing it into simpler and simpler parts. So, on the principle that even a small success works wonders for the ego, let's start by writing the code for S7. Look at the following:

```
(defun play ()
  (prog (won)
   loop
    (yourmove)
    (display)
    (mymove)
    (display)
    (cond ((not won)
           (go loop))
          (t (return nil))))))
```

For our purposes here, the essential things you should recall about the PROG construct are: (a) it has a slot for variables; and the values of these variables are set to NIL as the PROG is entered, and restored to any values they may previously have had when the PROG ends. Within the PROG, the value of any of those variables can be anything you care to make it. (b) PROG allows a LOOP arrangement similar to the GOTOs found in other languages. And (c) the loop can be halted at any time via a RETURN, whereupon the value returned by the whole PROG is that specified as the argument to RETURN. All of these things are to be found in PLAY.

PLAY's PROG has a local variable called WON, whose value on entering the PROG is as usual NIL. Control (what the computer is actually doing) then cycles round and round the loop until such time as something somewhere sets WON to T, at which point the conditional test RETURNs, the loop is therefore exited from, and the game stops. To restart, PLAY must be called again –

whereupon WON will again be initialised to NIL.

Now to what happens inside the loop – what happens over and over, in the same sequence, until the game ends. We're going to need three things, not necessarily in the order in which they are described here. First, a DISPLAY of the current state of the board, with all the appropriate Xs and Os appearing in the right places. DISPLAY will refer, in order to find out what should be printed where, to some kind of database, or internal representation of the board and the moves, and this representation will be continually updated by the routines YOURMOVE and MYMOVE.

Next, the function YOURMOVE, which will ask the human player to enter his/her next move. It will translate this entry into the form needed by the internal representation, and will update DISPLAY's database.

Then, a second DISPLAY, to reassure the human player that his/her move has been entered correctly, followed by MYMOVE. The latter is really a sort of sub-master-routine, since it will have its own set of subroutines which concern themselves with plausible-move generation, board-state evaluation – including checking for a win – and the updating of DISPLAY's database which must take place once the machine's move has been selected.

And that's it. If we can get all of that to work, we'll have a noughts and crosses program which will at least play responsively. Refining it so that it becomes difficult, or perhaps impossible, to beat is something which I hope you will feel able to tackle yourself by the end of this chapter.

5.3 The display

Now let's look at PLAY's subroutines in turn. DISPLAY is not only the first but in some respects the easiest. It needs to do two things at the same time: to print out a representation of the empty board, and to superimpose upon that any necessary Xs or Os. So, again, let's take the simpler problem first and generate a picture of the board alone. In other words, we want to display a cross-hatch of nine empty squares. Have a look around your keyboard to see what symbols look suitable. For the vertical lines, you'll see that you have a choice of ¦ or !. And for the horizontals there are the underline and the hyphen. But there are a couple of problems (of course!) here already. Both the vertical bar ¦ and the exclamation-mark ! can be special symbols in some Lisps, as the single quote should be in all of them. And it may be difficult to PRINT a special character. Have a look in your Lisp manual: it will tell you if either of these characters is special, or if your Lisp has a function – probably called PRINC – which will print them anyway. If all else fails, you'll have to make do with a capital I, I'm afraid!

As far as the horizontals are concerned, neither of the available lines looks convincing (try them), and the terminal won't let you put anything in the square immediately above either of them without special arrangements which for our purposes simply aren't worth the hassle. So what I suggest is that we leave out the horizontals altogether, but use the hyphen to denote the CENTRE of an empty square. This will result in a display which looks like this:

```
- ! - ! -
- ! - ! -
- ! - ! -
```

and later, with a few moves made in a game, it'll look like this:

```
- ! X ! 0
X ! 0 ! -
- ! - ! -
```

If you think that looks OK, read on. If not, have fun trying to do better!

Now then, in the computer's terms, the above empty diagram is composed of three sequential lines of type. Each consists of a hyphen, a space, an exclamation-mark, another space, another hyphen, another space, another exclamation-mark, another space, and another hyphen:

```
(print '(- ! - ! -))
```

But actually, that isn't really what we want, because later in the program we're going to require the same instruction (the same line of DISPLAY) effectively to be something like:

```
(print '(- ! X ! 0))
```

That's awkward. But the way to get around it is to make the hyphen – which will later be changed into an X or an O – the VALUE of a variable. So PRINT's argument will be a list which will consist of our three variables interleaved with the symbol "!". If we quote the latter but not the variable-names, the exclamation-marks will be printed verbatim, but the variables will be evaluated:

```
(print (list var1 '! var2 '! var3))
```

The PRINT in your Lisp may require you to insert some indication that there are spaces between the elements of the list. But there's one more thing we can usefully do before we actually write the code for DISPLAY. And that is to think ahead to how we're going to represent the various states of the board as the game progresses. Remember that we're going to insert the various Xs and Os by changing the values of var1, var2, var3 and so on. But we can't really expect our human players to type in things like (setq var1 'x). They're going to want to type something which obviously "means" the square onto which they intend to move, and they'll expect the machine to do the rest of the work. So let's, right here at the outset, simplify the job of any translating procedures we may need later by giving our nine variables (one for each square of the board) the very names that human players will type in. For example:

```
a1 ! a2 ! a3
b1 ! b2 ! b3
c1 ! c2 ! c3
```

That is, in order to specify the centre square, a player types simply "b2". So now we can put as the command in DISPLAY:

```
(print (list a1 '! a2 '! a3))
```

and all will be well. Here's the whole thing:

```
(defun display ()
  (print (list a1 '! a2 '! a3))
  (print (list b1 '! b2 '! b3))
  (print (list c1 '! c2 '! c3)))
```

A further refinement, whilst we're at it, would be to put an extra carriage-return before and after the clump of three program lines, so that successive activations of DISPLAY are clearly separated from one another. In my Lisp you can do that by calling the function TERPRI:

```
(defun display ()
  (terpri)
  (print (list a1 '! a2 '! a3))
  (print (list b1 '! b2 '! b3))
  (print (list c1 '! c2 '! c3))
  (terpri))
```

I have assumed here that your PRINT function does a carriage-return after printing. Otherwise, the fact that the three PRINT statements in the PROGRAM are on different lines doesn't automatically guarantee that they will be PRINTED on different lines!

By the way, don't be confused by the fact that each PRINT list, as well as the last board-diagram above, is longer than we actually want our printout to be. This is only because a1, for example, is longer than the single character (X, O or –) which is its VALUE, and which PRINT will actually print.

Anyway, assuming that you have discovered how to use your PRINT, I'd like you to type DISPLAY in, to set all the variables to some values (using SETQ) and to try it out. I think that to see the Xs and Os appear as you change the values of the corresponding variables will give you a better feel for what is to follow than any amount of description from me. If you've done that, it will probably occur to you that you won't want the bother of setting all nine variables to '– at the start of each game. And the golden rule of programming is: if you don't want to do something, get the machine to do it. So your first exercise in this chapter is to write a routine called SETUP which does exactly that (Exercise 5.1). Here's where it will go:

```
(defun play ()
  (setup)        <---
  (prog (won)
   loop
    (yourmove)
    (display)
    (mymove)
    (display)
    (cond ((not won)
           (go loop))
          (t (return nil))))))
```

The solution is at the end of this chapter, because I'd hate you to give up this project if you can't see how to do it. But do have a try on your own before peeping!

102

In the latest version of PLAY, there is no particular reason why SETUP appears before the PROG. It could just as effectively go inside it, just before the LOOP. But conceptually it is no part of the PROG, so to make its purpose and its relation to the loop easier to see by simple inspection, I've put it outside. At the same time, partly as a check that SETUP has operated correctly and partly because it's nice to start a game with a picture of an empty board, let's put an extra call to DISPLAY immediately after the call to SETUP:

```
(defun play ()
 (setup)
 (display)      <---
 (prog (won)
 loop
  (yourmove)
  (display)
  (mymove)
  (display)
  (cond ((not won)
         (go loop))
        (t (return nil))))))
```

And that's all of PLAY. You can try it out, if you like, by typing

```
(play)
```

SETUP should work, and if DISPLAY works as well you'll get a picture of an empty board. But of course the program will bomb out, and you'll get an error message from Lisp, as soon as it hits the call to YOURMOVE.

5.4 YOURMOVE

Compared to MYMOVE, which follows shortly, YOURMOVE is a doddle. So I'm going to get a lot of in-depth explaining out of the way in this section, in the hope that it'll make subsequent sections easier. All that YOURMOVE has to do is take the human player's input, set its value to X or to O as appropriate, and update some list of moves made so far. First, though, let's make a few arbitrary decisions which will make our job a bit easier. Most people seem to prefer to play X, so let's say that our machine is going to be very polite and will offer them X automatically. (That's another way of saying that we're not even going to allow them the choice.) Secondly, let's say that for similar reasons the human player always gets the advantage of the first move, and that therefore the order within PLAY of YOURMOVE and MYMOVE can stay as it is. I hope, anyway, that by the time you get to the end of this chapter you'll be expert enough to build into your program the necessary adjustments to make such choices available to its opponents. To worry about them now would just clutter us up with unnecessary details.

Have a look at this, as a first attempt at writing YOURMOVE:

```
(defun yourmove ()
 (prog (input)
```

103

```
(print (list 'please 'enter 'your 'move))
(setq input (read))
(set input 'x)))
```

Notice first of all that the PROG construct gives us a local variable, safely "isolated" from any other use which the same name may acquire in other parts of our overall program. This variable, INPUT, will serve merely as a convenient place to store the opponent's typed-in move so that we can do various things with it. The Lisp function READ reads in one S-expression (in this case an atom such as "a2") from the keyboard – and of course it can only do so once, which is why we need to "hold" whatever it returns in INPUT. When YOURMOVE is finished and working, computation will halt when it reaches the call to READ, and will wait for something (plus a carriage-return or – in some Lisps – a space) to be typed in at the keyboard. This is a part of what READ "does", so we won't have to make any special arrangements to achieve it. Also, what the opponent types in at this point doesn't need to be quoted. Remember the READ-EVAL-PRINT loop? There, READ does its stuff and is finished with long before EVAL ever gets its hands on whatever has been typed in. That is, READ does not normally evaluate things, so we needn't expect it to do so here. The result is that the opponent's move is typed in as the bare atom: no quotes, no double quotes, no brackets, no nothing. In case you're wondering, the reason for the variable INPUT is that we shall need to use its value again as YOURMOVE develops. Otherwise, the last two lines above could have been combined as:

```
(set (read) 'x)
```

Notice that the value-assignment instruction in the last line is SET and not SETQ. Why? Because in this case we don't want to bind the value 'X to the variable-name INPUT, but to INPUT's VALUE, which is something like "a1". Looking at it another way, we want EVAL to evaluate INPUT, putting "a1" in its place, before applying SET. So the SETQ shorthand is inappropriate here.

OK – that's the first part of YOURMOVE's job done. Now we need to update that aforementioned list of moves-so-far. Since we intend to use it as a representation of the current board state at any moment, let's call it simply BOARD. It'll be a list – or rather, BOARD will be a variable whose VALUE is a list. But, again thinking ahead, we need such a list for two purposes. The trivial one is to be able to point out the fact if the opponent tries to place a move on a square which has already been used; but the more interesting purpose of BOARD is to enable an evaluator (one we write ourselves – not to be confused with Lisp's EVAL) to calculate the machine's most effective reply to anything the opponent does. Therefore, it would seem only sensible to list not merely the moves, but which player made each of them. But in fact we needn't do that: all we need for BOARD is a list of moves made so far, because we've already arranged that the VALUE of each move (a2 etc.) shall be either X, O, or a hyphen. So we're straight away able to find out which player, if any, "owns" any particular square just by letting EVAL do its stuff on the name of the square. So, BOARD will be just a growing list of moves made so far:

```
(a1 b2 c3 ...)
```

Can you imagine how YOURMOVE might add appropriate elements to such a list? Here's one way:

```
(setq board (cons input board))
```

and here's another:

```
(setq board (append (list input) board))
```

Both of them create a new version of BOARD with the new move added onto the front – i.e. the first member of BOARD is the most recent move. If that strikes you as being back to front, there's nothing stopping you from swapping over the arguments to APPEND in the second version so that the new member goes onto the end of the list. So long as you understand what you've done, just in case the order of the members of BOARD should turn out to be important later, it doesn't matter at all.

Now let's put that list-building line into YOURMOVE:

```
(defun yourmove ()
  (prog (input)
    (print (list 'please 'enter 'your 'move))
    (setq input (read))
    (set input 'x)
    (setq board (cons input board))))   <---
```

That's fine. Notice that BOARD is what is known as a GLOBAL variable – as far as YOURMOVE and MYMOVE are concerned. Its value at any moment must be available to both of those routines and their subroutines if any. So what happens the very first time our new version of YOURMOVE tries to update it? At that point, BOARD will not previously have been assigned any value at all; in Lisp's terms, it will be (horrors) an UNBOUND VARIABLE, and you'll get an error message to that effect as soon as YOURMOVE tries to run. We'd better do something about that right away, whilst we have BOARD in our minds.

As I said, BOARD is a global variable. Its value will be updated throughout the game, every time YOURMOVE (or MYMOVE) is called. But once the game is over and a new game begins, we'll want BOARD to start off at NIL again. So the correct place to do that setting to NIL is just prior to the start of any game. And now that we know just where and when BOARD is to be initialised, a one-word change to PLAY will achieve it:

```
(defun play ()
  (setup)
  (display)
  (prog (won board)   <---
   loop
    (yourmove)
    (display)
    (mymove)
    (display)
    (cond ((not won)
```

```
                    (go loop))
                    (t (return nil)))))
```

That's almost all of YOURMOVE, and it would work as it stands, provided
that the human opponent never tried to put his/her X on a square which was
already occupied. That is to say, provided that the value of INPUT was never to
be found amongst the squares listed on BOARD. Remember what BOARD
looks like:

```
     (a1 b2 c3 ...)
```

It's a list, and each member of the list is the name of a square. Suppose that our
human opponent has entered "a1" to the "Please enter your move" prompt. How
is the machine to know that a1 is already a member of BOARD? By calling
MEMQ, which will return NIL if some S-expression is not a member of a given
list, and will return something other than NIL if it is.

```
     (memq 'a2 board)
```

is just what we need.

Now, do you remember the way in which the COND construct works
(Chapter 2)? It goes through a set of conditions, and if one of them evaluates to
non-NIL it performs the corresponding action. So:

```
     (cond ((memq input board))
           (print (list 'illegal 'move))))
```

So far so good, except that when the COND test succeeds (when an illegal
move has been entered) we want the human opponent to be re-cued for a
different, legal move. So we'll put in an instruction which makes control (what the
computer is actually doing) GO back round the LOOP if this condition arises.
Otherwise, it will proceed as before:

```
     (defun yourmove ()
       (prog (input)
       loop
         (print (list 'please enter 'your 'move))
         (setq input (read))
         (cond ((memq input board))                        <---
               (print (list 'illegal 'move))               <---
             (terpri)                                       <---
               (go loop))                                   <---
             (t (set input 'x)                              <---
                 (setq board (cons input board))))))))      <---
```

The TERPRI, by the way, is to make sure that when an illegal move happens, the
announcement to that effect and the subsequent "Please enter" prompt are
printed on the terminal with a blank line between them.

When you've typed in all of that, try calling PLAY again. This time, you
should be able to enter an "opponent's" move and see it displayed on the board
before the next error message interrupts PLAY's loop.

106

5.5 MYMOVE

Now the fun really begins. However, the 'skeleton' of MYMOVE is obviously going to be very similar to that of YOURMOVE, except that we won't need any protection against the machine trying to move onto a square which has already been used:

```
(defun mymove ()
  (prog (move)
    (set move 'o)
    (setq board (cons move board))))
```

Notice that I've avoided using the word 'mymove' as both the name of a function and the name of a variable. I personally find it a handy mnemonic that the purpose of a routine is to set or reset a variable of the same name, but many programmers abhor the very idea and have good reasons for doing so. Besides which, some Lisps won't let you do it.

I hope, however, that it's obvious to you by now that the "guts" of MYMOVE are going to come between the PROG and the SET above. Somewhere in there the machine has to be told how to generate its own next move. As I've said before, this will involve: (a) deriving from BOARD a list of plausible-moves — which in this tiny game can be the same thing as a list of unused squares; (b) evaluating the worth of each of them in terms of the overall board position; and (c) selecting the best to become MOVE. If you glance back for a moment to the list of program specifications, you'll see that we've already covered the easy ones, S7 and S6. Now we're occupied with S5, completely satisfying which is going to involve satisfying S4, S3, S2 and S1. Still taking these in reverse order, let's start with S4.

5.6 Plausible-move generation

This shouldn't take long. We already have in BOARD a note of every square which has been used during the game to date, and all we have to do is "subtract" this from a list of all nine possible moves. The second exercise in this chapter (Exercise 5.2) is to write the function PM-GEN, which takes two arguments: BOARD as above and ALL-SQUARES, which is simply a list of all nine squares a1, a2, a3 etc:

```
(pm-gen board '(a1 a2 a3 b1 b2 b3 c1 c2 c3))
```

PM-GEN needs to check through each member of ALL-SQUARES (use recursion and MEMQ) to see if (COND) it is a member of BOARD, and if not to save it up to be returned in a list with any other non-members when recursion unwinds. Don't forget to allow for the case when recursion has reduced one of the lists to NIL – that is, make sure that it will halt at some point!

There are several equivalent ways of achieving this. When you've written PM-GEN, check it by typing in various versions of BOARD and trying your routine out on each one. When you're happy with it, read on.

I mentioned before that in more complex games the plausible-moves generator has to do a great deal more than merely generate a list of unused squares. Hence its name. In Go-Moku, for example, the board is 19 squares by 19 – 361 vacant squares at the start of a game. And although that number may not seem very large in itself, particularly for a computer whose operating time is measured in millionths of a second, you'll see in the next section that the process of evaluating each square as a potential next move can involve a large amount of processing. Plausible-moves generators in larger games generally incorporate some more or less sophisticated method of selecting only those vacant squares which are somehow "within range" – under the rules of the game – of squares which have been played upon already.

5.7 Representation

This is in many respects both the most difficult and the most interesting aspect of designing a game-playing program: how can we give the machine the same kind of knowledge as we have ourselves and which enables us to decide what is and what is not a "good" move? The problem is really one of translation. The machine is only capable of handling certain kinds of knowledge STRUCTURES (for example, it handles lists very well), and what we have to try to do is express our knowledge in terms of those structures. In the next section we'll be trying to express our METHODS OF JUDGEMENT in the same terms, and when we've achieved both it won't be entirely irrational to say that we have given the machine an "analogous understanding" to our own. Of course, how accurately that understanding mirrors ours depends upon how accurately we do the translations; and one of the attractive things about game-playing programs is that such results can be directly assessed by how well the machine plays the game.

Therefore, the evaluation function I'm about to describe to you will be an almost absurdly simple one. At the end of the chapter I'll give you a few pointers as to how a better one might be designed, and I hope you'll have a go. In principle, noughts and crosses being such a limited game, a program which plays as well as any human is a possibility, given a sufficiently full description of each board-state.

First of all, let's dispose of the idea that there is any need to generate some huge list of all the "best" responses to each and every possible move made by the human opponent in all possible board configurations. The mere idea of trying to work out what all the permutations ARE should convince you that that's a dumb route to follow in Lisp (give it to the FORTRAN experts). I mentioned earlier one of the golden rules of AI programming: get the machine to do all the hard work. Another, almost as golden and almost contradictory, is: Don't Waste Computing Power. In this section I want to try to reduce the skills of playing noughts and crosses to a few simple, comprehensive rules which can be applied to any board configuration to produce a measure of the "worth" of playing on some particular square. I won't entirely succeed, but you'll get the general idea, which is the important thing.

5.8 "Describing" a single square

There are nine squares on the board. Consider any one of them – say a2. If at some point in the game that square is vacant but some others are not, how do we as humans know whether or not it would be a good idea to put our next move on a2?

One obvious starting-point is to refer to the rules of the game:

- (a)   three identical symbols in a straight line gives a win;
- (b)   the straight line may be vertical, horizontal, or diagonal.

Square a2 has two candidates for rule (b) passing through it: (a2 b2 c2) and (a1 a2 a3). Consider the former. As far as rule (a) is concerned if, say b2 and c2 both carry Xs, the machine should place its O on a2 at once in order to avoid defeat at X's next move. On the other hand, if b2 and c2 both carry Os, the machine should place its O on a2 in order to win. Therefore, if b2 and c2 both carry the SAME symbol, a2 is a "good" move; the only difference between the two cases being that in the former it is a good defensive move whereas in the latter it is a good attacking move.

```
a1 ! a2 ! a3      - ! * ! -     - ! * ! -     - ! * ! -     - ! * ! -
b1 ! b2 ! b3      - ! X ! -     - ! 0 ! -     - ! 0 ! -     - ! X ! -
c1 ! c2 ! c3      - ! X ! -     - ! 0 ! -     - ! - ! -     - ! - ! -
```

Similarly, if either b2 or c2 carries an O and the other square on that line is vacant, a2 might be a good move (or at least, not a bad move) if no winning position is to be found elsewhere on the board; and if either b2 or c2 carries an X that line is useless for O regardless of what the other square carries. Note that in this latter case a2 does not automatically become a "bad" move for O: its other line (a1 a2 a3) must be investigated before that can be said.

However, what is clearly a bad move for O – such as placing itself in a corner surrounded by three Xs – is not necessarily a "bad" move if X makes it. Finally, if both b2 and c2 are vacant, a2 is neither a good move nor a bad one, and to place an O upon it will be harmless provided that no better (or worse!) possibility exists along (a1 a2 a3) or elswhere on the board.

What all this boils down to is that a good move is a good move for either player, but a bad move is only bad for one specific player. Or, to put it another way, if we look at each available move on the board first from X's point of view and then from O's, the best move we find will be the best move for the machine to make.

So, one way in which the machine could describe square a2 is by means of the two lists (a2 b2 c2) and (a1 a2 a3) – given that it already "knows" from the information held by BOARD what moves if any have been made on the squares comprising those lists. To describe the overall status of square a2, it will be sufficient to obtain some kind of aggregate "worth" of all (in this case both) of the lines passing through it.

At this point we can introduce another simplification of the problem, based on the simple nature of noughts and crosses itself. In Go-Moku, it is more elegant to make the machine actually work out what squares are on the various lines passing through any given plausible-move, because there are so many possibilities; but in our case there are only eight possible lines in all, and only nine squares. So it's simpler just to create lists to represent their interrelations. For example:

```
(put 'a1 'lines '((a1 a2 a3) (a1 b1 c1) (a1 b2 c3)))
```

will put onto the property-list of the atom 'a1, under the property-name 'lines, a list of the three lines which pass through a1. The machine then has two distinct "meanings" which it can associate with "a1": the lines which pass through it, OR its value – which is, remember, a hyphen, an X or an O. The usefulness of this electronic double-entendre is that once the machine has used a GET to dig out a1's lines, it can then inspect the values of the squares (i.e. the atoms) comprising those lines in order to discover what Xs and Os are there. However, it is also pretty self-evident that all the lines passing though, say, a1 MUST contain a1 itself. So there's not much point in putting that redundant square into the lists on a1's property-list. Another exercise (5.3): add to your SETUP function the necessary PUT instructions to store all the lines associated with each of the nine squares.

5.9 Evaluating the lines

We are now in a position to design the algorithm for our scoring mechanism. The word "algorithm", remember, is computer terminology for a plan of what a function must achieve in order to satisfy its criteria. The criteria in this case were covered pretty accurately in the first five paragraphs of the last section. The algorithm is if you like the first stage of translation: we know what we want, and now we have to express it in terms of what the computer can do. Then, if we write code which conforms to the algorithm, its results should also satisfy our criteria.

The first thing we know is that we're going to consider each plausible-move in turn — and having produced some kind of score for each, we're going to select the best as the machine's next move — to be the value of MOVE, in fact. The second thing we know is that for each plausible-move, there are a number of lines passing through it each of which can be given a score as above. And the third thing we know is that on a given line, no score is possible for one player if the other player has already placed a move on that line. So here's the first version of our scoring algorithm:

    (a)   for each line through any given plausible-move:
        (1)   if an opponent's move is found on the line, set the score to zero and ignore the rest of the line;
        (2)   otherwise, score +1 for every own move on the line.

This algorithm would clearly work for either player. There is one refinement we can add, though. it is somewhat less useful to know what the score currently IS on a line than to know what it WOULD BE if the player concerned made his/her/its next move on the particular square being considered – i.e. on the plausible-move being evaluated. So we'll pretend that such a move has been made by starting the score off at 1 instead of 0 each time, which is equivalent to asking "what would happen if I went there?".

Whilst we're at it, it would be worth noticing that as we derive a score for each plausible move, we shall want to know if included in that score is the score for a winning LINE. In other words, a good way of deriving the score for a single plausible-move is not simply to add up the scores for each of the lines passing through it, but to score each of those lines separately and then to have our scoring function return the best of them. The machine's next move will then be the best of all the best found by taking each plausible-move in turn. That may seem a long-winded way of going about things, but it does allow quite a neat trick: we will later

110

be able to apply the scoring function just once to any opponent-entered move or to any machine-calculated move in order to detect wins. So our algorithm acquires a few additions:

    (a)   for each line through any given plausible-move:

        (1)   if an opponent's move is found on the line, set the score to zero and ignore the rest of the line;

        (2)   if there are no previous moves on the line, score 1;

        (3)   otherwise, score an additional 1 for every own move on the line;

        (4)   store that score somewhere.

    (b)   repeat for all lines through the plausible-move and return the best of the individual line-scores.

Notice step (1). Setting the score to 0 rather than 1 here makes a difference in principle, although it rarely will in practice. The zero expresses the fact that even INCLUDING the score of 1 for "pretending" to move onto the square under consideration, that line is useless for the player. It distinguishes a line which is useless from one which has no previous moves on it at all.

5.10 Scoring a line

Right. That's the algorithm. Now we can write the code which expresses this in Lisp:

```
(defun score (square player)
  (prog (opponent lines line maxscore score)
    (setq opponent (cond ((equal player 'x) 'o) (t 'x)))
    (terpri)
    (print (list 'square: square))
    (print (list 'player: player))
    (setq lines (get square 'lines))
    (setq maxscore 0)
    loop
    (and (null lines) (return maxscore))
    (setq line (mapcar 'eval (car lines)))
    (cond ((memq opponent line) (setq score 0))
          ((not (memq player line)) (setq score 1))
          ((equal line (list player player))
           (setq score 3))
          (t (setq score 2)))
    (and (greaterp score maxscore) (setq maxscore score))
    (print (list 'score: score))
    (setq lines (cdr lines))
    (go loop)))
```

No doubt that strikes you as pretty hairy. But it isn't really. Let's go through it and see what it all means. First, the PROG, which gives us as usual some local variables initialised to NIL – five of them. And the first thing we have to do is to re-initialise them to values which will be useful inside the following loop. It is obvious to you and me that if the PLAYER as specified in the call to SCORE was O, then the OPPONENT must be X and vice versa. But this isn't at all obvious to the machine – it doesn't, for example, even know that there are only two players.

So we have to tell it, via a COND which does the simple thing and assigns a value to OPPONENT which depends on what the value of PLAYER is. After that come a couple of PRINT instructions whose purpose is merely to let you see what happens as the program runs: you can take them out later, if you like.

Then we need the list of lines associated with SCORE's argument SQUARE. These can be retrieved from the property-list of SQUARE (you put them there yourself with SETUP, remember?). So GET returns that list and SETQ binds the local variable LINES to it. The variable LINE, which will be used further down to hold the current first member of LINES, can remain at NIL for now. After that MAXSCORE, which will eventually tell us the score of the best line passing through SQUARE from the point of view of the current PLAYER, is preset to zero; the variable SCORE will be set and reset as required for each line as iteration proceeds.

Now the loop, which actually does the work. The AND is the loop-halting instruction: stop if there are no more lines to be considered. The MAPCAR creates a list of the results of evaluating each square of the LINE in turn: that is, a list which shows which player if any has so far played on that square. If the CAR of LINES looked like this:

    (a1 a2 a3)

the MAPCAR might return this:

    (X 0 -)

Now a COND, which expresses the above scoring rules in Lisp. The first clause says "if the opponent has played on this line, it's no use to PLAYER, so score 0". The second says "if PLAYER has not played on this line it must (since the first COND clause has already happened) be empty, so score 1". The third clause says "if PLAYER already has two moves on this line, score 3". And the fourth says "in all other cases score 2".

If the resulting score for any line is greater than the previous best held in MAXSCORE, the latter is updated to be the same as the current line's score. And finally LINES is reset to its own CDR ready for the next iteration.

5.11 Choosing the best move

So far, we've designed SCORE, which handles all the lines passing through any one plausible-move. It returns the highest-scoring of all those lines. Now we need to write a much simpler routine which will apply SCORE twice to each member of the plausible-moves list (the list generated by the function you wrote), once as though it were X's turn to move and once as though it were O's turn. That is, once with X designated as the PLAYER, and once with O. We want to choose the highest of all the scores so found, which we can do by making it replace the current highest whenever appropriate, as was the case with MAXSCORE; but at the same time we'll need to keep a note of which SQUARE the current best score belongs to. There is one special case to cater for: the case where no "best" move is found because one or more squares score equally highly. In this case we'll arrange to take the earliest such best move found on the plausible-moves list; and in fact to make the thing completely watertight we'll initialise our "best move" variable to be the very first member of that list:

```
(defun choose (plausible-moves)
  (prog (bestscore bestmove temp)
    (setq bestscore 0)
    (setq bestmove (car plausible-moves))
    (setq temp 0)
    loop
    (and (null plausible-moves) (return bestmove))
--> (setq temp (score (car plausible-moves) 'x))
--> (cond ((greaterp temp bestscore)
-->        (setq bestscore temp)
-->        (setq bestmove (car plausible-moves))))
    (setq temp (score (car plausible-moves) 'o))
    (cond ((greaterp temp bestscore)
           (setq bestscore temp)
           (setq bestmove (car plausible-moves))))
    (setq plausible-moves (cdr plausible-moves))
    (go loop)))
```

CHOOSE takes the list of plausible-moves as its argument. The PROG sets up the two local variables mentioned above. Then, a loop again. I've given it its own local variable TEMP, which simply holds the result of SCORE because the subsequent COND needs to refer to that result twice, and it would be very wasteful to call SCORE twice when a TEMP will do. That's the kind of tradeoff which often comes up in programming: do you want your code to be easy for humans to read, or ultra-efficient? The choice is yours.

So, the SCORE for any given plausible-move is derived (remember, it's the best of the scores for the individual lines through the plausible-move) and compared with the current BESTSCORE, which is initially 0. If the new SCORE is greater than BESTSCORE, it becomes the new BESTSCORE, and at the same time the plausible-move itself replaces whatever is currently held in BESTMOVE. Notice that the arrowed section of the code is repeated, once for X and once for O.

Now we have found the best move on the board, and according to our theory that move remains the best whether we're talking from X's point of view or from O's. All we need now is to insert CHOOSE and PM-GEN into MYMOVE. Which will be taken care of in the next section.

5.12 Noticing a win

Just this one thing more is necessary, and if you've more or less coped with the above this one will seem almost trivial by comparison. It is the function which alters the value of the variable WON, way back in PLAY, to stop the game when a win occurs. The function looks like this, and shouldn't give you any headaches at all:

```
(defun win (player)
  (terpri)
  (terpri)
```

113

```
(cond ((equal player 'o)
       (print (list 'i 'win)))
      ((equal player 'x)
       (print (list 'you 'win)))
      (t (print (list 'drawn 'game))))
(setq won t))
```

Notice that there isn't much point in putting capital letters into the messages, because Lisp will change everything to upper case anyway. The third clause of the conditional (the 'T' clause) will operate when WIN is called with NIL as its argument. So the only remaining question about WIN is where and when it will be called. There are clearly three possible conditions in which it is desirable to call it: when X wins, when O wins, and when the game is drawn.

Now, it would be nice if we could keep things simple and call WIN from just one point in the program (one point in the PLAY loop) rather than scattering calls to it all over the place. And such a point occurs within MYMOVE, just after the machine's best move has been calculated. At that point the opponent's most recent move, which may have occasioned a win, is known; and furthermore MYMOVE makes a call to PM-GEN , so that a draw (= no more vacant squares left) can be detected here as well.

Catering for all of these factors at once is going to involve, as you might imagine, fairly drastic surgery to MYMOVE. But nothing that you, with your growing understanding of Lisp, can't handle:

```
(defun mymove ()
  (prog (move plausible-moves)                           <---
    (cond ((setq plausible-moves                         <---
             (pm-gen board '(a1 a2 a3 b1 b2 b3 c1 c2 c3)))) <---
           (print (list 'board: board))                  <---
           (setq move (choose plausible-moves))          <---
           (set move 'o)                                 <---
           (setq board (cons move board))                <---
           (cond ((eq (score (cadr board) 'x) 3)         <---
                  (win 'x))                               <---
                 ((eq (score move 'o) 3)                  <---
                  (win 'o))))                             <---
          (t (win nil)))))                                <---
```

OK, here we go. First of all, we need a PROG to initialise the local variables MOVE and PLAUSIBLE-MOVES to NIL, and then with a PRINT instruction as in SCORE there is a COND. This says "if I can SETQ the variable PLAUSI-BLE-MOVES to the result of calling PM-GEN...". That is, if the result of that call to PM-GEN is non-NIL, signifying that there is at least one plausible-move left at this stage in the game, go on to CHOOSE the best of the list of plausible-moves so found, and then set MOVE and BOARD as before. An inner COND checks for wins by either player. Otherwise, if there are NO plausible moves left, WIN is called to signal a drawn game.

114

If there is such a move (i.e. if there was still at least one PLAUSIBLE-MOVE for CHOOSE to choose) it is given its correct value of O and added to BOARD. At the same time we can use a COND to check for wins: now that the machine's latest MOVE is the CAR of BOARD, the opponent's latest move must be the CADR of BOARD. If either of these score 3, it is a winning move.

Finally, in the other condition – when there are no PLAUSIBLE-MOVES left – we need to stop the program via WIN.

And that's it. You should now have a fully working noughts and crosses program. The first thing you'll notice is that it doesn't play very well. Before we go on to discuss why not, please bear with a couple of digressions.

5.13 Criticising the program

First, the program runs rather slowly. You can effect a startling improvement if you are prepared to replace my PROG loops with your Lisp's looping construct, as mentioned in Chapter 3.

You'll probably have noticed one minor bug pretty quickly: that if the machine wins (if you let it win!) the program halts at once, whereas if you win it goes on to display the final board position for a second time. The reason for this is that the "stop" command for the whole thing is the RETURN in PLAY, and that only gets a chance to operate once every two moves – one move per player. The solution is to repeat the COND test in PLAY after YOURMOVE as well as after MYMOVE. But for this to work you'll also have to split up the COND in MYMOVE so that part of it occurs in YOURMOVE instead – otherwise WON will never be T immediately after YOURMOVE. If you think it's worth the trouble, by all means have a go.

As the program stands, YOURMOVE traps any attempt by the human opponent to enter the number of a square which has already been used. But something which is likely to occur quite often and which YOURMOVE doesn't guard against is the simple typing error, or the clever dick who thinks it funny to make your program bomb out immediately by entering "boo" or "kilroy woz ere". The modification is quite simple: and only requires adding a new first clause to the conditional in YOURMOVE:

```
(cond ((not (memq input '(a1 a2 a3 b1 b2 b3 c1 c2 c3))
       (print (list 'Illegal 'move))
       (terpri)
       (go loop))
      ((memq input board)
       (print (list 'Illegal 'move))
       (terpri)
       (go loop))
```

Don't type that in just yet. Notice first that the only genuinely new line is the very first. The calls to PRINT, to TERPRI, and recursively to YOURMOVE are identical in both clauses, which seems (and is) a bit wasteful of both the computer's memory and your time. One of the nice things about Lisp is that whenever you notice that sort of pattern in your code, you can do something about it. Often, what you would do is to set up an entirely new function (using DEFUN) whose sole purpose was to "do" the duplicated lines, and then you would call that function instead of the duplicated lines, wherever they occurred – in this case in each clause of the conditional. In simple cases such as ours there's an even easier solution:

```
(cond ((or (not (memq input '(a1 a2 a3 b1 b2 b3 c1 c2 c3)))
            (memq input board))
       (princ "Illegal move")
       (terpri)
       (go loop))
```

By the way, the person who types more than one S-expression in when cued for his/her move will now get as many "Illegal move" messages as there are S-expressions in the entry!

5.14 Improving the program's performance

You may think it a good idea to make the machine always grab the centre square, b2, if it can. And the way to do this is to make sure that if b2 ever occurs in the list of plausible-moves, it is moved smartly to the head of the list. Then the PROG in CHOOSE will make sure that that square is chosen unless there really is a better one. The "if" I just wrote should make you think "COND" at once: you'll need a COND to test whether or not b2 does occur in PLAUSIBLE-MOVES. If it does, you can use exactly the same method as I used when talking about CONS and DELETE, way back in section 1.7.

A genuine bug, equally obvious, is that this kind of position:

```
X ! O ! X
- ! - ! -
- ! - ! -
```

when it is the machine's move, always defeats it. It chooses b1, the head of the plausible-moves list, instead of b2. The crucial thing about this position is that after X's next move, on b2, he or she will always be left with a winning move regardless of what the poor machine does next. (This is the third backward stage in the "sequence of moves to an inevitable win" which I mentioned in section 5.2). And what fails at this point is the program's ability fully to DESCRIBE the potential of square b2. In fact the description, which we reduce to a single numeral, describes only a single line, the best line passing through the given plausible move b2, whereas what is needed here is a description of b2's TWO best lines. As the scoring algorithm stands, the score for all the three squares on the b-line is the same: 2. Hence CHOOSE selects whichever of them comes first on the plausible-moves list. What we need is a way of including in our description information about the second line passing through each square, so that the potential of the above position will not be ignored.

Simply adding up the two best line scores for any plausible-move won't do, because there are not the same number of lines passing through all squares, so that some scores would be unfairly "weighted" with respect to others. The effect of that would be, for example, that in positions like this one:

```
O ! - ! -
- ! X ! X
- ! - ! -
```

the machine would choose a3 (score 4 for X) rather than b1 (score 3 for X). What's more, you'd run into hairy complications because the score for a3 is actually higher than that required for a win. One (messy) solution is to alter the scoring algorithm so that the two line scores are added, but also so that any score higher than 3 is automatically reduced back to 3. But although it isn't obvious from the above diagram I still feel it in my bones that this would still lead to problems with false announcements of a win!

A more elegant method would involve changing SCORE so that, rather than being a single numeral as now, it returned a list of two numerals: one representing the score of the best line through the given square, and the other representing the second-best. CHOOSE would then select from these in two stages, firstly by the value of the first elements of all the lists returned by SCORE (the same procedure, effectively, as it uses now), and secondly by the value of the second element. This would obviate win-detection problems, because WIN would still only inspect the "best" scores – the first elements of the two-numeral lists – and any such score which equalled 3 would still represent a winning line; and it would also ensure that b1 was chosen rather than a3 in the example. In the previous example, b2 would be similarly selected in preference to either b1 or b3.

5.15 Answers to Exercises

Exercise 5.1

```
(defun setup ()
  (setq a1 '-)
  (setq a2 '-)
  (setq a3 '-)
  (setq b1 '-)
  (setq b2 '-)
  (setq b3 '-)
  (setq c1 '-)
  (setq c2 '-)
  (setq c3 '-))
```

In larger Lisps SETQ will take multiple arguments, like this:

```
(setq a1 '- b2 '- c3 '- ...)
```

Exercise 5.2

Here's my own solution, based on what you have learned so far:

```
(defun pm-gen (board all-squares)
  (cond ((null all-squares) nil)
        ((memq (car all-squares) board)
         (pm-gen board (cdr all-squares)))
        (t (cons (car all-squares) (pm-gen board (cdr all-squares))))))
```

Exercise 5.3

```
(defun setup ()
  (setq a1 '-)
  (setq a2 '-)
  (setq a3 '-)
  (setq b1 '-)
  (setq b2 '-)
  (setq b3 '-)
  (setq c1 '-)
  (setq c2 '-)
  (setq c3 '-)
  (put 'a1 'lines '((a2 a3) (b1 c1) (b2 c3)))
  (put 'a2 'lines '((a1 a3) (b2 c2)))
  (put 'a3 'lines '((a1 a2) (b3 c3) (b2 c1)))
  (put 'b1 'lines '((b2 b3) (a1 c1)))
  (put 'b2 'lines '((b1 b3) (a2 c2) (a1 c3) (a3 c1)))
  (put 'b3 'lines '((b1 b2) (a3 c3)))
  (put 'c1 'lines '((c2 c3) (a1 b1) (a3 b2)))
  (put 'c2 'lines '((c1 c3) (a2 b2)))
  (put 'c3 'lines '((c1 c2) (a3 b3) (a1 b2)))
```

Of course, the order of the lines for any given square isn't important, nor is the order of the squares within a line.

Chapter 6
Data structures

When you've practised on a few relatively simple programs (there are a couple of suggestions later in this chapter) and your programming ability has progressed to the point where you habitually think in terms of cons-cells and lambda-expressions, you'll certainly find that the programs you write need to operate with more complicated "chunks" of information than can easily be bound using the simple SETQ. This chapter will talk mainly about some of the possibilities for creating such "data structures".

6.1 Association-lists

These are generally known as ALISTS for short. The idea is this. Suppose you have a set of atoms with each of which you want to associate a different and possibly complex piece of data. Assume that the latter will itself be either an atom or a list. What you do is take each atom and LIST it together with its data; and then make a new list – the ALIST – out of the whole lot. Here is an ALIST in which each key atom (A, B, C or D) is associated with a piece of data which is either the atom 42 or the list '(X Y Z):

```
((a 42) (b (x y z)) (c (x y z)) (d 42))
```

You might find that easier to read with a bit of indenting:

```
((a 42)
 (b (x y z))
 (c (x y z))
 (d 42))
```

Getting information out of an ALIST is very easy, because there is a Lisp function intended for just that purpose. It is called ASSOC. If you bind L to the above list (using SETQ, of course) and then type:

```
*- (assoc 'c L)
```

[Check ASSOC in the Appendix]

119

Lisp will return:

```
(C (X Y Z))
```

that is, the WHOLE of that element of L whose CAR was equal to C (the "key"). So,

```
*- (cadr (assoc 'c L))
```

gives you the actual data associated with C. Incidentally, ASSOC uses EQUAL. So the KEYS can be lists rather than atoms if necessary.

Creating such an ALIST isn't so easy: Lisp doesn't provide any handy function for doing it, and so you have to write your own. But you can use a similar trick to one I showed you way back in Chapter 1. There, we effectively moved OCTOPUS from its position well down the list of ANIMALS (remember them?) to the head of the list, by using DELETE and CONS. We can do the same sort of thing to add new elements to an ALIST, except that instead of CONSing back on the DELETEd element, we CONS on a new one:

```
(defun alist-build (key datum al)
   (setq al (cons (list key datum)
                  (delete (assoc key al) al))))
```

Start from the ASSOC on the last line of this definition. ASSOC works its way down the ALIST element by element (in a similar way to MAPC), looking for an element whose CAR is EQUAL to the value of KEY. It returns the whole of any such element it finds – or NIL if it doesn't find one at all. If there is one, DELETE promptly removes it from the ALIST. And if there isn't, DELETE returns the ALIST unchanged. Then, onto the front of whatever ALIST may now be, CONS adds a list of the KEY and the DATUM – this being the specified form of each entry on the ALIST, as above. Finally, SETQ makes sure that from now on ALIST has this new value: the one with the old element deleted and the new one added on.

But suppose that previously ALIST had no value at all: that you were using ALIST-BUILD to create a new ALIST from scratch. Well, that's OK. In that case DELETE would inevitably return NIL; and remember that to Lisp the empty list signified by "()" and NIL are the same thing. So the CONS takes DELETE's NIL to be an empty list "( )" and adds into it the new (LISTed) item. In other words, what you get is this:

```
((<key> <datum>))
```

which is, of course, an ALIST as above but containing only one element. Experienced programmers quite frequently use (CONS <S-expression> NIL) instead of (LIST <S-expression>). It has the same effect, and is slightly faster in operation. LIST itself is then reserved for creating lists of more than one S-expression.

As things stand, ALIST-BUILD returns the value of the SETQ, that is to say the new value of the ALIST itself. You may think it neater to make it return only the new element you've just added; and that's quite simple to do. Remember that a function always returns the value of the last S-expression within it. So to make ALIST-BUILD return something else we simply give it an extra, final S-expression:

```
(defun alist-build (key datum al)
  (setq al (cons (list key datum)
                 (delete (assoc key al) al)))
  (list key datum))
```

Alternatively, to save it the trouble of re-computing the last line, you could decide that it would return only the datum:

```
(defun alist-build (key datum al)
  (setq al (cons (list key datum)
                 (delete (assoc key al) al)))
  datum)
```

If you think that looks odd, remember that as EVAL works its way through the definition, during execution of ALIST-BUILD, it evaluates each S-expression in turn. And the atom DATUM is just as much an S-expression as the previous complicated SETQ-CONS-DELETE-ASSOC combination. So, the value of DATUM gets returned.

Alists are useful when, say, the atoms you use as keys already have bound values in the normal way, and you want to associate with each of them only one other item of information. The alist becomes another "place", separate from the "place" where bound values are kept, in which to store the extra information relating to the key. But ASSOC takes time to search down the alist, pattern-matching each key with the one you specify until it finds a match. Long alists (of more than a dozen or so elements) are definitely not a good idea!

6.2 Using property-lists

Property-lists are the things to use when you want to associate more than one value with a given atom. Say you wanted to create a computerised address book. Well, one way to do it is first to decide on a unique atom to identify each person whose personal details are to appear in the book. Fairly obviously you should choose some standard abbreviation of the person's name – such as JOHN-S or J-SMITH – so that there's no risk of you later forgetting what atom you've chosen! Next, you use PUT to enter into the book all the data you want to keep there:

```
(put 'john-s 'phone 663595)
(put 'john-s 'address '(2007 willow close))
```

This has to repeated for each person; it takes quite a while, so if you intend to try to write yourself such an address book you'd better look in your manual first to see how to save all that hard work on tape or on disc.

The third stage is to write the function which will retrieve the data as and when you need it. And it is very simple:

```
(defun find (item person)
  (get person item))
```

When FIND is called and evaluated, ITEM and PERSON will also be evaluated (presumably they will be quoted atoms anyway) and these values will be supplied as the two arguments to GET. That is, to find the phone number of JOHN-S, you type:

```
*- (find 'phone 'john-s)
```

Alternatively, if you thought it fun to do so, you could write a whole series of little functions which would allow you to query the address book like this:

```
*- (address 'john-s)
```

to retrieve the appropriate information. Here is ADDRESS:

```
(defun address (person)
  (get person 'address))
```

You could even make them into FEXPRs, to save the bother of quoting the name each time:

```
(defun address person
  (get (car person) 'address))
```

Now, you just type

```
*- (address john-s)
```

and out comes the answer:

```
(2007 WILLOW CLOSE)
```

If you were now to do this:

```
*- (put 'john-s 'phone 653701)
```

JOHN-S's new phone number gets recorded and the old one is forgotten, because as I've mentioned already PUT overwrites any existing value under the same property. This overwriting isn't always convenient, so here is a function called ADDPROP. Rather than overwriting, ADDPROP makes a list out of any existing value and the new value, and stores that list under the property.

```
(defun addprop (id prop newval)
  (cond ((memq newval (get id prop)) nil)
        (t (put id prop (cons newval (get id prop))))))
```

Notice that ADDPROP always puts a LIST onto the property-list, even if it is a list of only one value, whereas PUT will put an atom there.

And that's really all you need to know about property-lists. They are very simple and very useful. The next two sections give you a flavour of how one type of data structure may be simulated using another.

6.3 Simulating property-lists with alists

Some Lisps do not allow you to make use of their property-lists, and so do not provide the usual functions PUT, GET and REMPROP. It is possible to simulate the property-list facility using alists to store the data, which ought to be easy because both property-lists and alists have essentially the same form: that of keys or property-names interleaved with their corresponding values. But (of course) there are drawbacks. Alists, if they are to have anything more than a transient existence, must be bound to some atom as its (SETQ'd) value. In the examples above, the atom was AL. That means that AL, or any other atom which "holds" an alist, cannot also be used as a variable to be bound via SETQ. The atom becomes a reserved word, like the name of a function. But that isn't all: the functions I'm about to show you and which simulate the effects of PUT, GET, REMPROP and ADDPROP will certainly fail, and cause an error message from Lisp, if the IDENTIFIER – the atom whose value will be an alist – is UNBOUND.

So, to simulate property-lists as they are simulated here, you need to ensure that two preconditions are met: (1) the IDENTIFIERs you use will be drawn from a set (i.e. a list) which you will specify in advance and which will not be used for any other purpose; and (2) that all of these identifiers are preset to NIL.

Given that, the rest is relatively painless. Here is an alist which would simulate one of the property-lists we developed above:

```
((address (2007 willow close))
 (phone 663595))
```

and, naturally enough, this alist would be kept at the value of the atom JOHN-S – in the terms of our simulation, JOHN-S is the IDENTIFIER. Now it is very easy to write a function which, used exactly as GET is used with real property-lists, will retrieve from the alist the information we want:

```
(defun pseudo-get (id prop)
  (cadr (assoc prop (eval id))))
```

PUT, GET etc. are EXPRs, taking quoted arguments, and so for consistency's sake we want our PSEUDO-functions to take quoted arguments as well. Therefore PSEUDO-GET will be expected to ASSOCiate PROP with the VALUE of ID. And, if you remember, ASSOC returns the WHOLE of the element it finds, so it is the CADR of that which PSEUDO-GET should return.

Now let's do PSEUDO-REMPROP:

```
(defun pseudo-remprop (id prop)
  (set id (delete (assoc prop (eval id)) (eval id))))
```

The ASSOC clearly returns the same element of the alist as it did above, and we need to DELETE that from the whole alist, i.e. from (eval id). I've used SET rather than SETQ because of course it is the value of ID – JOHN-S – and not ID itself which we want to have the modified alist bound to.

And, given those two functions, PSEUDO-PUT is a doddle:

```
(defun pseudo-put (id prop val)
  (and (pseudo-get id prop) (pseudo-remprop id prop))
  (set id (cons (list prop val) (eval id))))
```

It first checks with PSEUDO-GET to see if the PROP already has any VAL (remember, PUT always overwrites), and if so removes it with PSEUDO-REMPROP. Then it CONSes the new element of the alist onto the latter's existing value.

Finally, here is PSEUDO-ADDPROP. Since ADDPROP itself was created out of PUT and GET, PSEUDO-ADDPROP is exactly the same thing with all the PUTs replaced by PSEUDO-PUTs and all the GETs replaced by PSEUDO-GETs:

```
(defun pseudo-addprop (id prop newval)
  (cond ((pseudo-get id prop)
         (pseudo-put id prop (list newval (pseudo-get id prop))))
        (t (pseudo-put id prop (cons newval nil)))))
```

As before, PSEUDO-ADDPROP puts a LIST into the alist where PSEUDO-PUT would put an atom.

6.4 Simulating alists with property-lists

Supposing now that we were using a very odd Lisp which for some obscure reason would not allow alists to be created, although it did provide for the use of property-lists. (I don't suppose anyone will ever produce such a Lisp, but it's a fun exercise). What we would need is direct equivalents of ASSOC and of ALIST-BUILD, which actually stored the data on property-lists. These functions are even easier to write than those in the previous section:

```
(defun pseudo-assoc (key al)
  (list key (get al key)))

(defun pseudo-alist-build (key datum al)
  (put al key datum)
  datum)
```

Remember, this does not actually create any alists. If the identifier AL was unbound before these functions were called, it will be unbound afterwards.

```
*- (pseudo-alist-build 'a 42 'pseudo-alist)

42

*- (pseudo-alist-build 'b '(x y z) 'pseudo-alist)

(X Y Z)
```

will create a two-element pseudo-alist, which you can access using PSEUDO-ASSOC:

```
*- (pseudo-assoc 'a 'pseudo-alist)

(A 42)

*- (pseudo-assoc 'b 'pseudo-alist)

(B (X Y Z))
```

Naturally, the atom or atoms which appear where I have put PSEUDO-ALIST can have any names you like.

6.5 Arbitrary data structures

So, there are two basic facilities available in Lisp for creating data structures, and since as you've just seen they are with very little difficulty interchangeable, it should be possible to create data structures which are in part property-lists and in part some kind of alist. And of course, it is possible. In Lisp, you are free to use either property-lists or alists, or a combination of both, to create any data structure you choose. Later in this chapter I shall be showing you some of the standard data structures which have been developed in the course of Artificial Intelligence research, but first I want to talk about how you might decide what structure to create for a given purpose.

To go back to the address-book analogy for a moment, suppose you knew for sure that you would never want it to hold more than three items of information about any one person: that person's address, phone number and birthday. You could use property-lists, with a property-name and a value for each of these pieces of information; or you could use an alist of three elements, each element comprising the appropriate key and datum. But both of these methods are a bit wasteful of computer memory: since you already know that there will only ever be those three items to store, all you really need is a list of them, associated with each person's name. Provided that each such list has the same standard internal order, say:

(<address> <phone> <birthday>)

the "headings" — keys or property-names — become redundant. To access for example the phone number in such a list, you merely need to call CADR.

That is the basic principle underlying the use of data structures in Lisp. The structures themselves are sometimes referred to as "records", or "data types". The normal procedure is first to decide on some suitable standard structure, such as the above three-list. Next, you need to decide how THAT is to be stored – either on a property-list or as a bound value. And then you need to write a set of handy functions which will both create a new three-list (for a new entry in the address-book) and which will retrieve or update any desired item from the information stored there. Let's have a go.

We already have our structure decided upon: a three-list. That can either be stored as the value of the PERSON concerned, or on that PERSON's property-list as the value of some suitable property such as ADDRESSBOOK. In writing the necessary functions, I'll give you both alternatives all along the line.

The easiest starting-point, as above, is usually to assume that the desired data structure already exists, and to write the functions to access it. In our case, the functions to RETRIEVE any item are dead simple:

```
(defun address (person)
  (car (eval person)))
```

or

```
(defun address (person)
  (car (get person 'addressbook)))
```

```
(defun phone (person)
  (cadr (eval person)))
```

or

```
(defun phone (person)
  (cadr (get person 'addressbook)))
```

```
(defun birthday (person)
  (caddr (eval person)))
```

or

```
(defun birthday (person)
  (caddr (get person 'addressbook)))
```

Now we need a similar set of functions to UPDATE any existing item, or alternatively to insert it in an existing structure if the corresponding slot is empty:

```
(defun new-address (person address)
  (set person (cons address (cdr (eval person)))))
```

or

```
(defun new-address (person address)
  (put person
      (cons address (cdr (get person 'addressbook)))
      'addressbook))
```

Either function retrieves the whole of the existing data structure, and alters its CAR to be the new address. The remaining functions for updating do the same thing to their elements of the structure:

```
(defun new-phone (person phone)
  (set person (list (address person) phone (birthday person))))
```

or

```
(defun new-phone (person phone)
  (put person
      (list (address person) phone (birthday person))
      'addressbook))
```

and

```
(defun new-birthday (person birthday)
  (set person (list (address person) (phone person) birthday)))
```

or

```
(defun new-birthday (person birthday)
  (put person
      (list (address person) (phone person) birthday)
      'addressbook))
```

126

Now, to write the function which creates the data structure in the first place becomes very easy:

```
(defun new-person (address phone birthday)
  (set person (list nil nil nil))
  (new-address person address)
  (new-phone person phone)
  (new-birthday person birthday))
```

or

```
(defun new-person (address phone birthday)
  (put person (list nil nil nil) 'addressbook)
  (new-address person address)
  (new-phone person phone)
  (new-birthday person birthday))
```

and of course, if when calling NEW-PERSON you can't yet fill all of its three argument-slots, you just put NIL for now. Later, when the information becomes available, you can use one of the "NEW-" functions to insert it.

That is, in essence, how to use Lisp to create your own data structures. As you will see shortly, the structures can become very much more complex than the above simple three-list. But the principle is always the same: a suitable structure, some accessing functions, and a building function.

6.6 Search methods

6.6.1 Depth-first search

Data, particularly data concerning ROUTES from some known START state via unknown intermediaries to some recognisable GOAL state (such as finding a route on a map, or optimising a flow-chart) can often be organised into TREES. Such trees resemble family trees, and are therefore upside-down to botanical trees – with the ROOT at the top. As the branches spread out downwards, each junction is known as a NODE, and is assumed to be a stage in the search for a route to the goal:

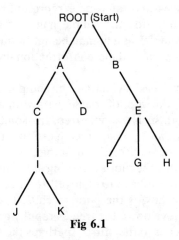

Fig 6.1

127

Nodes from which no further downward progress is possible (D, F, G, H, J and K) are called TERMINAL nodes. By analogy with a family tree, each node except the ROOT has a unique PARENT, and may have one or more OFFSPRING. The fact that any node other than the root has a unique parent is the distinguishing mark of a TREE. A link between B and D would change the above structure from a TREE into a NETWORK, with the concomitant possibility that any attempt to find a route through the network might get itself stuck in a loop ROOT-A-D-B-ROOT-A-D-... and so on; more about networks and what to do about the looping problem later.

A very important point to understand is that Lisp cannot contain any object which is physically identical to the above tree. The diagram is merely a convenient way of expressing the fact that certain things which can exist in Lisp – e.g. the atoms ROOT, A, B etc. – are linked in some way by pointers to each other, the latter also being able to exist in Lisp.

One way of representing such a tree in Lisp is to give each node, if it has any offspring, an OFFSPRING property on its property-list, and to insert the relevant offspring-nodes as the value of that property:

```
(put 'root 'offspring '(a b))
(put 'a 'offspring '(c d))
(put 'b 'offspring '(e))
(put 'c 'offspring '(i))
(put 'e 'offspring '(f g h))
(put 'i 'offspring '(j k))
```

The OFFSPRING properties then form the pointers referred to above. It is also possible to represent the tree as a single complex list:

```
(root (a (c (i (j k))
         (d))
      (b (e (f g h))))
```

but I shall concentrate on the former method because in this context it tends to result in simpler code.

The nodes themselves may of course represent arbitrarily complex data objects, just as in a family tree the simple name of a member of the family represents an object as complex as a human being. In this case the property-list of the node might contain a great deal more information under other properties than OFFSPRING.

Suppose that for some reason you want the computer to find for you the route from the start to node E. For you, of course, with your ability to see the world in three dimensions and with such a simple tree, the solution is obvious (although exactly how you found it is an interesting AI question). The computer has no such ability to see the whole tree at once. Sitting at the root node, it can see by looking at ROOT's property-list that the root's offspring are A and B. But it cannot see any further. To do that, it would have to "move" to A or B so as to be able to see that node's offspring. So how is the poor machine to find its way to node E?

One method is to move down the tree as rapidly as possible, taking at each node the branch which leads to the "first" (perhaps the leftmost) of its offspring.

That is, to move from ROOT to A, then to C, then to I and then to J. On reaching a terminal node (J) without finding the goal it is seeking, the program has to back up to the previous parent node (I), and then take the branch leading to the "first" of the remaining (so far untried) offspring of that node (if any). Which would take it to K. Then it would back up again, via C to A, before moving downwards again to D. Then back to A, back to the ROOT, and finally down through B to E. This is the algorithm for a type of search called a DEPTH-FIRST search.

Here is a function which, with its subroutine, will carry out a depth-first search of a tree, returning a list of the nodes which together form the most direct route it finds from the start to the goal:

```
(defun depth (start goal)
  (prog (paths current)
    (setq paths (list (list start)))
    loop
    (setq current (car paths))
    (cond ((null paths) (return nil))
          ((eq (car current) goal)
           (return (reverse current)))
          (t (setq paths (cdr paths))
             (setq paths (append (new-paths current) paths))))
    (go loop)))

(defun new-paths (path)
  (mapcar '(lambda (child)
             (cons child path))
          (get (car path) 'offspring)))
```

Look at the definition of DEPTH. The first instruction inside the PROG is to set the local variable PATHS to a list of a list of the starting-node. As execution of the program progresses, other paths will be added to this list. Each of them will itself be a list, and PATHS will be an overall list of the whole lot. Hence (LIST (LIST START)). Within the loop, the first instruction is to set another local variable called CURRENT to the first element of PATHS – which so far means to set it to a list of the starting node. CURRENT is merely a handy place to keep the CAR of PATHS. Then comes a COND. The COND says (take my word for it, for now): if I have explored all the paths through the tree and have not found the goal node, stop the loop and return NIL; or, if the first node in the CURRENT path is the goal node, stop the loop and return the REVERSE of the current path; otherwise, forget about the current path and replace it with a new set of paths – those through the offspring of the first node in the CURRENT path, as returned by NEW-PATHS.

To put that another way, the program says to itself at the start that the CURRENT path – the path it has followed so far – is (ROOT), and it investigates that path to see if the head of it is the goal node. Of course it isn't, so the program proceeds to investigate instead, one after another, the paths through ROOT's offspring, which are the paths (A ROOT) and (B ROOT). So the value of PATHS itself is then

```
((A ROOT) (B ROOT))
```

If on the next iteration it finds that the head of (A ROOT) isn't the goal node either (as it won't be), it replaces (A ROOT) with (C A ROOT) and (D A ROOT). The complete list of PATHS is then

    ((C A ROOT) (D A ROOT) (B ROOT)).

The paths are stored backwards — (C A ROOT) rather than (ROOT A C) simply because it is easier to inspect the CAR of a list than to inspect its last element. Hence also the REVERSE in the COND's second clause.

During the next two iterations, the value of PATHS will become successively

    ((I C A ROOT) (D A ROOT) (B ROOT)) and
    ((J I C A ROOT) (K I C A ROOT) (D A ROOT) (B ROOT)).

At this point there are no offspring of node J. So, since J is still not the goal node, the APPEND appends NIL onto the front of PATHS after the CAR of it has been removed. If you've ever tried APPENDing NIL to a list or vice versa, you'll know that APPEND takes the NIL as being the empty list ( ), and effectively removes it. That is, the value of PATHS becomes

    ((K I C A ROOT) (D A ROOT) (B ROOT)).

The effect of this is that the program, after investigating node J, goes on to investigate node K, just as we wanted it to. Failing to find the goal node there either, it truncates PATHS again, to

    ((D A ROOT) (B ROOT))

that is, it in effect backs up all the way to node A in order to investigate the downward branch via D. And after that, of course, it will "back up" to the ROOT itself in order to take the branch via B:

    ((E B ROOT))

This time, the first member of the CURRENT path (E B ROOT) is indeed the goal node, so the program returns the reverse of CURRENT, which is

    (ROOT B C)

Hooray.

NEW-PATHS does a very simple thing: it takes the node at the head of the CURRENT path and finds its offspring from the property-list. Then it uses MAPCAR to make a list of as many elements as there are offspring, each element comprising a list of one of the offspring CONSed onto the CURRENT path. For example, if the current path is

    (I C A ROOT)

Since J and K are the offspring of I, NEW-PATHS returns the list

    ((J I C A ROOT) (K I C A ROOT))

and this gets APPENDed onto the front of the truncated PATHS by the third COND clause in DEPTH.

6.6.2 Breadth-first search

Now, here's a neat trick. Suppose that instead of appending each set of new paths onto the FRONT of the existing ones, DEPTH had appended them onto the end. The effect of that would be that instead of going from ROOT to A and then to C, the program would go from ROOT to A and then to B. Subsequently it would investigate in turn nodes C, D and E; and in this particular example would reach the goal node slightly sooner:

```
(defun breadth (start goal)
  (prog (paths current)
    (setq paths (list (list start)))
    loop
    (setq current (car paths))
    (cond ((null paths) (return nil))
          ((eq (car current) goal)
           (return (reverse current)))
          (t (setq paths (cdr paths))
             (setq paths (append paths (new-paths current)))))   <--
    (go loop)))
```

Apart from that single change, DEPTH and BREADTH are identical; and both return (reasonably enough) the same path.

By the way, in case it hasn't occurred to you already, you can save yourself a lot of typing when defining near-identical functions by the following:

(a)   if your Lisp stores function-definitions as bound values,

```
(setq breadth depth)
```

(b)   or, if your Lisp stores function-definitions on property-lists,

```
(put 'breadth 'expr (get 'depth 'expr))
```

and in either case you just edit the change into BREADTH in the normal way.

6.6.3 Best-first search

It is probably all too clear that both depth-first and breadth-first searches are liable, depending upon the position of the goal node in any given tree, to do a good deal of fruitless searching. There are situations – for example, when the tree represents all the possible outcomes of alternate moves by you and your opponent in a game of chess – when it may be worth investigating all, or most, of the nodes in it. But more often there is a specific known goal node, and it is merely desirable to find the goal node as quickly as possible. Also, if the same node occurs several times in the tree – as is perfectly possible if the tree represents a map or the data for a flow chart – depth-first or breadth-first searching may not generate the optimum or shortest path.

Here is an imaginary map. You need to get from town S to town F:

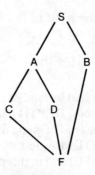

Fig 6.2

Clearly there are three routes, and depending upon the distances between the towns one of these routes may be shorter than the others. The map is clearly a network, and can be redrawn as a tree:

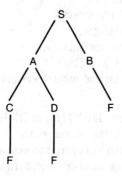

Fig 6.3

The node F now occurs three times – which is reasonable since in the original map there were three routes for which F was the terminal node. Now you can see at a glance that a depth-first search would take you to the left-hand of those Fs, whilst a breadth-first search would take you to the right-hand one. And of course, Sod's Law insists that therefore the shortest route would probably be the one via A and D to the middle F – for example, if all the distances between adjacent towns were ten miles, except that between D and F which was only five miles, and that between B and F which was twenty miles.

So we need a search algorithm to which we can give additional information concerning the "best" route as it makes its search. There are two pieces of extra information we could give it as it moves from node to node: how far away it currently is from the start, and a guess at how far it has still to go to reach the goal. The former enables the program, sitting at any given node, to select from amongst that node's offspring the one which is at the shortest total distance from the start. Obviously, if by the time it finds the goal node it has always taken the shortest distance in this way, it will inevitably have found the shortest route. And of course if it reaches the left-hand F, knowing that there are still some shorter routes remaining higher up the tree to be investigated, it can still back up and try again as before.

132

This will require some fairly drastic changes to the program, but nothing inherently difficult to do. Let's start by putting the necessary distances into the representation of the tree:

```
(put 's 'offspring '((a . 10) (b . 10)))
(put 'a 'offspring '((c . 10) (d . 10)))
(put 'b 'offspring '((f . 20)))
(put 'c 'offspring '((f . 10)))
(put 'd 'offspring '((f . 5)))
```

This represents the above tree-ified version of the map, with each node except the start-node now appearing as a dotted pair: its name and its distance from its own parent-node. So a PATH, instead of looking like this:

```
(C A S)
```

is going to look like this:

```
((C . 10) (A . 10) (S . 0))
```

This immediately requires two changes to BREADTH in order to turn it into BEST:

```
(defun best (start goal)
  (prog (paths current)
    (setq paths (list (list (cons start 0))))      <--
    loop
    (setq current (car paths))
    (cond ((null paths) (return nil))
          ((eq (caar current) goal)                <--
           (return (reverse current)))
          (t (setq paths (cdr paths))
             (setq paths (append paths (new-paths current)))))
    (go loop)))
```

The initial PATHS will need to look like this:

```
(((S . 0)))
```

and the check to see if the goal has been found yet will need to look at the CAAR of PATHS rather than at its CAR as before – its CAR will, of course, now be a dotted pair. And there are two more changes we need to make: instead of selecting merely the CAR of PATHS as the CURRENT path, we want the program to select the SHORTEST of them; and this in turn implies that once that path has been investigated it can't merely be CDR'd off (since it may NOT be the first) but must be DELETEd:

```
(defun best (start goal)
  (prog (paths current)
    (setq paths (list (list (cons start 0))))
    loop
    (setq current (shortest paths))                <--
    (cond ((null paths) (return nil))
```

```
          ((eq (caar current) goal)
           (return (reverse current)))
          (t (setq paths (delete current paths))          <--
             (setq paths (append paths (new-paths current)))))
      (go loop)))
```

NEW-PATHS also needs a minor change to enable it to cope with the dotted pairs:

```
(defun new-paths (path)
  (mapcar '(lambda (child)
             (cons child path))
          (get (caar path) 'offspring)))          <--
```

and that's that; so now we can worry about SHORTEST. It needs to look at all of the members of PATHS in turn, and to find the length of each of them – which it can do by simply applying PLUS to a list of all the CDRs of the dotted pairs therein. This instruction will do that:

```
(apply 'plus (mapcar 'cdr <path>))
```

SHORTEST finds the least of all the paths via a method which you first saw in a function called CHOOSE, in Chapter 6. The idea is that as SHORTEST works its way through all of the available PATHS, some temporary variable holds a note of the current LEAST distance found so far, against which each subsequent distance can be compared, and if one of these is LESS than that LEAST, it promptly becomes the new value of LEAST, ready for the next comparison. But of course, it's not much use if SHORTEST merely tells us what the shortest distance is – what we really want to know is which PATH that corresponds to. So the value of LEAST will be a list: of the shortest distance so far and of the corresponding path. It might look like this:

```
(20 ((C . 10) (A . 10) (S . 0)))
```

which may seem pretty horrible; but then only the machine, and not you, has to look at it!

So, SHORTEST is fed with the list of PATHS each time around the loop in BEST. It finds the corresponding distance from S for the first of these, and then uses its own loop to progressively compare that with the distances for subsequent paths in the list:

```
(defun shortest (paths)
  (prog (least hold)
    (setq least (cons (apply 'plus (mapcar 'cdr (car paths)))
                      (car paths)))
    (setq paths (cdr paths))
    loop
    (and (null paths) least (return (cdr least)))
    (and (lessp (setq hold (apply 'plus (mapcar 'cdr (car paths))))
               (car least))
         (setq least (cons hold (car paths))))
    (setq paths (cdr paths))
    (go loop)))
```

Notice the (SETQ HOLD...) trick to save the bother of calculating the distance twice inside the loop.

Now, BEST will return the path which leads to the middle one of the three Fs. Actually, it will return:

```
((S . 0) (A . 10) (D . 10) (F . 5))
```

but no doubt you can see how easy it would be to modify the COND in BEST so that it returned some nicer representation such as:

```
(THE SHORTEST ROUTE IS 25 MILES VIA A and D)
```

The order of the arguments to APPEND – the only difference, remember, between DEPTH and BREADTH – is no longer important in BEST. If you would like to, you could insert, inside the loop and just after the (SETQ CURRENT...) instruction, the new instruction (PRINT (CAAR CURRENT)). This will print out the names of the nodes that the function inspects; and if you try reversing the ordering of APPEND's arguments you'll see that it makes no difference at all. Because, of course, it is no longer the FIRST path which is being selected each time around the loop, but the SHORTEST.

Now consider the moment when the program has reached node A in the tree. If at that point the program could know which of the two routes via C and D was likely to bring it nearest to its goal, it could pick that through D and so save even more searching. This is the second kind of additional information I referred to above, and is analogous to you, trying to find your way through a map and having a compass to aid you: if the route via C happened to point AWAY from F, you would naturally select that via D.

The extra information could again be made use of by SHORTEST: instead of picking the route which represents the shortest distance so far from S, it could, if it had some means of guessing how far it currently was from the goal, pick the route corresponding to the shortest OVERALL distance – i.e. it could add together the distance so far and the remaining distance in each case, and pick the smallest total. This could be achieved by giving an extra argument to the PLUS inside the COND, so that it added in the returned result of some "guessing" function.

An alternative way to use the extra information of both types is to forget about SHORTEST altogether, replacing it with CAR as in DEPTH and BREADTH, and to employ instead a function to SORT the paths after APPEND has added in the NEW-PATHS. The sorting function must be written especially for the problem in hand, and makes an educated guess as to which of the available new paths is most likely to bring the program nearer to the goal. This algorithm is known as A*, pronounced ASTAR. For further information see Raphael (1976) and Hart, Nilsson and Raphael (1968).

6.6.4 Networks

Searching a network (see beginning of 6.6.1) requires exactly the same principles as above, but it also needs to avoid looping routes. All this means is that the program must not investigate any route in which the same node appears twice; and this is achieved by making NEW-PATHS delete any paths which do contain a duplicate node. In essence, what we have to do is alter the LAMBDA expression inside NEW-PATH's MAPCAR so that it returns NIL instead of a new path if the offspring-node it is about to make a new path with would already be a member of that path. Applying APPEND to the result of that will remove any NILs. The complications in the actual code arise merely because any CHILD is a dotted pair (the offspring-node being its CAR, of course), and because APPEND requires LISTS as its arguments:

```
(defun new-paths (path)
   (apply 'append
          (mapcar '(lambda (child)
                     (and (not (member (car child) (mapcar 'car path)))
                          (list (cons child path))))
                  (get (caar path) 'offspring))))
```

6.6.5 Frames

In the context of data structures, you may occasionally come across the idea of FRAMES. This refers to a suggestion first put forward by Minsky (1975) and combines both the notion of a standard structure for holding data as in 6.5 and the notion of a tree. Each node of the tree in a frame system is a complex data object – a structure: in Lisp terms a list or a property-list, or a combination of both. Exactly what the object looks like isn't important; what is important is that they are all the same standard "shape", so that the same access and retrieval functions can be used on them all, and that individual objects are connected into a tree via some standardised link or pointer. That is, each object will have a slot which carries information allowing that object's parent to be found, as well as zero or more slots allowing its offspring to be found. It is these data-objects which are referred to as FRAMES.

The customary example to show how a frame system works is to compare it to your own memory: you walk into a room, and you are at once aware not only that it IS a room – and therefore presumably shares some common attributes with every other thing that you would call a "room" – but perhaps also that it is a particular room, quite distinct in your mind from any other.

The idea is that you have in your own memory the equivalent of a frame, which represents the general concept "room". Perhaps all the rooms you know of have a floor, a ceiling, and four walls: the frame then has slots labelled "floor", "ceiling", "LH wall", "RH wall", etc. Because the real room matches this structure (in some unspecified way), you know that you are in a room and not in a field. However, the only data in the labelled slots are pointers to other frames: there will be a CEILING frame representing your generalised concept of a ceiling; a FLOOR frame representing your floor-concept, and so on. This process of subdivision of overall concepts into sub-concepts can continue indefinitely – one wall might contain a window, so that the "window" slot in your corresponding WALL frame would point to your generalised WINDOW frame – until the last frames reached contain sufficiently detailed data for the items they represent to be uniquely identified. These final frames in the sequence are known as TERMI-NAL frames. And of course once all the items comprising it can be uniquely identified, the original room is uniquely identified too.

When implemented on a computer, each frame in a frame system usually carries default values for its various slots – in case the corresponding data happens to be missing in a particular room (or whatever) – and special slots which contain purpose-built functions for moving data around from frame to frame as required. For further information on frame sytems refer to (Winston 1977) and (Winston and Horn 1981).

6.7 Search projects

The above programs represent general algorithms for solving search problems involving trees or networks. There follow now two practical examples of how particular tree-search problems may be solved: the first starting from the root of a tree and creating the offspring of each node as and when it needs them; and the second starting with a pre-existing network and finding its way around from any one node to any other.

6.7.1 The eight queens problem

The first problem is known as the eight queens problem: how can eight queens be placed on a chess-board so that none is threatened, under the rules of chess, by any of the others? The relevant rule of chess is that a queen threatens any square which is in a direct line with its own square: whether vertically, horizontally, or along either diagonal. For this project it will be helpful if your Lisp can handle small negative numbers (down to –7). See Chapter 4. You will also find PRINC, SPACES and LINES (Chapter 4) useful but not essential.

These four queens are safe from one another:

A normal chess board is eight squares by eight, but the problem of placing eight queens on such a board has no less than 92 solutions, so let's think of the program being applied to a smaller board — say, four squares by four, which has only two solutions. The problem will be the "same" problem if we try to place four queens on a 4 by 4 board, or N queens on an N by N board.

Each square will be represented by a list containing the square's ROW and COLumn, the rows being horizontal in the above diagram and the columns vertical.

(1) The program tries to place a queen on the square it is currently looking at. "Tries" involves checking to see if the square is safe given the presence of all other queens on the board. (At the start, the square will be in ROW 1 COL 1 and of course it will be safe since there are as yet no other queens on the board at all).

(2) If it is safe to place the queen there, the program does so by noting the queen's new square in a running list called BOARD. Since there can never be more than one queen on any given row, it then moves on to consider the first square in the next row, and tries again from (1). If there are no more rows left, it goes to (4), below.

(3) If it is not safe to place the queen, it moves to the next square (next COL) of the same row and tries via (1) again. But if there are no more squares in that row, it BACKTRACKS to remove the previous queen and to try again from (1) using the next square in that removed queen's row.

(4) At some point the program will run out of rows. Because of (3), this only happens if it has succeeded in placing a queen on every row of the board. So the current contents of BOARD can then be printed out as a solution. The program then returns to (3), trying to place a queen somewhere along a non-existent row (row 5 for a 4 by 4 board). But, because a queen in every row necessarily implies that there is also a queen in every column, none of the squares in row 5 is safe. So it eventually backtracks. Depending on the size of the board envisaged in the problem, it may backtrack right back to the first queen, whereupon because of (3) it tries again from the next square on that first queen's row, which must of course be safe since backtracking has now removed all the queens.

So, eventually, the program will have tried to solve the problem by starting from every square in the first row in turn. Since in any solution every row must contain a queen (four rows, four columns, four queens), it will by then have found all the solutions. In the final cycle, it will backtrack to a single queen on the last square of the first row. Because of (3), it will backtrack again; and in the BACKTRACK section of the program is an instruction which says "if there is no BOARD, halt the program".

Here is the program itself:

```
(defun queens (boardsize)
  (prog (row col board)
    (setq row 1)
    (setq col 1)
    loop
    (cond ((safe row col board)
           (setq board (cons (list row col) board))
```

138

```
                    (setq row (plus 1 row))
                    (setq col 1)
                    (and (greaterp row boardsize) (print (reverse board)))
                    (go loop)))
              trynext
              (setq col (plus 1 col))
              (cond ((greaterp col boardsize)
                     (go backtrack))
                    (t (go loop)))
              backtrack
              (cond ((null board) (return (print 'done)))
                    (t (setq row (caar board))
                    (setq col (cadar board))
                    (setq board (cdr board))
                    (go trynext)))))
```

It starts, reasonably enough, in ROW1 COL1, and this square is certain to be safe at this stage. So it inserts the queen, making BOARD look like this:

((1 1))

and moves to ROW2 COL1. This square is not safe becaue of the first queen, so control goes on past the TRYNEXT tag and into the next section of the program, so "moving" from ROW2 COL1 to ROW2 COL2 before going round the LOOP again. This square isn't safe either, so the program moves to ROW2 COL3. This one is safe, so it is noted into BOARD:

((2 3) (1 1))

and the next square to be looked at is ROW3 COL1:

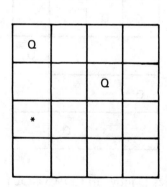

None of the squares on row 3 is safe, so eventually control goes from the TRYNEXT section to BACKTRACK. This resets ROW and COL to the co-ordinates of the previous queen as held in BOARD, and removes the queen by reducing BOARD itself to its own CDR:

((1 1))

Control then goes back to TRYNEXT. TRYNEXT moves the program's attention on to ROW2 COL4, which is a safe square since the only queen now on the board is that in row 1; and subsequently another safe square is found at ROW3 COL2:

Q			
			Q
	Q		

BOARD now looks like this:

   ((3 2) (2 4) (1 1))

But now no square in row 4 is safe, so again the program backtracks, removing the queen from row 3. None of the remaining squares in that row is safe either, so it backtracks again to remove the queen from row 2. And since there are no more squares at all in row 2, it backtracks a third time, removing the queen in row 1 and starting all over again from ROW1 COL2. (Notice that after removing the queen from row 1 control goes to TRYNEXT and then to LOOP. It is only when BACKTRACK is entered with an already-empty board that the program will halt.) This time, it will succeed in placing all four queens:

	Q		
			Q
Q			
		Q	

The program then tries to move to ROW5 COL1. But of course there is no row 5, so the AND instruction in the LOOP section prints out the current BOARD, which consists of those four squares (in reverse order because each one was CONSed into it). But nothing tells control not to go on to TRYNEXT as usual, so it does so. This involves trying all the squares in the hypothetical row 5; and of course none of them is safe because there is already a queen in every column. So the program runs out of squares on that row, causing another backtrack. This time backtracking proceeds right back to the first queen at ROW1 COL2. And the entire sequence begins again from ROW1 COL3.

Another solution is found starting from that square (see first diagram above), but no solution is subsequently found when starting from ROW1 COL4. So eventually a backtrack is attempted with no queen on the board at all, and this finally brings the program to a halt.

Here is the SAFE function (which is really a predicate, since it returns only T or NIL):

```
(defun safe (row col board)
  (prog ()
    loop
    (cond ((null board) (return t))
          ((or (eq row (caar board))
               (eq col (cadar board))
               (eq (plus row col)
                   (apply 'plus (car board)))
               (eq (difference row col)
                   (apply 'difference (car board))))
           (return nil))
    (setq board (cdr board))
    (go loop)))
```

It uses some arithmetical tricks to check whether or not any given square, represented by ROW and COL, is under threat from any queen noted in BOARD. Look at this representation of the board itself:

11	12	13	14
21	22	23	24
31	32	33	34
41	42	43	44

It's pretty obvious that if two squares are on the same ROW, the tens-digits of their numbers will be the same. Similarly, if two squares are on the same COLumn, the units-digits of their numbers will be the same. Remembering that each square is effectively represented as a LIST containing its tens-digit and its units-digit, that explains the first two lines of the complicated OR instruction in SAFE.

Considering any squares on a NE-SW diagonal, you can see by inspection that the SUM of each one's two digits is always the same. And for a NW-SE diagonal the DIFFERENCE between each one's two digits is always the same. Hence the remaining two lines of the OR, and hence my earlier warning about negative numbers.

So SAFE takes the ROW and COL of any square being checked, and makes sure that the square is not threatened by being on the same row, column or diagonal as any square in BOARD — i.e. as any square already containing a queen. If it gets all the way through BOARD without finding such a threat, it returns T. And that's that.

I'm a great believer in having complicated functions return clear, easily understood results. So here's a function to replace the PRINT instruction in QUEENS so as to display a reasonable representation of each solution it finds:

```
(defun print-board (board boardsize)
  (prog (row col)
    (terpri)
    (setq row 1)
    (setq col 1)
    loop
    (cond ((greaterp row boardsize) (terpri) (return t))
          ((member (list row col) board)
           (princ 'q) (spaces 3))
          (t (princ '-) (spaces 3)))
    (setq col (plus 1 col))
    (and (greaterp col boardsize)
         (lines 2)
         (setq col 1)
         (setq row (plus 1 row))
         (go loop))))
```

The overall program does a lot of work for each solution it generates. Finding all the solutions to the eight-queens version, by supplying 8 as the argument to QUEENS, may take some time! So you may like to include a counter to number each solution as it is churned out:

```
(defun queens (boardsize)
  (prog (row col board solcount)                            <--
    (setq solcount 0)                                       <--
    (setq row 1)
    (setq col 1)
    loop
    (cond ((safe row col board)
           (setq board (cons (list row col) board))
           (setq row (plus 1 row))
           (setq col 1)
           (and (greaterp row boardsize)
                (setq solcount (plus 1 solcount))           <--
                (print-board (reverse board) boardsize solcount)) <--
           (go loop)))
    trynext
    (setq col (plus 1 col))
    (cond ((greaterp col boardsize)
           (go backtrack))
          (t (go loop)))
```

142

```
backtrack
(cond ((null board) (return (print 'done)))
      (t (setq row (caar board))
         (setq col (cadar board))
         (setq board (cdr board))
         (go trynext)))))

(defun print-board (board boardsize solcount)      <--
  (prog (row col)
    (print (list 'solution solcount))      <--
    (terpri)
    (setq row 1)
    (setq col 1)
    loop
    (cond ((greaterp row boardsize) (terpri) (return t))
          ((member (list row col) board)
           (princ 'q) (spaces 3))
          (t (princ '-) (spaces 3)))
    (setq col (plus 1 col))
    (and (greaterp col boardsize)
         (lines 2)
         (setq col 1)
         (setq row (plus 1 row))
         (go loop))))
```

Finally, QUEENS does a depth-first search of the tree of possible next squares. It is certain to find the solutions in the end, since it has no concept of "shortest route" to worry about. But it is not particularly efficient – especially in its searching of the non-existent extra bottom row. It is possible to use the ASTAR algorithm on this problem to generate the solution much more quickly.

6.7.2 A simple inferencer

This project builds a system which has affinities with the frames mentioned in 6.6.5. It stores information only at points in the network where it is most generally true, rather than at each node where the information happens to be applicable. For example, addition is a kind of arithmetic, and both necessarily involve numbers. So if a part of our network looked like this:

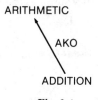

Fig 6.4

you could ask it, in effect, "does addition involve numbers?" and the correspond-

143

ing search program would look first at the node ADDITION and, not finding the information you wanted there, it would be able to follow the AKO link to ARITHMETIC, and on that node the information would be found. The advantage of such an arrangement is that each piece of information is stored only once, rather than perhaps many times. In large information systems, the functions required to handle the AKO links would occupy very much less memory-space than repeated entries of the same pieces of data.

Our inferencer is going to store triples (only) of information on property-lists. There is no particular reason for this, except that property-lists store triples very conveniently – the only access and retrieval functions required being PUT, GET and ADDPROP – and so make the rest of the code more transparent for you. We'll be able to type in triples such as the following:

```
(MAMMAL HAS HAIR)
(HUMAN ISA MAMMAL)
(JOHN ISA HUMAN)
```

and then ask

```
(JOHN HAS HAIR ?)
```

and the machine will infer the answer, returning

```
YES
```

Of course, you may know a John who self-evidently has no hair at all, but that does not detract from the interest of the program. We will also be able to type in statements such as:

```
(MARY ISA MAMMAL)
(MARY ISA HUMAN)
```

and the program will accept the first statement quite happily but, when you put in the second, it will realise that if Mary is a human she must also be a mammal (it already knows that from the statements above), and so the triple (MARY ISA MAMMAL) is redundant. The program will automatically delete that statement from its memory. The system therefore keeps its store of data to an absolute minumum, and in fact stores each triple at that node in a network where the statement is true of all "successor" nodes but not of any "predecessor" nodes:

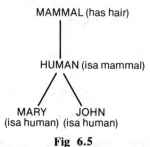

MAMMAL (has hair)

HUMAN (isa mammal)

MARY   JOHN
(isa human) (isa human)

Fig 6.5

Although this structure is clearly a tree, it will later grow into a network. Of course, there can be considerable amounts of other information stored in the form of triples at any node. The skeleton above has links which are ISA links: if you need to know the parent of any node, you look at its ISA triple to find out. Notice that each triple is of a standard form:

NODE RELATION NODE

although not all of the nodes mentioned in the triples (for example, HAIR) need appear as nodes in the network. Perhaps it is worth stressing at this stage that the "links" do not actually exists as explicit objects. But every node which is part of the network will have a triple involving ISA and whose third element is that node's parent-node, as in MARY ISA HUMAN. Diagrams like the above are just a handy way of representing that fact. Every node in the network will have a property-list: the node will of course be the IDENTIFIER, the relation from any associated triple will appear as a PROPERTY, and the second node (third element) of the triple will appear as that property's VALUE. Therefore, the property-list of any node in the tree will have an ISA property and a value (the node's parent) for that property.

For the sake of the following explanation, assume that these instructions have been entered into Lisp and have been evaluated:

```
(addprop 'mammal 'has 'hair)
(addprop 'human 'isa 'mammal)
(addprop 'john 'isa 'human)
```

Since these are ADDPROP instructions, the VALUE on any of the property-lists so created will not be an atom but a LIST. This fact will be important. The network now looks like this:

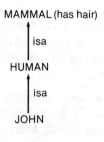

Fig 6.6

The program will also automatically insert for itself "reverse-ISA" links, symbolised by the atom "<-isa" in the relation position (i.e. as a PROPERTY on the node's property-list). For example, when we tell it that MARY ISA HUMAN, the program will store that triple and will also create the additional triple HUMAN <-ISA MARY. In that way it will be able to discover, when it needs to, all the nodes which have . . . ISA HUMAN as the body of their triples. But as I say, all of that happens behind the scenes.

The first (easy!) stage is to build a top-level loop which will accept your statements and your questions, and which will print back to you the system's replies:

```
(defun infer ()
  (prog (input)
    loop
    (print '>>)
    (setq input (read))
    (cond ((equal input '(bye)) (return 'bye))
          (t (print (parse input))))
    (terpri)
    (go loop)))
```

There are two things here which you haven't seen before: the RETURN of an atom BYE and the PRINTing of a function's (PARSE's) returned value. The purpose of the function RETURN is, as you well know, to halt the loop. The VALUE which is returned can be anything you like, so long as it is printable by the PRINT in Lisp's READ-EVAL-PRINT loop. Usually one wants to RETURN the value of some function, or a logical value (T or NIL). But a quoted atom has a value – the atom itself – which is just as printable as any other value. So that's OK. The PRINT line is almost the opposite process: usually you have seen things like (PRINT (LIST ... ...)). And in fact, of course, it is the returned VALUE of LIST which gets printed. So there's no reason why we shouldn't print PARSE's returned value instead. As a matter of fact, PARSE will itself return quoted atoms most of the time!

The prompt which is printed right at the start of the loop is optional, naturally. I just picked a likely-looking symbol, but more or less anything will do.

Notice that I've used READ to take in your actual input to the program. And READ insists on being given a valid Lisp S-expression, which in this case – since we're going to be entering mainly triples – will have to be a list. If you don't like that, LINEREAD is a viable alternative: it accepts anything on a line up as far as the first carriage-return, and makes a list out of it. LINEREAD, if your Lisp has it, will save you having to type the brackets.

Now to PARSE. The name is a bit pretentious, since a real parser would be happy to accept sentences like:

"Forget what you know about humans being mammals."
"Can you please tell me if John has hair?"
"I want you to understand that Mary plays golf."

and would be able to comprehend them well enough to turn them all into their underlying triples if we wanted it to do so. Our poor little parser will only be able to understand three very strict formats: an instruction to the program to FORGET a triple it was previously told; a question concerning the data it currently holds; and a new triple which it is expected to learn: that is, to enter at the appropriate point into the network. From the user's point of view, these three formats will be:

```
(FORGET JOHN ISA HUMAN)
(JOHN HAS HAIR ?)
(MARY PLAYS GOLF)
```

Notice that in the middle example, the question, we aren't even allowed to write the question-mark, as one normally would, directly at the end of HAIR. Both the FORGET instruction and the question-form have to be four-element lists. Right. So here's how PARSE works:

```
(defun parse (input)
  (cond ((eq (car input) 'forget)
         (forget (cadr input) (caddr input) (car (cdddr input))))
        ((eq (car (cdddr input)) '?)
         (cond ((find (list (car input))
                      (cadr input)
                      (caddr input))
                'yes)
               (t 'no)))
        (t (learn (car input) (cadr input) (caddr input)))))
```

All those CDDDRs and things look truly horrible, don't they? Whenever I see such things I itch to redefine them like this:

```
(defun second (L)    (defun third (L)    (defun fourth (L)
  (cadr L))            (caddr L))          (car (cdddr L))
```

just to make the code more readable. You can easily do that if you want to, although this is the only function in this particular program which needs them. Rewritten using those little routines, PARSE would look like this:

```
(defun parse (input)
  (cond ((eq (car input) 'forget)
         (forget (second input) (third input) (fourth input)))
        ((eq (fourth input) '?)
         (cond ((find (car input) (second input) (third input))
                'yes)
               (t 'no)))
        (t (learn (car input) (second input) (third input)))))
```

which is far less nerve-racking.

PARSE looks at the input typed by the user of the system and decides which of the three permissible formats it represents. If the first word of the input is FORGET, PARSE calls a function of the same name to do just that with the remainder of the input. If the last "word" of the input is a question-mark, PARSE calls FIND to deal with it. FIND will be able to search through the network of nodes looking for a triple which matches the remainder of the input, and will be able to make any necessary inferences as above. So if FIND succeeds we'll arrange for it to return T, so that PARSE itself returns YES to the PRINT instruction in INFER; and if FIND fails it will return NIL so that PARSE returns NO.

If the input is neither a FORGET instruction nor a question, it must (should!) be a new triple of information to be learned, so PARSE calls the function LEARN to do so. A nice improvement to PARSE would be to include an extra first clause

147

to its COND, which made sure that no error messages came from Lisp if some user clumsily entered an impermissible format:

```
((or (lessp (length input) 3)
      (and (eq (length input) 4) (not (eq (fourth input) '?))
           (not(eq(car input)'forget)))
      (greaterp (length input) 4))
  'eh?)
```

Let's now go through the three functions called by PARSE, starting with FIND – since that is the easiest:

```
(defun find (id rel val)
         (cond ((null id) nil)
               ((member val (get (car id) rel))
                (list (car id) val rel))
               ((get (car id) 'isa)
                (find (get (car id) 'isa) rel val))))
```

FIND is asked to find out if, for example, JOHN HAS HAIR. In fact the first argument to FIND is made into a list by PARSE, for reasons which will become clear later. Within FIND, the first clause of the COND fails. So does the second, because HAIR is not on JOHN'S property-list under the property HAS. However, JOHN has an ISA property, so the third COND-clause recursively calls FIND again with the arguments (HUMAN), HAS, and HAIR. In other words the original input question is no longer being asked concerning JOHN, but is being asked concerning HUMAN. During this recursive call to FIND the same thing happens again, so that the question is effectively being asked about MAMMAL. This time the second clause of the COND is activated, so that FIND returns non-NIL and hence PARSE returns YES. As you can see, FIND actually returns a list of the final form of the question (MAMMAL HAS HAIR) rather than the atom T. Again, the reasons for this will be clear in a minute.

But suppose that the part of the network which FIND was asked to search looked like this:

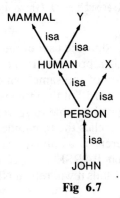

Fig 6.7

It doesn't matter what the extra nodes X and Y are, merely that they are there. FIND now needs to do a depth-first (UPwards) search of the network in order to find MAMMAL; and this is quite easy to arrange using recursion:

```
(defun find (id rel val)
  (cond ((null id) nil)
        ((member val (get (car id) rel))
         (list (car id) val rel))
        ((get (car id) 'isa)
         (or (find (get (car id) 'isa) rel val)
             (find (cdr id) rel val)))))
```

The GET in the third clause of the COND will always return a list (hence the ADDPROPs earlier), and if this list has several members the same clause will call FIND to check out the first member of the list as usual, and then again if that check returns NIL to deal with the CDR of the list. So that's why the first argument to FIND is always a list, even if it is a list of only one element.

Suppose now that the user of the system wants to add a new triple to the network, such as MARY ISA HUMAN. As soon as that is typed in, PARSE calls the function LEARN:

```
(defun learn (id val rel)
  (prog (triple)
    (cond ((setq triple (find (list id) rel val))
           (cons 'known: triple))
          (t (addprop id rel val)))))
```

If it is already known that MARY ISA HUMAN or if FIND can infer it, LEARN returns a statement to that effect, which is duly returned by PARSE. Otherwise, the new information is simply ADDPROPped onto MARY's property-list. The fact that FIND returns the triple it finds, rather than T, enables us to use that SETQ trick in the first COND clause, which avoids having to call FIND to do the same job twice.

However, here comes a nasty complication: suppose that the network looked like this:

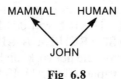

Fig 6.8

and suppose that the new triple to be entered is HUMAN ISA MAMMAL. In order to keep the network to a minimum and to remove redundant links, the program needs to be able to see that the link between JOHN and MAMMAL is no longer required; it can be inferred now. But how is the program to know that there IS a link between JOHN and MAMMAL? JOHN is not referred to in the new input (HUMAN ISA MAMMAL). So, unless the program is to keep a running list of all the nodes it knows about, and to search the whole list every time a change is made to the network, it needs some way of inferring from that input triple that MAMMAL has a link FROM somewhere else.

And that last statement is the clue: we put in for every ISA link, as triples are added to the network, an equivalent "reverse-ISA" link:

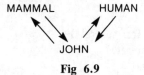

MAMMAL   HUMAN

JOHN

Fig 6.9

Now, given the input triple HUMAN ISA MAMMAL, the program can go straight to MAMMAL and from there follow the reverse-isa link back down to JOHN. It can then, by removing redundant links of both types (ISA and reverse-ISA), reorganise the network as we would like:

MAMMAL

HUMAN

JOHN

Fig 6.10

So LEARN needs some additions:

```
(defun learn (id val rel)
  (prog (triple)
    (cond ((setq triple (find (list id) rel val))
           (cons 'known: triple))
          ((eq rel 'isa)
           (search-link-kill id val)
           (link-search-kill id val)
           (addprop val '<-isa id)
           (addprop id 'isa val))
          (t (addprop id rel val)))))
```

At first sight it might seem pretty obvious what the two new functions SEARCH-LINK-KILL and LINK-SEARCH-KILL will do. But I'm afraid nothing is as simple as it seems. Let's look at SEARCH-LINK-KILL first. In a real case, rather than in the simple example above, the network might look something like this at the moment when the new triple HUMAN ISA MAMMAL is entered:

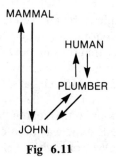

MAMMAL

HUMAN

PLUMBER

JOHN

Fig 6.11

150

The new link between HUMAN and MAMMAL still incurs the removal of the link between JOHN and MAMMAL. So SEARCH-LINK-KILL is going to need to be able to chase down the series of reverse-ISA links from HUMAN to JOHN; and only when it gets to JOHN and finds JOHN's ISA link back up to MAMMAL will it be safe for it to remove anything:

```
(defun search-link-kill (id val)
  (cond ((member val (get id 'isa))
         (print (list 'redundant id 'isa val))
         (forget id 'isa val))
        ((get id '<-isa)
         (search-link-kill id val))))
```

FORGET does the actual deletion of the links, as you'll see shortly. But even that isn't all: as SEARCH-LINK-KILL chases down the reverse-ISA chain, it may well find that some parent-node has several offspring, and at such points it must be able to investigate the chains from each of those offspring – it has no way of knowing in advance which of them will eventually lead to JOHN and hence back to MAMMAL. So a mapping function is needed, to enable it to chase down several chains in turn:

```
(defun search-link-kill (id val)
  (cond ((member val (get id 'isa))
         (print (list 'redundant id 'isa val))
         (forget id 'isa val))
        ((get id '<-isa)
         (mapc '(lambda (pred)
                  (search-link-kill pred val))
               (get id '<-isa)))))
```

Phew. Here's FORGET:

```
(defun forget (id rel val)
  (put id rel (delete val (get id rel)))
  (and (eq rel 'isa)
       (put val '<-isa (delete id (get val '<-isa)))))
```

It simply retrieves the current value of ID's REL property (the REL may not be ISA – see below), deletes VAL from it, and puts the remainder back again. When the REL is ISA, it does the same thing for the corresponding reverse-ISA link.

LINK-SEARCH-KILL is somewhat simpler, and exists to cover the opposite kind of network change: that where the link up to MAMMAL already exists, and the new one is to a node which is also already linked to MAMMAL; such as, given the network below, inserting a new link MARC ISA PLUMBER:

151

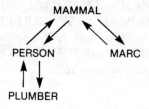

Fig 6.12

Here is LINK-SEARCH-KILL:

```
(defun link-search-kill (id val)
  (mapc '(lambda (succ)
           (cond ((find (list succ) '<-isa val)
                  (print (list 'redundant id 'isa succ))
                  (forget id 'isa succ))))
        (get id 'isa)))
```

The GET supplies as argument to the MAPC a list of any ISA links which MARC has, in this case a list of MAMMAL. FIND then chases down the chain of reverse-ISA links from MAMMAL, and if at any point it encounters PERSON, it knows that the original ISA and reverse-ISA links between MARC and MAMMAL are redundant, and so can be deleted.

These two KILL functions are named so as to remind you of what they do: SEARCH-LINK-KILL searches until it finds a certain link, and then deletes it. LINK-SEARCH-KILL follows a single link first, then searches, and if the search succeeds deletes the link it started with. Notice that "link" can mean either an ISA/reverse-ISA pair or a single link such as HAS. Notice also that the abbreviation PRED (for PREDECESSOR) could as well have been called SUCC (for SUCCESSOR), depending on which of the two ISA-type links you choose to regard as dominant!

One final refinement to the system: since it is now able to perform automatically such complex rearrangements of ISA-type links, it will be easy to give it a similar ability for non-ISA links. Thus, inserting MAMMAL HAS FEET into the following network should ensure that the redundant PLUMBER HAS FEET triple is removed:

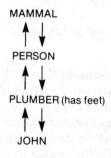

Fig 6.13

That is a LINK-SEARCH-KILL kind of operation, and indeed the function is very similar:

```
(defun rel-search-kill (id rel val)
  (cond ((member val (get id rel))
         (print (list 'redundant id rel val))
         (forget id rel val))
        ((get id '<-isa)
         (mapc '(lambda (pred)
                  (rel-search-kill pred rel val))
               (get id '<-isa)))))
```

And that's the lot. Now you can play with it, inserting various triples at various points on the network, and watching what the inferencer does. You will find that every time you add or delete a triple, PARSE returns to you the result of the corresponding ADDPROP or PUT in LEARN or FORGET. So what you see is the new value of the node's property, after your addition or deletion. You might like to modify LEARN and FORGET so that they return a clearer form of that message.

Chapter 7
Pattern matching

7.1 Eliza

ELIZA is a famous AI program (Weizenbaum 1965) which makes the computer seem to engage in a sensible conversation with the user. It works by noticing keywords in (your) typed input, from which it can compute and print back a reasonable-looking answer. For example, if you typed in

```
*- (I think my brother hates me)
```

it would notice the keywords "brother" and "hates", and might respond with:

```
(TELL ME MORE ABOUT YOUR FAMILY)
```

If you typed:

```
*- (What would you know about it?  You are only a computer)
```

the machine might ask:

```
(ARE YOU AFRAID OF COMPUTERS)
```

By giving the program a richly varied set of possible responses, you can make it behave with apparent intelligence.

Of course, it isn't intelligent really, which is what makes this an interesting program from the Artificial Intelligence point of view. The intelligence lies in a clever pattern matching algorithm which can pick the keywords out of input sentences; in the set of keywords itself, which clearly embodies some notion of how a sentence is understood by a human listener; and in the set of responses which the machine can generate when it reads those keywords. All that the machine does is what it always does: it takes from you a series of symbols by READing your input; it manipulates those symbols by EVALuating one or more function-definitions with the symbols as arguments; and it PRINTs back the result. That is essentially no more intelligent than when it prints the value of ANIMALS at your request.

And yet a good Eliza program can genuinely be said to hold conversations with human beings which make sense. Alan Turing was the first to suggest what is really a philosophical point about the meaning of "person". Here is my allegorical version of the same point:

You are taken to a house wherein lives a chronic invalid. This person has total allergy syndrome, and acquired immune deficiency syndrome as well. Not even minimal physical contact is possible. So you are introduced, and chat, via a microphone and loudspeaker. And you really get to like this invalid. He or she (sex doesn't come into this story) is bright, articulate, amusing, sensitive – all the things you most admire in other people. And you haven't yet read this book, so that when one day they take the screens away, you are genuinely amazed to find that your sick friend is a healthy computer. Until that moment there had been not the slightest reason to suppose that he/she wasn't as human as you are. So what do you say, when they invite you to switch off the power?

To develop that analogy, it is not a particularly impressive achievement to be able to build huge calculating engines, which can analyse the voting patterns of a nation or do an oil company's annual accounts in a matter of seconds. It's impressive enough the first time you see such a program in action, but overall it is far less exciting than, say, the first fire must have been to our ancestors. The more exciting question is this: since machines can do that kind of thing, which until recently ONLY human beings could do, is there a limit on the extent to which the machine could copy our (mental) abilities? Will there always be a logically necessary dividing line between machines and people? And this of course raises a whole host of concomitant questions, from What is a Person? through What is Intelligence? to What is a Logically Necessary Dividing Line? And that is what is interesting about AI, not what is interesting about Lisp.

The importance of Eliza in this context is the apparent ease with which we can give the machine an indefinable but unmistakable air of human-ness.

I don't propose to write out a whole Eliza program for you – a really good one would fill most of this book. But I'll show you how the pattern matching program is written, and how to write the loop which will read your input into Eliza. But except for the bare minimum of necessary examples, I leave the question of which keywords it shall pick up on, and what it shall say in response to them, up to you. In other words, I'll contribute the "mechanical" part, and the impressive bit – the "personality" of your Eliza will be added by you. A friend of mine once wrote an Eliza which had an unfortunate tendency, on occasion, to be very rude indeed.

7.2 Pattern matching

Here are two lists:

(a b c)   (a b d)

Whether they "match" or not depends on what criterion you use. The normal instinctive response is to say no, they don't match because the atom C and the atom D are different. But if your only requirement for a match was that each element should always be an atom (i.e. not a list), then they would match. Both of these ways of looking at the question are types of pattern matching. Presumably a pattern matching algorithm to test that the corresponding elements of both lists were atoms would involve the predicate ATOM. And in principle there's no reason why you shouldn't have a predicate called LEX which checked that corresponding elements were lexically identical. The instinctive response is only one kind of pattern matching. But let's see how to do it.

We will assume the presence of a pattern list such as (a b c), and write a function which will take that together with any other list, returning T if they are lexically the same and NIL otherwise. The obvious way to do it is to go through both lists simultaneously, element by element, checking at each stage that the CARs of the two lists are EQUAL. I hope you're already thinking "recursion". So here is the simplest possible pattern matcher other than EQUAL itself:

```
(defun match (patt inp)
  (cond ((and (null patt) (null inp)))
        ((or (null patt) (null inp)) nil)
        ((equal (car patt) (car inp))
         (match (cdr patt) (cdr inp)))))
```

This function, in English, says: if both patterns are empty, we must have matched all the elements of each, so the answer is T. If either list is empty and (because of the previous clause of this COND) the other is not, they don't match and the answer is NIL. Otherwise, and if the CARs of the two lists are EQUAL, go on to match their CDRs. (In case you've forgotten: the absence of an "action" S-expression in the first COND-clause entails that if the test succeeds, its value is returned. And when AND succeeds, it returns T.) If none of the conditions is true, the COND returns NIL – i.e. the value of its last argument.

This is what we've achieved so far:

```
*- (match '(a b c) '(a b c))

T

*- (match '(my cat hates me) '(my cat loves me))

NIL
```

But what about these two lists:

```
(footballs are round)   (footballs are balls)
```

There could clearly be cases where you would want to say that those two do match. So let's extend the power of our matcher by specifying that the atom –ANY–, if it appears in the pattern, can "match" the corresponding element of the input, no matter what that element is. But let's say that there must be such an input element, so that

```
(a -ANY- c)
```

will not match

```
(a c)
```

In order to do this, the matcher simply has to check at each stage of the recursion that either the CARs of the two lists are the same, OR the CAR of the pattern is −ANY− :

```
(defun match (patt inp)
  (cond ((and (null patt) (null inp)))
        ((or (null patt) (null inp)) nil)
        ((or (equal (car patt) '-ANY-)
             (equal (car patt) (car inp)))
         (match (cdr patt) (cdr inp)))))
```

Notice that the recursive call to MATCH only occurs if at least one of the new OR's arguments evaluates to T. If neither does, OR returns NIL and so the COND returns NIL. Now MATCH can do things like:

```
*- (match '(my -ANY- hates me) '(my canary hates me))

T
```

See? It can be ironic already! However, the matcher isn't nearly good enough yet. In order to be able to pick out keywords in input sentences, it will need to be able to say that the pattern list

```
( ... love ... )
```

matches the input list

```
(the fire has gone out of our love since Friday)
```

If it can do that, it can detect the keyword LOVE no matter how much other stuff surrounds it in the input. So we need something analogous to −ANY−, but which will "match" with one or more input atoms. (The above pattern list would, of course, also match with the input "I love strawberries". But you can face that problem when you come to it).

Let's call the new atom for our patterns −MANY−. Whenever −MANY− is encountered in the pattern as MATCH works its way down the lists, there are two possibilities to cater for:

pattern	input
(young men see -MANY-)	(young men see visions)
(old men -MANY-)	(old men dream dreams)

157

That is, cases where –MANY– has to "match": (1) one atom; or (2) more than one atom. Another way of looking at this is to say that the remainder of the input list after EQUAL atoms have been removed from both pattern and input lists as above (1) matches the pattern – in this case –MANY– is allowed to have the same effect as –ANY– ; or (2) would match the pattern if the input's first atom were removed and the recursive calls were allowed to repeat this process as many times as are necessary:

```
pattern                    input

(-MANY-)                   (visions)
(-MANY-)                   (dream dreams)
```

In the next version of MATCH a third clause is added to the existing COND. It detects the presence of –MANY– in the pattern, and then uses a second COND to handle the above two cases:

```
(defun match (patt inp)
  (cond ((and (null patt) (null inp)))
        ((or (null patt) (null inp)) nil)
        ((or (equal (car patt) '-ANY-)
             (equal (car patt) (car inp)))
         (match (cdr patt) (cdr inp)))
        ((equal (car patt) '-MANY-)
         (cond ((match (cdr patt) (cdr inp)))    <-- (1)
               ((match patt (cdr inp)))))))       <-- (2)
```

The first clause of the COND removes the CAR of both lists and proceeds to try to match their CDRs, thus making –MANY– work like –ANY–. And the second clause allows the matcher to discard the first member of the input list and try to match the full pattern list, whose CAR remains –MANY– to the remainder.

We're now in a position to make a start on the function MICRO-ELIZA itself. The first point is that it wouldn't seem like much of a conversation if the human participant had to keep hassling with quote-marks, calls to MATCH and so on. What we really need is a function which, whilst MICRO-ELIZA is running, will sit waiting for the user to type something in, just as at normal Lisp top level the function READ sits waiting for you to type something in. In fact, READ is the function we're going to use, embedded in a loop which iterates until you have had enough of talking to MICRO-ELIZA:

```
(defun micro-eliza ()
  (prog (input)
    loop
    (setq input (read))
    (cond ((equal input '(bye)) (return nil))
          ((match '(<pattern1>) input) (print <response1>))
          ((match '(<pattern2>) input) (print <response2>))
          ..... )
    (go loop)))
```

158

Incidentally, if your Lisp has the function LINEREAD, use it instead of READ in MICRO-ELIZA. The difference is that whereas READ expects an S-expression (i.e. you have to type brackets around what you say), LINEREAD reads anything up until the next carriage-return, and then makes a list out of it. You should find that the normal method of deleting and retyping mistakes still works, whichever of these two functions you use.

But, there's more to come yet. Suppose you typed in:

```
*- (I am afraid of the dark)
```

it would be nice if MICRO-ELIZA could reply with something like:

```
(WHAT IS IT THAT MAKES YOU AFRAID OF THE DARK)
```
where MICRO-ELIZA has matched the pattern

```
(I AM AFRAID -MANY-)
```

against your input, but has "remembered" the matching part so as to repeat it in the reply.

One way to do this would be to bind "OF THE DARK" to –MANY– as the latter's value. But this would entail that you could only have one –MANY– in any given pattern, which could be an inconvenience. OK then, let's use some other atom(s) to bind the matched bits to: atoms which will behave just like –MANY– in all other respects.

Somehow, the matcher has to be able to tell that a given atom in the pattern is one of these new special atoms. So here's a neat trick: at any point where we need binding to occur we write into the pattern not just the special atom, but a list. A very simple list, of only two elements. The first element is like a flag, and serves merely to tell the matcher that the second element is: a special atom. Let's say that the flag is to be the atom –BIND–. Here is a possible pattern using it:

```
(the cat (-BIND- XX))
```

MATCH is then called:

```
(match '(the cat (-BIND- XX)) '(the cat wants to go out))
```

MATCH returns T, and the special atom XX is bound to the list

```
(WANTS TO GO OUT).
```

The special atom should, of course, be one that is extremely unlikely ever to occur as an element of any input.

To make this work, the main COND in MATCH needs a new clause whose condition part says "If the CAR of the pattern is not an atom (i.e. if it is one of our new two-lists) and if the CAR of that is –BIND–, go on to do the following action-part". And, as with –MANY–, there are two cases to cover in the action-part: (1) where XX matches to one atom; and (2) where it matches to several atoms. We

159

adopt the same approach as before to handle these two cases, but with extra instructions to effect whatever binding is required: (1) bind the special atom to the CAR of the input; or (2) add the current CAR of the input to a "running total" list to which the special atom will eventually be bound:

```
(defun match (patt inp)
  (cond ((and (null patt) (null inp)))
        ((or (null patt) (null inp)) nil)
        ((or (equal (car patt) '-ANY-)
             (equal (car patt) (car inp)))
         (match (cdr patt) (cdr inp)))
        ((equal (car patt) '-MANY-)
         (cond ((match (cdr patt) (cdr inp)))
               ((match patt (cdr inp)))))
        ((and (listp (car patt))
              (equal (caar patt) '-BIND-))
         (cond ((match (cdr patt) (cdr inp))
                (set (cadr (car patt)) (cons (car inp) nil)))
               ((match patt (cdr inp))
                (set (cadr (car patt))
                     (cons (car inp) (eval (cadr (car patt))))))))))
```

You should put as many XX-type variables as you are ever likely to need into the variables-slot of MICRO-ELIZA's PROG. That way, the variables are kept tidily local to the MICRO-ELIZA program. They are also preset to NIL at the start, which is crucial because otherwise the call to EVAL inside the CONS would immediately issue an error message about one of them being unbound.

Now to an example – more a broad hint, really – as to how your final MICRO-ELIZA might look:

```
(defun micro-eliza ()
  (prog (input xx yy zz)
    (print (list '(hello - what seems to be the trouble today?)))
    loop
    (print '-->)
    (setq input (read))
    (cond ((atom input) (print '(brackets please)))
          ((equal input '(bye)) (return nil))
          ((equal (length input) 1)
           (print '(please do not be so short with me)))
          ((match '(-many- my (-bind- xx) hates me) input)
           (cond ((member (car xx)
                          '(husband wife mother father sister brother))
                  (print '(tell me more about your family)))
                 (t (print '(why should that bother you?)))))
          ((or (match '(-many- machine) input)
               (match '(-many- machine -many-) input)
               (match '(computers -many-) input))
```

160

```
            (print '(are you afraid of computers?)))
         (t (print (list 'you 'were 'talking 'about 'your (car xx)))))
   (go loop)))
```

As it stands, you have to be a bit selective about the things you say to it! But the beginnings of a conversation are possible:

```
*- (micro-eliza)

(HELLO - WHAT SEEMS TO BE THE TROUBLE TODAY?)

*- (I think my mother hates me)

(TELL ME MORE ABOUT YOUR FAMILY)

*- (No)

(PLEASE DO NOT BE SO SHORT WITH ME)

*- (You are only a machine)

(ARE YOU AFRAID OF COMPUTERS?)

*- (No)

(PLEASE DO NOT BE SO SHORT WITH ME)

*- (Okay okay)

(YOU WERE TALKING ABOUT YOUR MOTHER)
```

Chapter 8
Implementing another language

I have frequently said that one of the joys of Lisp is the ease with which, if you don't like the way it behaves, you can make it behave differently. You have already seen examples of how system functions can be defined or redefined to suit the purposes of this book. But much more is possible: extrapolating the idea of "changing Lisps's behaviour", we should be able to make it behave as though it were not Lisp at all, but some other programming language. Within certain limits (imposed only because I can't be sure which, if any, of Lisp's more advanced facilities will exist in your microcomputer dialect) this chapter will show you how to write a program which does exactly that. You will need the function READ, and you will need to have understood how to use your Lisp's PRINTing functions as discussed in Chapter 4. You may also need a new version of APPEND, and a new version of MAPCAR. I'll show you how to write them when the need arises. And finally, it would be nice if you had defined SECOND and THIRD from PARSE in section 6.7.2. Otherwise, you'll have to use CADR and CADDR respectively in the program below.

This is the biggest project I shall ask you to undertake.

8.1 LSOLO

The language I'm going to introduce you to, and which in the course of what follows you will write in Lisp, is called LSOLO. It is a variant of a genuine programming language called SOLO (Eisenstadt 1982) which is used to teach the principles of AI programming – as distinct from teaching an actual programming language – to undergraduate students who are assumed to have no prior experience of computers at all. LSOLO is very, very simple compared with what you've been learning in this book. But it is an interactive language like Lisp: you type in an instruction, and SOLO responds in some meaningful way.

SOLO (and hence LSOLO) is a database-dependent language. That is, it relies on a store of data which the user can modify and/or query. SOLO programs are very much like Lisp programs, except that instead of inspecting and operating upon each other's returned values they inspect and operate upon the contents of the database.

Only one type of data-unit is permitted in SOLO's database: a data structure or record called the relational triple. For example:

```
(FIDO ISA DOG)
```

is such a triple, in which two nouns or "nodes" are thought of as being connected together via the one-way relation ISA. Here is another triple:

```
(FIDO BROTHER ROVER)
```

It records the information that FIDO has a brother called ROVER. But, because the relation is specified as being one-way, it does not imply the reverse fact that ROVER also has a brother called FIDO. That is what "one-way" means in this context. In terms of the data structures you read about in Chapter 6, the relational triple is like a parent-node from a tree connected to just one of its offspring.

LSOLO functions can call each other and can take formal parameters as in Lisp; the language permits both conditional expressions and recursion. (If you've been having trouble understanding recursion, this chapter is the one you've been waiting for: you're actually going to build the mechanism whereby recursion in LSOLO achieves its effects!) LSOLO has no direct equivalents of bound variables other than formal parameters, nor of the loop construct, although SOLO itself has both.

8.2 The LSOLO system functions

In fact LSOLO has only eight top-level functions: NOTE, FORGET, DE-SCRIBE, CHECK, PRINT, TO, LIST and BYE. We shall now work through them one by one. At each stage I shall tell you how the function is used and what it does, how to define it in Lisp, and how to integrate that definition into a growing overall LSOLO system. What you will end up with is an implementation of LSOLO which you can use, say, to demonstrate to a computer-mad child the differences between BASIC and a proper AI language.

8.3 The three basic functions

In LSOLO, NOTE is used for adding new triples to the database. It doesn't overwrite any existing triples, so removing them from the database has to be done explicitly using FORGET. You may well have guessed already that the way we're going to create LSOLO's database is by using Lisp's property-lists:

```
(FIDO ISA DOG)    -->    (<id> <prop> <val>)
```

But, since the specification of NOTE says that the function doesn't overwrite, we'll need ADDPROP rather than PUT:

```
(defun note (triple)
   (addprop (car triple) (second triple) (third triple)))
```

This will work already, although of course it isn't the final version of NOTE:

```
*- (note 'fido 'isa 'dog)

(DOG)

*- (note 'tiddles 'isa 'cat)

(CAT)
```

So the property-lists that we use will, together, form LSOLO's database. There will eventually be any number of nodes that LSOLO knows about, and each of them will be a (Lisp) identifier having the corresponding relation as its property-name and the remaining node from the LSOLO triple as that property's value. Notice that although LSOLO could already retrieve the information about FIDO, which is an identifier, the other node DOG is not an identifier. As far as LSOLO is concerned that is equivalent to there being "no information" about DOG. LSOLO only knows about the items which appear in the first position of its triples, and this restriction preserves the specified "one-way" nature of the relations. Inverse relations such as (ROVER BROTHER FIDO) have to be NOTEd explicitly.

In order to give you the flavour of what LSOLO will finally look like, let's now write its top level; that is, its equivalent of Lisp's READ-EVAL-PRINT loop. Here is a very simple version:

```
(defun lsolo ()
  (prog (input)
    (terpri)
    loop1
    (terpri)
    (print 'solo:)
    (setq input (read))
    (and (equal input '(bye)) (return nil))
    (print (eval input))
    (go loop1)))
```

As you can see, control iterates round and round the loop, printing a different prompt from the Lisp one, but otherwise doing the same as Lisp itself does: printing the value of whatever you type in. When you want to exit from LSOLO and back to Lisp you type (in brackets) the word "BYE". The TERPRIs are there merely to make the printouts a bit prettier. But now you can do the following:

```
*- (lsolo)

SOLO: (note '(fido isa dog))
```

[you type the NOTE instruction once the SOLO: prompt has appeared]

```
(DOG)

SOLO:
```

See? It's beginning to be a real interactive language already! But the display is spoiled a bit by that all-too-obvious returned value from ADDPROP. And that is there because we told LSOLO to PRINT the value of any input. That can come

164

out again straight away:

```
(defun lsolo ()
  (prog (input)
    (terpri)
    loop1
    (terpri)
    (print 'solo:)
    (setq input (read))
    (and (equal input '(bye)) (return nil))
    (eval input)
    (go loop1)))
```

The trouble now is, as you'll see if you make that change and try LSOLO out again, that although NOTE works, just as before, LSOLO doesn't tell you so – it merely goes back to its top-level prompt. And I did say that LSOLO was to be an interactive language, not a stolid unresponsive clod. And a similarly small change to NOTE will make it say something when it has done its stuff:

```
(defun note (triple)
  (addprop (car triple) (second triple) (third triple))
  (terpri)
  (print (cons 'noted: triple)))
```

That's better:

```
*- (lsolo)

SOLO: (note '(fido isa dog))
(NOTED: FIDO ISA DOG)
SOLO: (bye)
NIL

*-
```

We'll make some more improvements to that in a minute, but first let's write the function FORGET, which removes that database triple concerning FIDO. Do this:

```
*- (lsolo)

SOLO: (note '(fido isa friend))
(NOTED: FIDO ISA FRIEND)
SOLO: (bye)

*-
```

and, if you look at FIDO's property-list, you'll see that the property-name ISA now has a LIST of DOG and FRIEND as its value. The new function FORGET needs to be able to remove just one of those – we want to type something like:

```
SOLO: (forget '(fido isa friend))
```

to remove our most recent database entry but to leave all others (such as FIDO ISA DOG) intact. REMPROP would be too coarse for our purposes: it would remove all of the ISA values from FIDO. So we'll use a trick you've seen before – that of retrieving the whole list of values, DELETEing the unwanted one, and PUTting the whole thing back again:

```
(defun forget (triple)
  (terpri)
  (put (car triple)
       (second triple)
       (delete (third triple) (get (car triple) (second triple))))
  (terpri)
  (print (cons 'forgotten: triple)))
```

That PUT instruction, translated into English and with the triple given as FIDO ISA FRIEND, says: get the list which is the value of FIDO's ISA-property, delete FRIEND from it, and put the result back as FIDO's new ISA-property.

Before you try out FORGET, there's a nice refinement to add. And that is to have FORGET tell the user if ever he or she tries to FORGET a triple which actually wasn't present in the database to start with. As things stand, you could go on FORGETting FIDO ISA FRIEND till the cows came home, and FORGET would faithfully say that it had forgotten it each time. All we need is a COND which checks to see whether or not the triple is present:

```
(defun forget (triple)
  (terpri)
  (cond ((memq (third triple) (get (car triple) (second triple)))
         (put (car triple)
              (second triple)
              (delete (third triple) (get (car triple) (second triple))))
         (terpri)
         (print (cons 'forgotten: triple)))
        (t (print (list 'no 'such 'description 'of (car triple))))))
```

Now you can do this:

```
*- (lsolo)

SOLO: (forget '(fido isa computer))
(NO SUCH DESCRIPTION OF FIDO)
SOLO: (forget '(fido isa friend))
(FORGOTTEN: FIDO ISA FRIEND)
SOLO: (forget '(fido isa friend))
(NO SUCH DESCRIPTION OF FIDO)
SOLO: (bye)
NIL

*-
```

Yes, that's coming along nicely. But it's still not interactive enough. It's a bit like a Lisp all of whose functions invariably returned either T or NIL: not very informative. In LSOLO there are no returned values to print out, so to make it match Lisp in this respect we need something else, and this could well be a "description" of the node concerned – a description which would appear automatically whenever a user NOTEd or FORGETted any triple with that node in its first position (e.g. any triple about FIDO). And of course that is exactly what the LSOLO function DESCRIBE does. It's available to the user as a top-level function, and is also automatically called from within both NOTE and FORGET. I'm afraid there have to be two different versions of DESCRIBE, for different types of Lisp. The normal one, for Lisps which store data on their property-lists as a list of alternate properties and values, is:

```
(defun describe (node)
  (prog (pairs)
    (terpri)
    (setq pairs (plist node))
    loop
    (and (null pairs) (return t))
    (mapc '(lambda (v)
             (print (list node (car pairs) v)))
          (second pairs))
    (setq pairs (cddr pairs))
    (terpri)
    (go loop)))
```

But, for Lisps which store data on their property-lists as dotted pairs:

```
(defun describe (node)
  (prog (pairs)
    (terpri)
    (setq pairs (plist node))
    loop
    (and (null pairs) (return t))
    (mapc '(lambda (v)
             (print (list node (caar pairs) v)))
          (cdr (car pairs)))
    (setq pairs (cdr pairs))
    (terpri)
    (go loop)))
```

This sets the local variable PAIRS to the whole of (e.g.) FIDO's property-list, and then iterates round a loop. On each cycle of the loop, it prints out the NODE followed by the current CAR of PAIRS – which will be a property-name – followed by one of that property-name's values. The MAPC ensures that all of the property-name's values are printed out in this way. Thus, if you NOTE back the

167

FRIEND triple for FIDO:

```
SOLO: (describe 'fido)
(FIDO ISA DOG)
(FIDO ISA FRIEND)
SOLO:
```

Incidentally, there is no special reason why I've made DESCRIBE return T rather than NIL when it has finished. Now, to add it to NOTE and FORGET:

```
(defun note (triple)
  (addprop (car triple) (second triple) (third triple))
  (terpri)
  (print (cons 'noted: triple))
  (describe (car triple)))              <--

(defun forget (triple)
  (cond ((memq (third triple) (get (car triple) (second triple)))
         (put (car triple)
              (second triple)
              (delete (third triple) (get (car triple) (second triple))))
         (terpri)
         (print (cons 'forgotten: triple))
         (describe (car triple)))       <--
        (t (terpri)
           (print (list 'no 'such 'description 'of (car triple))))))
```

Now you should find that any call to either function results in a neat display of the effect that call has had on the corresponding part of LSOLO's database:

```
SOLO: (note '(fido has fleas))
(NOTED: FIDO HAS FLEAS)
(FIDO HAS FLEAS)
(FIDO ISA FRIEND)
(FIDO ISA DOG)
SOLO: (forget '(fido isa dog))
(FORGOTTEN: FIDO ISA DOG)
(FIDO HAS FLEAS)
(FIDO ISA FRIEND)
```

Exercise 8.1

Some Lisps store function-definitions on the property-lists of function-names. Lisp system functions are stored under the SUBR or FSUBR properties, and user-defined functions as EXPR or FEXPR properties. Add a trap to DESCRIBE so that the corresponding values (the definitions) will not be printed out. (If you're SURE that you Lisp stores definitions as ordinary bound values, you're excused this exercise.)

8.4 The LSOLO interpreter

Right. That's the easy part of the implementation of LSOLO done. The next step, though innocuous-looking, is a momentous one.

Programming languages such as Lisp and SOLO are "interpreted" languages. That is to say, the computer doesn't directly understand such things as CAR or CDR. They, and all the other Lisp system instructions your machine "knows", have to be translated (or interpreted) into memory-addresses at which the appropriate machine-code routine is stored. When you load your Lisp tape, it puts all the necessary machine-code routines in place, and also creates the Lisp interpreter – which you can visualise as being rather like an ordinary Lisp function. From then on, when you type (CAR ...) the interpreter says "ah, yes, I need machine-code routine so-and-so to do this" and retrieves it from wherever it has been put by the tape.

You are now going to make a start on writing the LSOLO interpreter. Of course, since LSOLO is written in Lisp, its interpreter only has to translate from LSOLO instructions to Lisp instructions; the supporting Lisp system's own interpreter will then translate the resulting Lisp into machine instructions. You will see two important changes in LSOLO immediately: (1) you will no longer need the quotes in front of everything, although I'm afraid the opening and closing brackets around each LSOLO expression will still be necessary; and (2) LSOLO will bomb out (giving a Lisp error message, of course, since they are the only ones the system has at the moment) if you try to enter anything other than legal LSOLO expressions. From the latter point of view, it is the interpreter which makes LSOLO a different language from its supporting Lisp.

```
(defun interpret (input)
  (cond ((eq (car input) 'note) (note (cdr input)))
        ((eq (car input) 'forget) (forget (cdr input)))
        ((eq (car input) 'describe) (describe (second input)))))
```

INPUT will have been bound (in the top-level loop) to the WHOLE expression that you type in – not merely to the triple. Notice that the COND clause involving DESCRIBE supplies as DESCRIBE's argument the SECOND element of IN-PUT – not the CDR as is the case with the other two LSOLO functions. The following are the kinds of things INTERPRET will see as the values of INPUT:

```
(note fido isa dog)
(describe fido)
```

and these are also the things you actually type to the "SOLO:" prompt. The job of INTERPRET is then to call NOTE with the argument '(FIDO ISA DOG), or DESCRIBE with the argument '(FIDO) – which is what you used to have to type to the prompt.

Clearly, it is now highly undesirable that your inputs should be evaluated before being passed to INTERPRET: you don't want Lisp to be continually complaining that, say, FIDO is an unbound variable! So INTERPRET goes into LSOLO's top-level loop IN PLACE OF the call to EVAL:

```
(defun lsolo ()
  (prog (input)
    (terpri)
    loop1
    (terpri)
    (print 'solo:)
    (setq input (read))
    (and (equal input '(bye)) (return nil))
    (interpret input)                        <--
    (go loop1)))
```

BYE stays where it is because we need it to stop the loop by RETURNing NIL. In any case, although RETURN can be nested deep inside any S-expression which is also a part of the PROG, it wouldn't work from inside INTERPRET, which is a SEPARATE function.

Notice what has been achieved: we've got a top-level loop which completely bypasses the normal Lisp READ-EVAL-PRINT loop. It calls READ for itself as and when it needs to; INTERPRET replaces EVAL, and we have in effect our own PRINTing arrangement in NOTE and FORGET which prints special LSOLO-oriented messages rather than Lisp-type values. All of this is built "on top of" the existing Lisp in the sense that LSOLO decides for itself what Lisp is to do with what parts of your input. You may type (NOTE FIDO ISA DOG), but all Lisp gets is a call to ADDPROP and a PRINT instruction.

Later on you will make some substantial changes to the function LSOLO, and INTERPRET will acquire an important assistant called INSTANTIATE. These three functions are the core of LSOLO, without which it would be no more than a collection of Lisp routines called NOTE, FORGET etc. It is common, though a touch imprecise, to refer to the whole group of three as "the interpreter".

8.5 The more advanced LSOLO functions

Now we come to the remaining four LSOLO system functions. Two of them are difficult and two of them are easy. After that will come the really hard-core stuff: making LSOLO handle user-written functions and recursion.

First, CHECK. It is the most complex of LSOLO's functions from the user's point of view. So let's start with the simplest use of it, which is simply as a retriever of stored triples, analogous to Lisp's GET:

```
SOLO: (check fido isa dog)
PRESENT
SOLO: (check fido isa computer)
ABSENT
```

Here's that simple version of CHECK:

```
(defun check (line)
  (prog (vals)
    (setq vals (get (car line) (second line)))
    (cond ((memq (third line) vals)
           (terpri) (print 'present))
          (t (terpri) (print 'absent)))))
```

The reason why LINE rather than TRIPLE is suddenly more mnemonic will become clear later. This time, the PROG is there only to give us a handy local variable VALS; there won't be any need for a loop. CHECK works like this: when you say, in effect, "is the triple FIDO ISA DOG present in my database?", GET retrieves the whole list of values which FIDO has under its property ISA. That list is held as the value of VALS. Then the COND merely checks to see if DOG is included in the list. Now let's add CHECK to LSOLO's repertoire of functions by including it in the interpreter:

```
(defun interpret (input)
  (cond ((eq (car input) 'note) (note (cdr input)))
        ((eq (car input) 'forget) (forget (cdr input)))
        ((eq (car input) 'describe) (describe (second input)))
        ((eq (car input) 'check) (check (cdr input)))))
```

CHECK will now work as in the example above. Try it.

It may have struck you that the PRESENT and ABSENT which CHECK prints are very like Lisp's T or NIL. And when CHECK is used not from top level as above but as one of the instructions within a user-defined LSOLO function, it does indeed behave as a very simple, two-clause COND: a pure IF-THEN-ELSE. You haven't yet seen how to define functions in LSOLO, but essentially the procedure is much the same as in Lisp: you simply bundle together a set of system functions (and/or other user-defined functions) and give them an overall name. A very simple LSOLO function (you won't be able to get this to work yet) might look like this:

```
TO DEMO
(NOTE FIDO ISA DOG)
(DESCRIBE FIDO)
(FORGET FIDO ISA DOG)
(DESCRIBE FIDO)
```

When used within such a function, CHECK has the following syntax:

```
(CHECK <triple>
    <action if triple is present>    <control-statement>
    <action if triple is absent>     <control-statement>)
```

and might actually look like this:

```
(check fido isa dog (describe fido) (exit) () (cont))
```

Which means: IF the triple FIDO ISA DOG is present, DESCRIBE FIDO and then EXIT from this function. ELSE (i.e. if the triple is absent) do nothing and continue to the next line of this function. Only the two alternative control-statements EXIT and CONT are allowed; EXIT is analogous to RETURN used within a PROG, but there is no direct Lisp equivalent of CONT – as you know, Lisp automatically goes on to the next line of a function anyway. In LSOLO, users are required to state explicitly where control should go after a CHECK <action> has been executed. Users are NOT allowed to put another CHECK instruction as one of the <actions> in a CHECK line. Notice that in LSOLO every instruction is surrounded by its own pair of brackets: even the instruction to do nothing, on the If Absent branch.

The above CHECK instruction is equivalent to the following Lisp code:

```
(prog ()
 (cond ((retrieve '(fido isa dog))
        (describe 'fido)
      (return t))
     (t nil))
 ... )
```

Forgetting about those mysterious control-statements for a moment, a CHECK which would either execute the DESCRIBE or not, depending on the presence or absence of the triple, would look like this:

```
(defun check (line)
 (prog (vals)
   (setq vals (get (car line) (second line)))
   (cond ((memq (third line) vals)
          (terpri) (print 'present)
          (interpret (nth 4 line)))        <--
        (t (terpri) (print 'absent)
          (interpret (nth 6 line)))))))    <--
```

When an LSOLO user-defined function is running, each line of it is fed in turn to the interpreter. In the above example INTERPRET would see a CHECK instruction and would call CHECK to handle it; and CHECK, as you can see, would then recursively call INTERPRET to deal with the DESCRIBE. Once the latter call to INTERPRET was finished, control would return to this CHECK, and then via the previous call to INTERPRET back to the top level. And that's fine. I want to leave CHECK for a while now, because you'll only be able to understand it fully when you've seen how the process of interpreting user-defined functions is managed. First, let's clear up some more of the easy stuff.

LSOLO needs a PRINT function. In LSOLO, PRINT takes any number of arguments. It first does a carriage-return, and then prints the arguments all on the same line, with a space between each. There is an added complication: it wouldn't be desirable for the LSOLO interpreter to call a Lisp function named PRINT and defined according to that specification, because that would necessarily involve redefining your Lisp's own PRINT. The easiest way out is simply to write the guts of the definition directly into the interpreter:

```
(defun interpret (input)
 (cond ((eq (car input) 'note) (note (cdr input)))
       ((eq (car input) 'forget) (forget (cdr input)))
       ((eq (car input) 'describe) (describe (second input)))
       ((eq (car input) 'check) (check (cdr input)))
       ((eq (car input) 'print)
        (terpri) (mapc '(lambda (i)
                          (prin1 i) (spaces 1))
                     (cdr input)))))
```

But please remember the things you discovered in the course of Chapter 4 about your Lisp's printing functions.

The next requirement is harder, though not a brain-twister. It is the function TO, which allows LSOLO users to define their own functions. And of course in order to see how that is to work you need to know the format in which such functions are stored inside LSOLO.

Remember that LSOLO does not have bound values in the Lisp sense: it has instead its database, which we have simulated using Lisp's property-lists. So we're going to store LSOLO user-defined functions (UDFs from now on) also on Lisp property-lists. This is something that many Lisps do with their own UDFs — that is, with the Lisp functions that you write for yourself. But there will be no chance of confusion because your Lisp, if it stores your functions in this way, will use property-names such as EXPR and FEXPR, whereas the LSOLO functions are going to be stored under the property name UDF.

So: the identifier is the LSOLO function's name (naturally), and the property-name is UDF. Defining a new LSOLO function is then a matter of PUTting its definition onto the property-list of its name under the property UDF. The LSOLO system function TO does this, and so is directly equivalent to DEFUN in Lisp. The other thing you need to know is what the VALUE – that is, the definition itself – looks like. Let's start with the simple function DEMO, from a few pages back:

```
TO DEMO
(NOTE FIDO ISA DOG)
(DESCRIBE FIDO)
(FORGET FIDO ISA DOG)
(DESCRIBE FIDO)
```

That could be stored like this:

```
((10 (NOTE FIDO ISA DOG))
 (20 (DESCRIBE FIDO))
 (30 (FORGET FIDO ISA DOG))
 (40 (DESCRIBE FIDO)))
```

In other words, if that list were PUT as the UDF property of DEMO, the function-definition would be thereby stored. The line-numbers have appeared because, as you'll soon see, LSOLO needs them in order to retrieve individual lines from the definition during execution of DEMO.

However, looking ahead to something we'll need to do later, the ability to write functions would be pretty dull if the only thing the functions could do was execute a string of instructions which you might just as well have entered by hand, from top level. We're going to want to give arguments – and hence formal parameters – to UDFs. So let's make a slot for the latter, by making the above the first element of a list, the second element being a so-far empty slot:

```
(((10 (NOTE FIDO ISA DOG))
  (20 (DESCRIBE FIDO))
  (30 (FORGET FIDO ISA DOG))
  (40 (DESCRIBE FIDO)))
 NIL)
```

That format is a bit reminiscent of a LAMBDA expression, isn't it? In fact, Lisps which store their UDFs on property-lists do store them as LAMBDA expressions, very similarly to the above. Continuing the analogy with Lisp, let's say that when a function-definition is printed out on the terminal it will look something like this:

```
(TO <function-name>
    (<list of formal parameters>)
    <body>)
```

more or less exactly as in Lisp. And TO is going to be an LSOLO system function, just as DEFUN is in Lisp. But TO is going to be more helpful to the user than DEFUN is: it is going to prompt him or her to type in the correct kind of thing. Like this:

```
SOLO: TO DEMO
VARIABLES-LIST: ()
--> (note fido isa dog)
--> (describe fido)
--> (forget fido isa dog)
--> (describe fido)
--> (done)
SOLO:
```

The user types only the parts in brackets, and TO itself prints the rest automatically, as each bracketed line (i.e. each Lisp S-expression, but the user doesn't know that!) is entered.

The function TO prompts first for the formal parameters, and expects a list – whether or not the list has any variable-names in it. You, with your growing Lisp expertise, are well aware that you could type NIL in place of the above empty list. But LSOLO users aren't supposed to know that either: they know only the universal rule that ALL entries into LSOLO are surrounded by a single pair of brackets.

Subsequently, TO repeatedly prompts with "-->" for each line of code; and when the definition is complete the user types the keyword "DONE" – but, again, since it is effectively an LSOLO instruction, it has its own brackets. DONE is actually the signal to TO that it should do its stuff, that is it should assemble the definition into the correct format as above and PUT the whole onto the appropriate property-list. Here is TO:

```
(defun to (udf)
  (prog (formals line-number input code)
    (setq line-number 0)
    (terpri)
    (print 'variables-list:)
    (terpri)
    (setq formals (read))
    loop
    (setq line-number (plus 10 line-number))
```

174

```
(print '-->)
(setq input (read))
(cond ((eq (car input) 'done)
       (put udf 'udf (list (reverse code) formals))
       (return t))
      (t (setq code (cons (list line-number input) code))))
(go loop)))
```

Imagine that TO was being used as above to define DEMO. The PROG's list of local variables are: FORMALS, which will hold the list of DEMO's formal parameters as read from the keyboard by READ – in this case, NIL of course; LINE-NUMBER will start off at zero and will be updated each time around the loop, so as to number the lines of DEMO successively; INPUT will hold one line of DEMO (i.e. one Lisp S-expression) as read in by the READ within the loop; and CODE will be progressively augmented each time around the loop so that when DONE finally appears CODE holds the whole body of the definition.

Now go on to the line following the line with PROG in it. On that line the initial value of LINE-NUMBER is reset from NIL to 0. Next comes a TERPRI, which prints an extra carriage return just before the "VARIABLES-LIST" prompt. Then READ takes in whatever S-expression the user types in response to that prompt and binds it to the variable FORMALS. After that a second TERPRI inserts another carriage return, and then the loop is entered. Each time around the loop, the following happens.

First, LINE-NUMBER is updated to be ten more than its current value. Then the "-->" prompt is printed, and another call to READ binds the next typed-in S-expression to INPUT. A COND checks to see if this new value of INPUT is equal to '(DONE). If not, a list of the current value of LINE-NUMBER and the value of INPUT is CONSed onto CODE. This cycle repeats with every line the user types in, causing CODE to grow by one element each time, until "DONE" is typed. Then the first clause of the COND is activated: it reverses CODE, so that the lowest-numbered line of DEMO is at the head of it, rather than the highest-numbered; it makes a list of that together with FORMALS; and PUTs the whole lot onto the property-list of DEMO under the property UDF. The COND then calls RETURN to stop the loop and to exit from TO. Phew.

Now it's necessary to put TO into the interpreter:

```
(defun interpret (input)
  (cond ((eq (car input) 'note) (note (cdr input)))
        ((eq (car input) 'forget) (forget (cdr input)))
        ((eq (car input) 'describe) (describe (second input)))
        ((eq (car input) 'check) (check (cdr input)))
        ((eq (car input) 'print)
         (terpri) (mapc '(lambda (i)
                           (prin1 i) (spaces 1))
                        (cdr input)))
        ((eq (car input) 'to) (to (second input)))))   <--
```

And next comes something very easy: the definition of LIST, which will display the definition of any function written via TO. But notice that it is called

175

SLIST, to avoid confusion with your Lisp's own LIST function.

```
(defun slist (udf)
  (terpri)
  (print 'to)
  (princ udf)
  (print (second (get udf 'udf)))
  (terpri)
  (mapc 'print (car (get udf 'udf))))
```

If you have no equivalent of PRINC for line 2, just use PRINT. The only difference will be that TO and the UDF-name appear on successive lines rather than on the same line.

And this has to go into the interpreter too: in LSOLO the function call is (LIST..), which the interpreter passes to Lisp as (SLIST..):

```
(defun interpret (input)
  (cond ((eq (car input) 'note) (note (cdr input)))
        ((eq (car input) 'forget) (forget (cdr input)))
        ((eq (car input) 'describe) (describe (second input)))
        ((eq (car input) 'check) (check (cdr input)))
        ((eq (car input) 'print)
         (terpri) (mapc '(lambda (i)
                           (prin1 i) (spaces 1))
                        (cdr input)))
        ((eq (car input) 'to) (to (second input)))
        ((eq (car input) 'list) (slist (second input)))))     <--
```

So far so good. LSOLO can now accept and store function-definitions. But it still has no idea how to execute them. INTERPRET's COND has no clause telling it what to do with a call to DEMO; so if you tried to run the function now, control would simply drop off the end of the COND, and the "SOLO:" prompt would reappear. Ultimately, we want LSOLO's functions to be able to pass the values of formal parameters to each other, and to recurse, just like Lisp functions. To show you how that is going to work will require a substantial digression, but it will be worthwhile because the way in which LSOLO achieves these things will be a very good partial model of how Lisp itself achieves the same things.

Suppose you had a (Lisp) function which took two formal parameters:

```
(defun foo (x y)
  <body>)
```

and suppose that you called that function to do its stuff, supplying as arguments the values ME and YOU:

```
(foo 'me 'you)
```

Now, as you know, inside FOO and throughout the time that its <body> is being executed, X is bound to the atom ME and Y is bound to the atom YOU. So, the

176

first thing our LSOLO interpreter has to do in order to run a similar function is to bind those variables. And although that may have seemed a mysterious process until now, it can be achieved quite easily. For example, LSOLO could maintain a special list, called VARIABLES or something, on which was a series of pairs. Of each pair, one element would be the variable-name and the other would be its "bound" value. In LSOLO, these pairs are actually dotted pairs. This has two advantages: (1) it is more efficient in its use of memory-space (one cons-cell instead of two for each pair); and (2) it slightly simplifies coding because the second half of a cons-cell is its CDR, whereas the second element of a two-element list is its CADR. Thus, VARIABLES might have a value which looked like this:

```
((X . ME) (Y . YOU))
```

so that whenever LSOLO needed to know the value of X or Y, it could do a quick ASSOC on that list and retrieve the CDR of the appropriate element.

Here is an LSOLO function, written using TO:

```
TO FOO
(X Y)
10 (PRINT X)
20 (PRINT Y)
```

Now, in order to execute either of FOO's two lines, LSOLO has to replace the X or the Y with its bound value, so that the call

```
SOLO: (foo me you)
```

will, as desired, have the effect

```
ME
YOU
SOLO:
```

So here is LSOLO's (very, very primitive!) evaluator:

```
(defun soloeval (line)
  (prog (temp)
    (mapcar '(lambda (e)
               (cond ((setq temp (assoc e variables))
                      (cdr temp))
                     (t e)))
           line)))
```

The MAPCAR goes through each element of LINE (e.g. through PRINT and then X). Since it IS a MAPCAR, and not a MAPC, it will return a list of its results. And because of the COND, each element of that result-list will be EITHER the bound value of the original item if the item is on the VARIABLES list, OR the item itself. That is, in this case:

```
(PRINT ME)
```

OK – so once we have given it the mechanism whereby it CAN work its way line by line through any UDF you call, LSOLO will be able to evaluate each instruction so as to replace any references to formal parameters with their bound values.

I said in the discussion of LAMBDA lists in Chapter 3 that when Lisp is asked to evaluate a function-call, it replaces the function's NAME with its LAMBDA definition. LSOLO doesn't do exactly the same thing as Lisp does, but it achieves a very similar effect, as follows. When you type into LSOLO the instruction (FOO ME YOU), the top-level loop passes that instruction directly to the interpreter. But as things stand the interpreter doesn't know what to do with it. So let's specify that when the interpreter sees an instruction whose first element is the name of a UDF, it shall take special action:

```
(defun interpret (input)
  (cond ((eq (car input) 'note) (note (cdr input)))
        ((eq (car input) 'forget) (forget (cdr input)))
        ((eq (car input) 'describe) (describe (second input)))
        ((eq (car input) 'check) (check (cdr input)))
        ((eq (car input) 'print)
         (terpri) (mapc '(lambda (i)
                           (prin1 i) (spaces 1))
                        (cdr input)))
        ((eq (car input) 'to) (to (second input)))
        ((eq (car input) 'list) (slist (second input)))
        ((get (car input) 'udf) (instantiate input))))    <--
```

The new Lisp function, INSTANTIATE, cheats. It sets up a situation which makes the top-level loop think that it is handling not a single instruction from you, but a whole string of them; and the loop duly passes these one by one back to INTERPRET. Naturally, that string of instructions is identical to the body of, in this case, FOO. Neat, eh?

In order for this to be possible, we need to give the top-level loop the ability to handle more than one instruction at a time. That's not very hard. Imagine that what INSTANTIATE does is make a list of all the line-numbers in the definition of FOO, and that the top-level loop is able to go through this list, passing each corresponding line (also retrieved from the definition) to INTERPRET until the list is exhausted:

```
(defun lsolo ()
  (prog (input udf steps variables)                       <--
    (terpri)
    loop1
    (terpri)
    (print 'solo:)
    (setq input (read))
    (and (equal input '(bye)) (return nil))
    (interpret input)
    loop3                                                  <--
    (cond ((null steps) (setq variables nil) (go loop1))  <--
          (t (interpret (soloeval (get-line (car steps) udf))))  <--
```

178

```
        (setq steps (cdr steps))              <--
        (go loop3)))))                         <--
```

The new sequence of events is that you type (FOO ME YOU) to the
"SOLO:" prompt. The first call to INTERPRET (just above "loop3" in LSOLO)
passes that same thing to INTERPRET. And the new line in INTERPRET,
recognising FOO as a UDF, calls INSTANTIATE to handle it. INSTANTIATE
in fact does three things. It creates the list of line-numbers (called STEPS); it
binds the variable UDF to the UDF-name, FOO; and it sets up the VARIABLES
list of dotted pairs as above. Notice that all three of these variables are now
specified as being LOCAL to the function LSOLO. As far as any of LSOLO's
subroutines are concerned, they are GLOBAL. So whatever value they are set to
by INSTANTIATE is also seen by the COND in LSOLO's LOOP3.

If you're wondering why it is called LOOP3 rather than LOOP2, it is because
things are shortly going to get even more complex!

Anyway, INSTANTIATE having done those three things, the call to IN-
TERPRET ends, and execution of the code in LOOP3 begins. Obviously STEPS
is not empty, because INSTATIATE has just filled it. So the first clause of the
COND in LOOP3 fails. STEPS looks like this:

    (10 20)

since FOO has only two lines, and they have those line-numbers.

In the T-clause of the COND, a function called GET-LINE retrieves that line
of FOO corresponding to the CAR of STEPS – i.e. FOO's line 10 – and
SOLOEVAL replaces the X in it by ME before the result is passed back to
INTERPRET. This time, INTERPRET executes line 10 quite normally. The
next instruction in LOOP3 is to chop the head off STEPS and to go back round the
same loop, so that line 20 also gets executed. The third time around, STEPS is
empty and so control goes back to LOOP1, restoring the "SOLO:" prompt ready
for your next top-level entry.

Should that next entry be to an LSOLO system function such as:

    SOLO: (describe fido)

it gets executed as usual by the earlier of the two calls to INTERPRET. But
INSTANTIATE doesn't get called this time (because, of course, DESCRIBE
isn't a UDF and therefore has no UDF property). So the first clause in the COND
of LOOP3 operates straight away, sending control back to LOOP1 and restoring
the normal prompt as before.

Thus, UDFs are handled quite differently from simple top-level calls to
system functions, and there is a very real sense in which one can say that the
LSOLO interpreter effectively replaces a UDF call by that UDF's definition; the
latter being executed line by line (the LSOLO equivalent of S-expression by
S-expression) in place of the one-line UDF call.

Here's GET-LINE:

```
(defun get-line (step fn)
  (second (assoc step (car (get fn 'udf)))))
```

179

And here's the first version of INSTANTIATE:

```
(defun instantiate (input)
  (setq udf (car input))
  (setq steps (mapcar 'car (car (get (car input) 'udf))))
  (setq variables (mapcar2 '(lambda (d f)
                              (cons f d))
                           (cdr input)
                           (second (get (car input) 'udf)))))
```

Notice the (SETQ VARIABLES...) line. It uses MAPCAR2, and I'm afraid that isn't a misprint.

8.6 MAPCAR2

Look closely at the offending line in INSTANTIATE. Notice that the LAMBDA expression inside the MAPCAR2, and MAPCAR2 itself, each have two arguments. The principle of MAPCAR2 is simple: whereas the ordinary MAPCAR does its thing to successive elements of a list, MAPCAR2 does something (in this case a CONS) to successive elements of two lists at once. In other words, the CAR of one list gets CONSed onto the CAR of the other; then the two CADRs are CONSed together, and so on. The end result, by analogy with MAPCAR, is a LIST of the results of all those conses. MAPCAR2 is in fact only an extension of the MAPCAR you know already, and is defined like this:

```
(defun mapcar2 (fn L1 L2)
  (cond ((or (null L1) (null L2)) nil)
        (t (cons (eval (list fn
                             (list 'quote (car L1))
                             (list 'quote (car L2))))
                 (mapcar2 fn (cdr L1) (cdr L2))))))
```

If you glance at the definition of MAPCAR in the Appendix, you'll see the similarities between the two functions.

8.7 Implementing recursion

This is not going to be as hard as you think. If you remember the discussion of recursion in Chapter 2, you'll recall that when one function contains a recursive call to itself (or a call to some other function), execution of the outer call is "suspended" until the inner one is complete. For the sake of example, visualise a function like this:

```
(defun blah (n)
  (cond ((zerop n) nil)
        (t (print n)
           (blah (difference n 1))
           (print n)
           t)))
```

and imagine this call to it:

```
(blah 1)
```

The result will be:

```
1
NIL
1
T
```

Clearly, this will require only one level of recursion. "Suspension" of the outer call to BLAH involves, as you know, saving away not only the so-far unexecuted portion of it, but also the value of its formal parameters N. The latter is restored to N when execution of the inner call to BLAH has been completed; whereupon the remainder of the outer call is executed. As with the previously-mentioned binding of variables, this is an essentially simple process once you know how to do it.

The secret in our case is yet another PROG variable which is local to the function LSOLO but global to the rest of the program – in particular it is global to INSTANTIATE. This variable is called PDL, short for PUSH-DOWN LIST. The push-down list is also sometimes referred to as the "stack". The standard analogy given in AI text-books (I don't like it) is to the arrangement found in many cafeterias for the supply of clean plates. Instead of the pile of plates being ON the counter, it is kept in a cylindrical hole IN the counter. At the bottom of the hole, under the pile of plates, is a spring. So that as the top plate is removed the whole pile rises up slightly to bring the next plate clear of the counter itself. Concomitantly, if a fresh plate is placed on the top, its weight pushes the pile down slightly. The net effect being that at all times only the top plate – the most recent addition to the pile – is available. A cumbersome and somewhat inaccurate comparison for what is essentially a very simple idea.

In LSOLO, the push-down list – the pile of plates, springs, and other paraphernalia – is simply a list. It is a "push-down" list because we take care that adding a new element to it is done only by CONSing that element onto the head of the list, and that removing an element from it is done only by chopping off the CAR of the list. We will also allow ourselves to inspect the rest of the list and to make use of what we find there.

Consider the point in time, during execution of the outer call to BLAH, where the first PRINT instruction has been done and the recursive call to BLAH is about to be set up. At that point, a kind of "snapshot" of the current state of affairs is made and CONSed onto the PDL. This snapshot could consist of the remaining unexecuted expressions in the outer BLAH, plus a record of N's value at that time. The outer call to BLAH is then completely forgotten about whilst the inner one, with its new value for N, is executed. But once the inner call comes to an end, the snapshot can be taken back off the PDL. The previous value of N can thus be restored, and execution of the outer call to BLAH can proceed as though no inner call had happened.

Now consider the case where the original top-level call to BLAH is given an argument of 2, as the starting value for N. Exactly the same thing happens, except that an extra level of recursion is involved: in the middle of what was formerly the inner call to BLAH. a third call has to be executed. So a snapshot of the current state of the SECOND call is CONSed onto the PDL, which therefore has two elements where before it had one. "Unwinding" the recursion when the inner-most BLAH is completed is simply a matter of removing these elements (the snapshots) from PDL, taking the most recent entry first, and executing them in turn – rebinding N each time.

I hope it is clear that this process could continue no matter how deep the recursion went; and that even if the sequence of calls were not recursive, but consisted of functionA calling functionB calling functionC and so on, exactly the same principle could be applied, and would have the same effects.

Clearly the snapshots themselves must contain all the information necessary to continue the execution of any "suspended" function-call. In LSOLO this entails that any snapshot shall be a list of three elements: the name of the "suspended" UDF; a record of its unexecuted steps so that GET-LINE can later retrieve them for execution; and a record of the current values of any formal parameters the UDF may have:

    (\<name> \<steps> \<variables>)

The push-down list in a language like Lisp is, naturally, a rather more complicated affair. But the principle is the same.

There. That was relatively painless, wasn't it? Now to the question of how to implement it: as I've already hinted, INSTATIATE and LSOLO itself are the crucial functions. Let's start with LSOLO. That function can already take a UDF call from you and run each of that UDF's lines in sequence until the end is reached. Now we'd like to extend that ability so that LSOLO can do the same thing for any snapshot it finds on the PDL, and can repeat the same process for any further snapshots until the PDL is empty. Here is the latest version of LSOLO:

```
(defun lsolo ()
  (prog (input udf steps variables pdl)                    <--
    (terpri)
  loop1
    (terpri)
    (print 'solo:)
    (setq input (read))
    (and (equal input '(bye)) (return nil))
    (interpret input)
  loop2                                                    <--
    (cond ((null pdl) (go loop1))                          <--
          (t (setq udf (caar pdl))                         <--
             (setq steps (second (car pdl)))               <--
             (setq variables (varsearch pdl))))            <--
  loop3
    (cond ((null steps)                                    <--
           (setq variables nil) (setq pdl (cdr pdl)) (go loop2)) --
```

182

```
                (t (interpret (soloeval (get-line (car steps) udf))))
                (setq steps (cdr steps))
                (go loop3)))))
```

The flow of control has changed slightly from the previous version. When
LOOP3 has iterated through all the steps of any given UDF, instead of going back
to LOOP1 and to top level as before, it now goes to LOOP2 to see if there are any
other partly-executed UDFs waiting on the PDL. If not, LOOP2 itself sends
control back to LOOP1 and hence to top level. Otherwise, LOOP3 is as it was
before, except for the additional instruction, executed at the END of a UDF, to
set the PDL to its own CDR. LOOP2 is very similar to LOOP3; if the PDL is not
empty, it re-binds the three variables UDF, STEPS and VARIABLES to the
values held in the first element of the PDL. LOOP3 will then iterate through all
the steps so retrieved from the PDL, with any formal parameters appropriately
re-bound. Here's VARSEARCH:

```
(defun varsearch (pdl)
  (and pdl (apply 'append (mapcar 'third pdl))))
```

If there is some PDL (there's no point in bothering otherwise) and if a MAPCAR
list of the third elements of all its stored snapshots comes to something other than
a list of NIL, it APPENDS the members of that list together to make one list. At
times the PDL may well hold more than two snapshots, so that APPEND has to be
able to take more than two arguments. But that's OK – if the APPEND in your
Lisp won't already do that, redefine it as two functions according to the Appendix.
  Now see what will happen if you call some UDF. The first call to IN-
TERPRET, in LOOP1, will call INSTANTIATE. Then LOOP2 will be entered,
and if there is no PDL (as there won't be unless either INTERPRET or INSTAN-
TIATE creates one) control will return immediately to LOOP1. So one of the
things a new version of INSTANTIATE is going to have to do is create a PDL
record (snapshot) of ANY called UDF, regardless of whether it is recursive or
not. And this will of course have to be done AFTER it has established the values
of UDF, STEPS and VARIABLES for that new UDF:

```
(defun instantiate (input)
  (setq udf (car input))
  (setq steps (mapcar 'car (car (get (car input) 'udf))))
  (setq variables (mapcar2 '(lambda (d f)
                              (cons f d))
                           (cdr input)
                           (second (get (car input) 'udf))))
  (setq pdl (cons (list udf steps variables) pdl)))        <--
```

Given that, when control enters LOOP2 there is a non-NIL value for PDL, so
the second clause of the COND is executed, using the PDL to bind UDF, STEPS
and VARIABLES as I've said. This re-binding will not of course alter the values
at this stage. The code in LOOP2 is executed only once during the downward part
of the recursive spiral; on the way back up – during unwinding – its re-binding of
the three variables will make a difference.

Control then enters LOOP3: there are some STEPS, since LOOP2 has just made sure of that, so again it is the second COND clause which gets executed. If the UDF has no nested calls to other UDFs, its lines (steps) are interpreted one by one until STEPS runs out, whereupon PDL is reset to its own CDR (which will be NIL) so that the snapshot is removed. VARIABLES is also reset to NIL so that any bindings used by the UDF are forgotten. Control then returns via LOOP2 to LOOP1 and top level.

So far so good. Now consider the next most complicated case: that where UDF1 calls UDF2, but neither calls anything else. As far as LOOP3, exactly the same things happen as before. But during the iteration of LOOP3, the call to UDF2 is encountered. This causes INSTANTIATE to cheat as usual, arranging that the next iteration round LOOP3 will start interpreting UDF2 rather than UDF1.

But during this call to INSTANTIATE it is desirable to save the remainder of UDF1 by putting a suitable snapshot onto the PDL. There already is a snapshot of UDF1 on the PDL, of course, and it needs to be there for the reasons I've just been giving. But it is a snapshot of the WHOLE of UDF1, not the partial snapshot (of the unexecuted part only) which we need now. So we get INSTANTIATE to update the existing snapshot, by altering the CAR element of PDL. Luckily, the only change necessary will be to the STEPS slot of that element. Subsequently, INSTANTIATE will add a complete snapshot of UDF2 to the PDL, as it did for UDF1 the last time around.

```
(defun instantiate (input)
    pdl (setq pdl (cons
                                                       <--
                        (caar pdl) (cdr steps) variables)  <--
                        pdl))))                            <--
        udf (car input))
        steps (mapcar 'car (car (get (car input) 'udf))))
        variables (mapcar2 '(lambda (d f)
                                f d))
                        input)
                    (get (car input) 'udf))))
    pdl (cons (list udf steps variables) pdl))))
```

The AND in the new line checks to see if PDL has any snapshots in it: if not, the current UDF just arrived from INTERPRET isn't nested inside any outer UDF, and so the rest of the line needn't be done.

But here comes a nasty complication. Look what happens in LOOP3, immediately after the call to INTERPRET/INSTANTIATE which effects the cheating. STEPS is set to its own CDR. So the first line of UDF2 would be lost. This didn't happen with UDF1, or with the single non-nested UDF above, because their first lines were interpreted in LOOP1. Only UDFs at level 2 and below have this problem. The solution is simple, albeit a bit ugly: if there is more than one snapshot on the PDL at the end of INSTANTIATE, we'll get the latter to add a dummy step to STEPS. Then LOOP3 can CDR it off again without any harm being done:

```
(defun instantiate (input)
  (and pdl (setq pdl (cons
                        (list (caar pdl) (cdr steps) variables)
                        (cdr pdl))))
  (setq udf (car input))
  (setq steps (mapcar 'car (car (get (car input) 'udf))))
  (setq variables (mapcar2 '(lambda (d f)
                              (cons f d))
                          (cdr input)
                          (second (get (car input) 'udf))))
  (setq pdl (cons (list udf steps variables) pdl))
  (and pdl (cdr pdl) (setq steps (cons 'dummy steps))))    <--
```

The new AND, before checking to see if there is more than one element on the
PDL, has to check to see if there is any PDL at all, because some Lisps are not
smart enough to realise that the CDR of NIL must also be NIL, and would bomb
out if the PDL were empty.

Yeucchh. How one has to suffer for one's art.

Oof. Nearly there. The only other thing to worry about as far as recursion is
concerned is what happens to the values of formal parameters. By analogy with
Lisp, we'd like the values of the formal parameters of any UDF to be available to
any subroutines that UDF might have. But the converse should not be true. For
example:

```
TO FOO              TO BLAH
(A)                 (X)
(PRINT A)           (PRINT A X)
(BLAH TONY)
(PRINT X)
```

When FOO is called with some argument, it should of course print that
argument. Then it calls BLAH with the argument "TONY". BLAH binds its
formal parameter X to "TONY". The bound value of A is also available to it from
FOO, so it prints both quite happily. But when control subsequently returns to
FOO, it would not be correct if FOO could then print the value of X. This type of
binding is known as "dynamic" binding.

This means that all the way DOWN the recursive spiral (that is, every time
INSTANTIATE is called), we need to augment any current VARIABLES list
with the bindings due to the latest UDF:

```
(defun instantiate (input)
  (and pdl (setq pdl (cons
                        (list (caar pdl) (cdr steps) variables)
                        (cdr pdl))))
  (setq udf (car input))
  (setq steps (mapcar 'car (car (get (car input) 'udf))))
  (setq variables (append (mapcar2 '(lambda (d f)         <--
                                      (cons f d))
                                  (cdr input)
```

```
                              (second (get (car input) 'udf)))
              variables))                                      <--
   (setq pdl (cons (list udf steps variables) pdl))
   (and pdl (cdr pdl) (setq steps (cons 'dummy steps))))
```

This ensures that at any moment during downward recusion, values from previous
— higher — levels are still bound (as far as SOLOEVAL is concerned) to their
corresponding formal parameters. And the easiest way to cope with the unwinding process is to say that as each and any UDF comes to an end all variables are
unbound (i.e. VARIABLES is set to NIL), and the bindings we still want – those
of UDFs which occurred higher in the recursion and so have not yet been
completed – are restored from the records on the PDL. Which, luckily, is exactly
what the latest version of LSOLO does for us already.

   And that's how recursion can be implemented in LSOLO.

8.8 The remainder of LSOLO

You may remember that several pages ago we were talking about CHECK, and I
said that I'd have to leave it for now whilst I made a digression. Well, recursion
was the digression, and now I can finish off CHECK. To recap, the syntax of
CHECK in LSOLO is:

```
(CHECK  <triple>
    <action if triple is present>    <control-statement>
    <action if triple is absent>     <control-statement>)
```

and a CHECK line might actually look like this:

```
(check fido isa dog (describe fido) (exit) () (cont))
```

   It is now a simple matter to include in the definition of CHECK a couple of
lines to make the control statements work properly. Remember: EXIT means
stop executing this UDF altogether (i.e. return to the next higher one if this one
was nested, or return to top level); and CONT means continue to the next line of
this UDF. A further point is that CHECK's calls to INTERPRET now need to
include a SOLOEVAL so that any formal parameters in the line get properly
evaluated. Here are the changes:

```
(defun check (line)
(prog (vals)
  (setq vals (get (car line) (second line)))
  (cond ((memq (third line) vals)
         (terpri) (print 'present)
         (and (equal (nth 5 line) '(exit)) (setq steps 'dummy))  <--
         (interpret (soloeval (nth 4 line))))                    <--
        (t (terpri) (print 'absent)
           (and (equal (nth 7 line) '(exit))                     <--
                (setq steps 'dummy)))))                          <--
              (interpret (soloeval (nth 6 line))))))             <--
```

186

Notice that if a control-statement slot has NIL in it, it defaults to CONT. Concomitantly, if there are no further UDF lines to continue to, a CONT will default to EXIT.

Notice also the insertion of 'DUMMY into an otherwise empty STEPS list. It is to prevent the loss of subroutine first lines, as in INSTANTIATE in the previous section. Like INSTANTIATE, CHECK operates during a call to INTERPRET, in LOOP3 of LSOLO. And that call is inevitably followed by an instruction to set STEPS to its own CDR.

The above Lisp function CHECK also contains its own calls to INTERPRET, intended to handle the If Present and If Absent instructions within an LSOLO CHECK line. And these instructions might well be LSOLO subroutine calls. The sequence of events would then be:

LOOP3 in LSOLO calls INTERPRET.
    INTERPRET, seeing an LSOLO CHECK line, calls CHECK.
        CHECK calls INTERPRET again to handle the If Present instruction.
            INTERPRET, seeing a UDF call, calls INSTANTIATE.
                INSTANTIATE resets the variables UDF, STEPS and VARIABLES.

After all that, control returns (like recursion unwinding) stage by stage back to the original point in LOOP3, and because of the effect of INSTANTIATE the loop proceeds to execute the LSOLO subroutine. Clearly, if this is to work properly, the effect of INSTANTIATE must override any other change to STEPS introduced by the presence in the SOLO code of an EXIT control statement. Hence the order of the corresponding instructions in the above definition of CHECK.

The LSOLO instruction CHECK has one more useful attribute, although again it is one which can only be used when the CHECK itself is within a UDF. Within a UDF, you can write something like:

```
(CHECK FIDO ISA ?)
```

whereupon CHECK will bind the atom "?" to the third element of any database triple which fits the (FIDO ISA...) pattern. Often, it is DOG. Only one such "wildcard" is allowed in any CHECK triple, and it must appear in the third position of that triple. If it happens that there are several matching patterns for the triple, CHECK picks the one most recently entered. Thus, if (DESCRIBE FIDO) would produce this:

```
(FIDO ISA FRIEND)
(FIDO ISA DRUNK)
```

the atom "?" would be bound to FRIEND. Now: the scope of that binding is restricted to the CHECK line itself. That is, any system function or UDF which occurs in the If Present or If Absent slots of the CHECK can refer to it (but their subroutines if any can't – its value would have to be passed explicitly as the value of a formal parameter as in the example below). And by the time the NEXT line of the UDF containing the CHECK comes to be executed, the binding is lost. For example, either of these will work:

187

```
TO FOO
(A)
(CHECK FIDO ISA ? (FOO ?) (EXIT) () (EXIT)
TO BLAH
(A)
(CHECK FIDO ISA ? (PRINT ?) (CONT) () (EXIT)
(PRINT FINISHED)
```

but this will not:

```
TO GORT
(A)
(CHECK FIDO ISA ? () (CONT) () (EXIT)
(PRINT ?)
```

In order to achieve this very handy addition to LSOLO, we need yet another global variable in the PROG of LSOLO itself:

```
(defun lsolo ()
  (prog (input udf steps variables pdl checkvars)          <--
    (terpri)
    loop1
    (terpri)
    (print 'solo:)
    (setq input (read))
    (and (equal input '(bye)) (return nil))
    (interpret input)
    loop2
    (cond ((null pdl) (go loop1))
          (t (setq udf (caar pdl))
             (setq steps (second (car pdl)))
             (setq variables (varsearch pdl))))
    loop3
    (cond ((null steps)
           (setq variables nil) (setq pdl (cdr pdl)) (go loop2))
          (t (interpret (soloeval (get-line (car steps) udf)))
             (setq steps (cdr steps))
             (go loop3)))))
```

and we need a new clause in CHECK to handle the "?" symbol and the new CHECKVARS variable:

```
(defun check (line)
  (prog (vals)
    (setq vals (get (car line) (second line)))
    (cond ((memq (third line) vals)
           (terpri) (print 'present)
           (and (equal (nth 5 line) '(exit)) (setq steps 'dummy))
```

```
                (interpret (soloeval (nth 4 line)))
                ((and vals (eq (third line) '?))                    <--
                 (and (equal (nth 5 line) '(exit)) (setq steps nil))   <--
                 (setq checkvars (cons (cons '? (car vals)) checkvars)) <--
                 (interpret (soloeval (nth 4 line)))                <--
                 (setq checkvars nil))                              <--
                (t (terpri) (print 'absent)
                   (and (equal (nth 7 line) '(exit))
                        (setq steps nil))
                   (interpret (soloeval (nth 6 line)))))))))
```

As you can see, CHECKVARS will only ever hold a single item: a dotted pair of one variable-name ("?") and one value, just like a single member of VARIABLES itself. And the reason for this similarity is that we can now make a very simple change to SOLOEVAL so that "?" gets evaluated properly:

```
(defun soloeval (line)
   (prog (temp)
      (mapcar '(lambda (e)
                  (cond ((setq temp (assoc e variables))
                         (cdr temp))
                        ((setq temp (assoc e checkvars))   <--
                         (cdr temp))                       <--
                        (t e)))
              line)))
```

So, anything seen by CHECK's new call to INTERPRET will be evaluated with the ?-binding in force. That means anything which is in the "if present do this" or the "if absent do that" slot on the LINE. But CHECKVARS is reset to NIL as soon as that single call to INTERPRET has been completed, so that the ?-binding is lost for any subsequent lines of the UDF concerned. This kind of binding is known as LEXICAL binding.

There is just one more thing, and then LSOLO really will be finished, so that you can sit back and play with it. And it's a relatively trivial thing: the business of modifying TO so that it helps users to enter CHECK lines properly. Since this is quite a cumbersome business, though easy, we'll add another line to the definition of TO which calls a new subroutine as and when required:

```
      (defun to (udf)
         (prog (formals line-number input code)
            (setq line-number 0)
            (terpri)
            (print 'variables-list:)
            (terpri)
            (setq formals (read))
            loop
            (setq line-number (plus 10 line-number))
            (print '-->)
            (setq input (read))
            (cond ((eq (car input) 'done)
```

```
            (put udf 'udf (list (reverse code) formals))
            (return t))
        ((eq (car input) 'check)                              <--
         (setq code (cons                                     <--
                    (list line-number (entercheck input))     <--
                    code)))                                    <--
        (t (setq code (cons (list line-number input) code)))))
    (go loop)))
```

The new function, ENTERCHECK, merely creates a proper CHECK-formatted list out of items for which it prompts the user:

```
(defun entercheck (input)
    (prog (output)
        (print (list 'if 'present:))
        (setq output (list (read)))
        (print (list 'exit 'or 'cont:))
        (setq output (append output (list (read))))
        (print (list 'if 'absent:))
        (setq output (append output (list (read))))
        (print (list 'exit 'or 'cont:))
        (setq output (append output (list (read))))
        (setq output (append input output))
        (return output)))
```

and I doubt if you'll now have any problems understanding that!

8.9 Using LSOLO

8.9.1 Here is a summary of LSOLO:

All LSOLO instructions are enclosed in a single pair of brackets. The binding of formal parameters in LSOLO functions is dynamic. The binding of CHECK wildcards is lexically restricted to the line in which the CHECK itself appears.

NOTE <triple> adds the triple to the database. It does not overwrite.

FORGET <triple> deletes the triple from the database.

DESCRIBE <node> prints all the database triples associated with the node.

CHECK <triple> used from top level, prints PRESENT if the triple is present in the database, otherwise ABSENT.

CHECK <triple> <actionA> <csA> <actionB> <csB> used from within a user-defined function, executes <actionA> followed by <csA> if the triple is present in the database, otherwise it executes <actionB> followed by <csB>.

The third element of the <triple> may be the wildcard "?", which is bound to the third element of the most recently entered matching database triple, if any.

PRINT <itemA> <itemB> <itemC>... takes each item in turn, printing its value if it has one, otherwise printing the item verbatim.

190

TO <UDF-name> permits the definition of a user-defined function.
LIST <UDF-name> prints the existing definition of a user-defined function.
BYE ends a session with LSOLO.

8.9.2 Editing LSOLO functions

As you've seen, LSOLO has no editor of its own. But with luck you should be able to use your Lisp's editor (or whatever editor you normally use) via one of the following:

(a) If your Lisp stores function-definitions as the BOUND VALUES of the function-names:

```
(defun soloedit (udf)
  (setq soloeditfn udf)
  (<edit> soloeditfn)                <--line X
  (setq soloeditfn nil))
```

(b) If your Lisp stores function-definitions on the property-lists of the function-names:

```
(defun soloedit (udf)
  (put 'soloeditfn 'expr (get udf 'udf))
  (<edit> soloeditfn)                <--line X
  (remrprop 'soloeditfn 'expr))
```

In either case, the LSOLO definition is temporarily made to be a Lisp "function-definition". Then <edit> (the name of your normal editing instruction) is called to work on it. Some <edit> functions are FEXPRs, in which case line X should read "(eval (list <edit> soloeditfn)). If you're happy with this arrangement, you can of course add EDIT as an LSOLO instruction:

```
(defun interpret (input)
  (cond ...
        ((eq (car input) 'print)
         (terpri) (mapc '(lambda (i)
                           (prin1 i) (spaces 1))
                        (cdr input)))
        ((eq (car input) 'to) (to (second input)))
        ((eq (car input) 'list) (slist (second input)))
        ((get (car input) 'udf) (instantiate input))
        ((eq (car input) 'edit) (soloedit (second input)))))) <--
```

You will probably now be able to add new instructions to an existing LSOLO function: before, between or after existing lines. The LSOLO interpreter will of course execute them in numerical order as usual.

8.9.3 The Tower of Brahma

There is a famous AI problem variously known as the Tower of Brahma or the Tower of Hanoi. Legend has it that somewhere in the Mysterious East is a holy temple wherein teams of brown-robed monks spend their lives in solving the problem. And predictably, when they eventually succeed the world will end. We can help to bring that merciful day a little closer using an LSOLO program to solve the problem.

A simplified version of the Towers of Brahma is sometimes seen as a child's toy. It consists of a horizontal base on which are mounted three vertical pillars, and on one pillar is a pile (tower) of rings or discs of decreasing size, the smallest at the top:

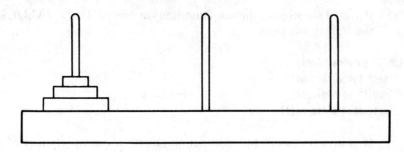

Fig 8.1

The problem is to move the whole pile of discs from its present pillar to one of the other pillars. But: (a) only one disc may be moved at a time; and (b) no disc may ever be placed on top of a disc smaller than itself.

The recursive process, as you have seen, progressively breaks a problem down into smaller and smaller chunks until the answer to each chunk can be found, and then as it unwinds it assembles all the part-solutions into an overall solution. A recursive approach to the above problem says: try to move the largest disc (No.3) from its present pillar to the goal pillar. If you can't do that (because there are smaller rings on top of it) try to move the next-largest disc (No.2) out of the way – i.e. to the spare pillar – making it possible to move No.3 as desired. Then move No.2 from the spare pillar to its target position on top of No.3.

Of course, it isn't possible to move No.2 either, because it has No.1 on top of it, so the recursive process tries again, reading No.2 for No.3 and No.1 for No.2. Here is such a program in LSOLO:

```
TO BRAHMA
(N FROM TO SPARE)
(10 (CHECK N MEANS STOP () (EXIT) () (CÒNT)))
(20 (CHECK N SUB1 ? (BRAHMA ? FROM SPARE TO) (CONT) () (EXIT)))
(30 (PRINT N FROM TO))
(40 (CHECK N SUB1 ? (BRAHMA ? SPARE TO FROM) (EXIT) () (EXIT)))
```

and here, for comparison, is the Lisp equivalent:

```
(defun brahma (n from to spare)
    (cond ((zerop n) nil)
          (t (brahma (difference n 1) from spare to)
             (print (list n from to))
             (brahma (difference n 1) spare to from))))
```

192

The corresponding database, entered via a series of NOTEs, is:

```
(ZERO MEANS STOP)
(THREE SUB1 TWO)
(TWO SUB1 ONE)
(ONE SUB1 ZERO)
```

We're obliged to replace numbers by words in these triples because PUT and ADDPROP won't accept numbers as identifiers. If in your Lisp they will, you can use numbers in the triples. The first triple allows us to put a recursion-halting condition into BRAHMA at line 10. That line means: if there are no more discs to handle, exit from this call to BRAHMA; otherwise, continue. The formal parameter N is the number of discs, which is of course the same thing as the "name" of the largest disc. So the program, given the problem of moving three discs from one pillar to another, tries to move only two of them out of the way, onto the spare pillar as above (line 20 of the program). If it were able to succeed in that attempt, it would print out (line 30) the fact that the largest disc could now be moved to the target pillar, and would then try (line 40) to move the previous two from the spare pillar to the target pillar. But of course in trying to move two discs at once the program is recalling itself recursively (line 20 and, later, line 40). In doing that, it will call itself again to move just one disc. And during that call it will succeed, because both line 20 and line 40 will call BRAHMA with N set to ZERO, which halts the recursion.

Notice the order of the arguments to BRAHMA. The top-level call asks it to move THREE discs from FROM to TO, with the remaining pillar designated as the SPARE. On line 20 it is asked to move TWO discs from FROM to SPARE, with what was the TO pillar counted as spare. And on line 40 it is asked to move TWO discs from SPARE to TO without using FROM. Which says the same thing as the descriptive paragraph just before the above function-definition. In terms of the diagram of the toy, the program says: try to move three discs from A to B. If you can't, try to move two discs from A to C; then move the largest disc from A to B; and finally move the two discs from C to B.

There is a very useful addition which you can make to your LSOLO to help you see how this function reaches the required solution. Make the following changes to LSOLO and to INSTANTIATE (as usual, you may have to fiddle a bit with the printing functions in the latter):

```
(defun lsolo ()
  (prog (input udf steps variables pdl checkvars traceflag)    <--
    (terpri)
    loop1
    (terpri)
    ... ))
(defun instantiate (input)
  (cond (traceflag (terpri)                            <--
                   (spaces (times 2 (length pdl)))     <--
                   (print (cons 'entering input))))    <--
    (setq udf (car input))
```

```
(setq steps (mapcar 'car (car (get (car input) 'udf))))
(setq variables (append (mapcar2 '(lambda (d f)
                                     (cons f d))
                          (cdr input)
                          (second (get (car input) 'udf)))
                 variables))
(setq pdl (cons (list udf steps variables) pdl))
(and pdl (cdr pdl) (setq steps (cons 'dummy steps)))))
```

The idea is that the global flag TRACEFLAG, if set to T, will cause the new COND in INSTANTIATE to do a carriage-return, then to print a number of spaces proportional to the current length of the PDL (i.e. proportional to the current depth of recursion), and then to print something like

```
(ENTERING BRAHMA TWO A C B)
```

This will happen every time a new call to BRAHMA or any other UDF is set up by the interpreter. To make this useful, you want to be able to turn it on and off at will. Which means giving LSOLO a couple of simple new commands, TRACE and UNTRACE:

```
(defun interpret (input)
  (cond ...
    ((eq (car input) 'print)
     (terpri) (mapc '(lambda (i)
                       (prin1 i) (spaces 1))
               (cdr input)))
    ((eq (car input) 'to) (to (second input)))
    ((eq (car input) 'list) (slist (second input)))
    ((get (car input) 'udf) (instantiate input))
    ((eq (car input) 'edit) (soloedit (second input)))
    ((eq (car input) 'trace) (setq traceflag t))        <--
    ((eq (car input) 'untrace) (setq traceflag nil))))  <--
```

Having made those changes, you can now run BRAHMA with TRACE turned on:

```
SOLO: (TRACE)
SOLO: (BRAHMA THREE A B C)
```

You will see a printout in which those calls to BRAHMA occurring at the same depth of recursion are printed vertically beneath one another: other intervening calls will be shifted horizontally to the left or the right.

By the way, the correct solution to the problem involving three discs only, and assuming that the top-level call to BRAHMA was as shown is:

```
(ONE A B)
(TWO A C)
(ONE B C)
```

```
(THREE A B)
(ONE C A)
(TWO C B)
(ONE A B)
```

The poor monks have 64 discs to move, and for all they know one of their ancestors may have made a mistake, back during the Ming dynasty. But I wouldn't advise you to try the program out on the 64-disc problem. Even though your computer probably has enough spare memory to handle 64 levels of recursion, you and I would be very old indeed by the time it had finished. The world might even have ended by itself, before then.

(For those who itch to know such things, the number of moves required is 2 to the power N, minus 1 for the starting-state. At the rate of one move per second, it would take something like 584 billion years...)

8.10 Improvements to the program

8.10.1 Reducing its verbosity

You may already have noticed that if an LSOLO program includes NOTEs or FORGETs, their printouts and those provided by the automatic call to DE-SCRIBE – which are useful when working with NOTE or FORGET from top level – can become a bit of a trial. Suppressing them is no problem. You'll need yet another global variable in LSOLO's PROG: a variable called RUNFLAG and which is set to T while any UDF is being executed but is otherwise set to NIL:

```
(defun lsolo ()
  (prog (input udf steps variables pdl checkvars traceflag runflag) <--
    (terpri)
    loop1
    (terpri)
    (print 'solo:)
    (setq input (read))
    (and (equal input '(bye)) (return nil))
    (interpret input)
    loop2
    (cond ((null pdl) (setq runflag nil) (go loop1))          <--
          (t (setq runflag t)                                 <--
             (setq udf (caar pdl))
             (setq steps (second (car pdl)))
             (setq variables (varsearch pdl))))
    loop3
    (cond ((null steps)
           (setq variables nil) (setq pdl (cdr pdl)) (go loop2))
          (t (interpret (soloeval (get-line (car steps) udf)))
             (setq steps (cdr steps))
             (go loop3)))))
```

Then make the following changes to NOTE, FORGET and CHECK:

```
(defun note (triple)
  (addprop (car triple) (second triple) (third triple))
  (cond ((not runflag)                              <--
         (terpri)
         (print (cons 'noted: triple))
         (describe (car triple)))))

(defun forget (triple)
  (cond ((memq (third triple) (get (car triple) (second triple)))
         (put (car triple)
              (second triple)
              (delete (third triple)
                      (get (car triple) (second triple))))
         (cond ((not runflag)                       <--
                (terpri)
                (print (cons 'forgotten: triple))
                (describe (car triple)))))
        (t (cond ((not runflag)                     <--
                  (terpri)                          <--
                  (print                            <--
                   (list 'no 'such 'description 'of (car triple))))))))

(defun check (line)
  (prog (vals)
    (setq vals (get (car line) (second line)))
    (cond ((memq (third line) vals)
           (cond ((not runflag) (terpri) (print 'present)))   <--
           (and (equal (nth 5 line) '(exit)) (setq steps 'dummy))
           (interpret (soloeval (nth 4 line))))
          ((and vals (eq (third line) '?))
           (and (equal (nth 5 line) '(exit)) (setq steps 'dummy))
           (setq checkvars (cons (cons '? (car vals)) checkvars))
           (interpret (soloeval (nth 4 line)))
           (setq checkvars nil))
          (t (cond ((not runflag) (terpri) (print 'absent)))  <--
             (and (equal (nth 7 line) '(exit))
                  (setq steps 'dummy))
             (interpret (soloeval (nth 6 line)))))))
```

Don't forget to make sure the brackets balance after inserting the new bits! By the way, I've used COND rather than AND because TERPRI returns NIL.

8.10.2 Automatic LISTing

In a similar vein, it is useful to have an automatic LISTing of any UDF as soon as it is defined:

196

```
(defun to (udf)
  (prog (formals line-number input code)
    (setq line-number 0)
    (terpri)
    (print 'variables-list:)
    (terpri)
    (setq formals (read))
    loop
    (setq line-number (plus 10 line-number))
    (print '-->)
    (setq input (read))
    (cond ((eq (car input) 'done)
           (put udf 'udf (list (reverse code) formals))
           (terpri)                                        <--
           (slist udf)                                     <--
           (return t))
          ((eq (car input) 'check)
           (setq code (cons
                        (list line-number (entercheck input))
                        code)))
          (t (setq code (cons (list line-number input) code)))))
    (go loop)))
```

8.10.3 Error traps

I won't go into many of these in detail, because one could go on adding them more
or less ad infinitum. But you may like, for example, to add traps here and there to
prevent people from entering ATOMIC (i.e. non-bracketed) things – which are
almost certain to produce error messages from the supporting Lisp. Here's how it
can be done for LSOLO:

```
(defun lsolo ()
  (prog (input udf steps variables pdl checkvars traceflag runflag)
    (terpri)
    loop1
    (terpri)
    (print 'solo:)
    (setq input (read))
    (cond ((and input (atom input))                       <--
           (terpri)                                        <--
           (print (list 'brackets 'please)) (go loop1))   <--
          ((equal input '(bye)) (return nil))             <--
          (t (interpret input)))                          <--
    loop2
    ... ))
```

It is (AND INPUT...) because of course if the user enters "( )", that is the same
thing as entering NIL, which is an atom. Similar traps could also be put into TO

197

and ENTERCHECK, although you would also need to add a PROG and several LOOP tags to ENTERCHECK, so that it re-cues the user for the correct version of any erroneous entry.

Unfortunately, most users will enter several atoms at once rather than just one, so that if the opening bracket is missing they'll get as many "brackets please" messages as soon as they press the carriage-return! If your Lisp has LINEREAD (see Chapter 4) there is a much nicer solution, which is to replace all calls to READ in the whole program by calls to LINEREAD. There aren't many of them: one in LSOLO itself, two in TO and four in ENTERCHECK. This will have the effect of removing the requirement that all LSOLO instructions have to be enclosed in brackets; in fact brackets will become taboo except as an alternative for NIL. If your LINEREAD is the same as mine, everything else will still work normally. The above error trap then becomes redundant.

You could also remove the brackets around LSOLO's printouts by defining the function PRINL to print them. PRINL takes a single list as its arguments and uses MAPC to print the contents of the list one by one, with a space after each:

```
(defun prinl (L)
   (mapc '(lambda (e)
            (prin1 e) (spaces 1))
       L))
```

(N.B. The function is called PRINL. MAPC applies PRIN1 to the list).

A similarly useful trap makes sure that users, when calling UDFs from top level, supply the right number of arguments. It could go into the same new COND:

```
(defun lsolo ()
   (prog (input udf steps variables pdl checkvars traceflag runflag)
      (terpri)
      loop1
      (terpri)
      (print 'solo:)
      (setq input (read))
      (cond ((atom input)
              (terpri)
              (print (list 'brackets 'please)) (go loop1))
            ((and (get (car input) 'udf)
                  (not (equal (length (cdr input))
                              (length (second (get (car input) 'udf))))))
              (terpri)
              (print (list 'wrong 'number 'of 'arguments))
              (go loop1)))
            ((equal input '(bye)) (return nil))
            (t (interpret input)))
      loop2
      ... ))
```

The new clause simply ensures that the LENGTH of the list of entered arguments – (CDR INPUT) – is the same as that of the arguments-list in the function -definition.

A fairly disastrous error, which may cause (may have caused?) your computer to crash, is that of endless recursion. It is quite easy to trap, provided that you are willing to put some arbitrary limit (say, ten levels) on the permissible depth of recursion for UDFs. All you require is a test in INSTANTIATE which, if the length of the PDL exceeds that limit, sets both the PDL and STEPS to NIL. This ensures that the "SOLO:" prompt reappears at once:

```
(defun instantiate (input)
  (cond (traceflag (terpri)
                   (spaces (times 2 (length pdl)))
                   (print (cons 'entering input))))
    (and pdl (setq pdl (cons
                          (list (caar pdl) (cdr steps) variables)
                          (cdr pdl))))
    (setq udf (car input))
    (setq steps (mapcar 'car (car (get (car input) 'udf))))
    (setq variables (append (mapcar2 '(lambda (d f)
                                        (cons f d))
                                     (cdr input)
                                     (second (get (car input) 'udf)))
                            variables))
    (setq pdl (cons (list udf steps variables) pdl))
    (and pdl (cdr pdl) (setq steps (cons 'dummy steps))
    (cond ((greaterp (length pdl) 10)                <--
           (print (list 'recursion 'limit/'exceeded)) <--
           (setq pdl nil) (setq steps nil)))))        <--
```

And so on. The thing to do, of course, is to see what kind of errors you or your users most often make, and then to devise traps for them. A good one, if you fancy trying it, is a trap to prevent nested CHECKs being entered via ENTERCHECK.

8.11 Other example programs

BRAHMA is actually quite a clever program to write in such a simplified language as LSOLO. Here are a few others which are more typical of the uses to which SOLO itself is put.

8.11.1 SOBTEST

SOBTEST is, as you'll soon realise, an LSOLO equaivalent of the AND/OR constructs which you can create in Lisp. The database contains a number of nodes (people's names) about which certain information is known. For example:

```
(URSULA IN LOVE)  (URSULA LOVEDBY MICKEY)
(PETER IN LOVE)  (PETER ISA EGOTIST)
(JOHN IN LOVE)
```

The program will decide the following about any of these nodes:
X is happy if
      (a) X is not in love; or
      (b) X is in love and is loved by someone else; or
      (c) X is an egotist.
X is broken-hearted if
      (a) he/she is in love; and
      (b) is not loved by anyone; and
      (c) is not an egotist."

Here's the program:

```
TO SOBTEST
(X)
(10 (CHECK X IN LOVE () (CONT) (PRINT X IS HAPPY) (EXIT)))
(20 (CHECK X LOVEDBY ? (PRINT X IS HAPPY) (EXIT) () (CONT)))
(30 (CHECK X ISA EGOTIST (PRINT X IS HAPPY) (EXIT)
                            (PRINT X IS BROKEN-HEARTED) (EXIT)))
```

Try it on URSULA, PETER, JOHN and MARY (yes, MARY).

8.11.2 KEEPITDARK

KEEPITDARK recursively "propagates an inference" along a chain of database triples. Such as this chain:

```
(MICKEY TELLS PETER)
(PETER TELLS JOHN)
(JOHN TELLS MARY)
(MARY TELLS URSULA)
```

Here's the program:

```
TO KEEPITDARK
(X)
(10 (NOTE X KNOWS SECRET))
(20 (CHECK X TELLS ? (KEEPITDARK ?) (EXIT) (SHOW) (EXIT)))
```

It has a subroutine, SHOW:

```
TO SHOW
NIL
(10 (DESCRIBE MICKEY))
(20 (DESCRIBE PETER))
(30 (DESCRIBE JOHN))
(40 (DESCRIBE MARY))
(50 (DESCRIBE URSULA))
```

Now, suppose you have a secret, which you reveal to Mickey, saying to him:

```
SOLO: (KEEPITDARK MICKEY)
```

You'll find that all of those people immediately know your secret. It's nice to use TRACE again on this one. Incidentally, if URSULA also tells MICKEY, whom she loves (and tells via the appropriate database triple, of course) the program will recurse for ever unless you've put in the trap mentioned in the previous section.

8.11.3 TELLIF

TELLIF searches a tree of triples, from the terminal nodes upwards, in much the same way as does the inferencer in Chapter 6. The idea is that you ask it a (rather stilted!) question about one of its terminal nodes. If the information you want is stored directly as one of that node's triples, it is printed out. If not, the program selects a special triple (which is present for all nodes except the one at the very top of the tree) to find out what kind of thing the node is. For example, a COD is a kind of FISH:

```
(COD IS DELICIOUS)
(COD IS FRIED)
(COD AKO FISH)
```

Having followed the A-Kind-OF link, the program calls itself recursively to see if the information you want is stored on the FISH node. If not, the process repeats until the information is found or until there is no more tree to explore. Here's some more data, so that the program will do something:

```
(FISH CAN SWIM)
(FISH HAS SCALES)
(FISH AKO CREATURE)
(CREATURE HAS SOUL)
```

And here's the program:

```
TO TELLIF
(A B C)
(10 (PRINT QUESTION: A B C))
(20 (CHECK A B C (PRINT YES: A B C) (EXIT) () (CONT)))
(30 (CHECK A AKO ?) (TELLIF ? B C) (EXIT) (PRINT NO) (EXIT)))
```

Try it:

```
SOLO: (TELLIF COD HAS SOUL)
QUESTION: COD HAS SOUL
QUESTION: FISH HAS SOUL
QUESTION: CREATURE HAS SOUL
YES: CREATURE HAS SOUL
```

Which proves that fish and chips has (have?) feelings, too. A nice refinement to this program involves writing TELLIF2, which is similar to TELLIF but takes an extra argument. This argument will eventually be bound to the first node in the actual question-as-entered (i.e. COD) so that the final answer can be:
YES: COD HAS SOUL

```
TO TELLIF2
(X A B C)
(10 (PRINT IT B IF: A B C))
(20 (CHECK A B C (PRINT YES: A B C SO X B C) (EXIT) () (CONT)))
(30 (CHECK A AKO ?) (TELLIF2 X ? B C) (EXIT) (PRINT NO) (EXIT)))
```

TELLIF2 is called from TELLIF in place of the original recursive call:

```
TO TELLIF
(A B C)
(10 (PRINT QUESTION: A B C))
(20 (CHECK A B C (PRINT YES: A B C) (EXIT) () (CONT)))
(30 (CHECK A AKO ? (TELLIF2 A ? B C) (EXIT) (PRINT NO) (EXIT)))
```

Before going on to write yourself a huge database, try the program out on a few more questions, such as:

```
SOLO: (TELLIF FISH HAS WINGS)
```

or

```
SOLO: (TELLIF I AM GOD)
```

8.12 ANSWER TO EXERCISE
Exercise 8.1

The modification is the same for both versions of DESCRIBE:

```
(defun describe (node)
  (prog (pairs)
    (terpri)
    (setq pairs (plist node))
    loop
    (and (null pairs) (return t))
    (and (not (member (car pairs) '(expr fexpr subr fsubr)))   <--
         (mapc '(lambda (v)
                   (print (list node (car pairs) v)))
               (second pairs)))
    (setq pairs (cddr pairs))
    (go loop)))
```

Chapter 9
Production systems

9.1 Production systems

The production system is a computational technique, whose effect is to make the computer into a more or less expert problem-solving machine. Programs referred to as "expert systems" are frequently based on production systems. The concept is an extension of the idea of a programming loop, in the sense that a PS iterates continuously until some exit condition – the solution to the problem – is satisfied. However, it does not iterate through a normal sequence of S-expressions as does a PROG loop (although a PS can be created out of a PROG loop). What a PS iterates through is a set of IF-THEN rules, each consisting of a left-hand side (its condition) and a right-hand side (its actions). One of the rules will contain as its left-hand side the exit-condition, and until this rule "fires" – until its conditional LHS is satisfied and its RHS actions are executed – the system iterates repeatedly through the entire set of rules, one or more of which may have its LHS conditions satisfied during any one cycle. The set of rules is known as the PRODUCTION MEMORY.

But a production system is not like a big COND inside a PROG loop. The circumstances under which any given rule's LHS will be satisfied are much richer in content than is a simple yes-no predicate. In fact the LHS of a rule contains a set of data-objects, and perhaps also functions. The data objects, which can be atoms, bindings, or simple data structures, are "matched" using techniques similar to those discussed in Chapter 7 (MICRO-ELIZA) against the contents of a database called the WORKING MEMORY. If there are functions in a rule's LHS, they are used to select or modify the actual matching process.

When the matching succeeds – that is, when the data in a rule's LHS can be successfully matched to the contents of working memory – the rule is said to be INSTANTIATED. If it happens that more than one rule is instantiated during any one cycle, a set of fixed and predetermined criteria are employed to select just one of them as the one whose RHS shall be executed. This process is called CONFLICT RESOLUTION, and the chosen rule is said to have FIRED, this implying execution of its RHS. Unless the rule's LHS specifies the exit condition, the effect of the RHS is to modify the contents of working memory so that a different rule or rules will be instantiated during the next cycle. The cycle is therefore referred to as the RECOGNISE-ACT CYCLE.

These four elements, PRODUCTION MEMORY, WORKING MEMORY, RECOGNISE-ACT CYCLE and CONFLICT RESOLUTION, are the basic components of a production system; but simpler systems – systems intended to solve simpler problems – can often do without conflict resolution, since they can be designed so that it is impossible for more than one rule to fire during any one cycle.

You may have heard of the two-person game called Mastermind. In it, your opponent sets up a secret pattern of four coloured pegs. Each peg may be of one of a set of six known colours, and it is permissible to have two or more pegs of the same colour in the pattern. Your objective, of course, is to discover the pattern; and this you do via a series of informed guesses: you guess by putting four pegs of the appropriate colours into the board, and your opponent gives you a "reply". The reply consists of a black peg for every peg in the pattern which matches one of your pegs in both position and colour; and a white peg for any other peg in the pattern which matches one of your pegs as to colour only. Then you guess again, and so on.

At first sight the game seems fiendishly complex. But it is surprising that most human players, after a little practice, can almost invariably reach the correct solution well within the permitted maximum of eight guesses. With a little luck to help you, you can often get there in four, or even three guesses. What is even more interesting is that most players cannot tell you the details of the strategies they use, although they evidently both know them and can use them.

As you might expect, it is possible to reduce those strategies to a set of rules which, taking the set of guesses and replies to date as a basis, can determine the next guess to be made. The rules progressively refine the guesses until the correct solution is reached. In this case the WORKING MEMORY is represented by the board, with the previous guesses and replies visible on it. In other words, a player might be thinking: "because of that particular sequence in my previous guesses and their replies, I know that the pattern has a red peg in its third position". That kind of knowledge can be represented as a production rule whose RHS action simply puts a red peg in position 3 of the next guess. But its LHS would be a very complex matching process.

Production systems are attractive, intriguing and effective for two main reasons: (1) the knowledge they contain is explicitly laid out in the rules rather than hidden away piecemeal in complex functions or data structures; and (2) although the rules themselves are conceptually clean and precise, the order in which they might fire throughout, say, an entire game of Mastermind can be very tortuous indeed, and so a production system can appear to play the game just as "intelligently" and mysteriously as does a human player.

The knowledge I have just referred to is knowledge about the problem domain – about the game of Mastermind. It is held in the rules – i.e. in PRODUCTION MEMORY. But the PS also holds a different kind of knowledge: knowledge of how to "be" a production system. That knowledge is integral to the loop which creates the RECOGNISE-ACT cycle, to the matcher which compares the LHS of each rule with the current WORKING MEMORY, and to the CONFLICT RESOLUTION techniques if any. The functions which together do these jobs are collectively known as the production system's INTERPRETER.

Esssentially, production systems are working models of complex PRO-CESSES. To the extent that a process is a means to attaining a goal, a PS is both an expert system and a problem-solver. Production systems are also used in pure research as, for example, working models of some current hypothesis, which can be tested against counter-examples and difficult cases in order to improve or to disprove the hypothesis itself. The advantage here is that the hypothesis remains clearly expressed in the set of rules, and cannot become lost or confused amidst a myriad of ad hoc functions devised to cope with this or that special-case failure of the model.

In a pure PS the lexical order of the rules would not matter at all, because in principle any rule may fire during any one cycle. But simpler production systems, in order to avoid the complexities of conflict resolution, often employ an implicit ordering – for example by specifying the positions of rules within the RECOG-NISE-ACT cycle, or by allowing the RHS actions of one rule to put into working memory temporary tags whose effect is to inhibit the firing of certain other rules.

Conflict resolution is in any case a somewhat arbitrary business, quite out of keeping with the overall clarity of the PS concept. For example, one might specify that if several rules are instantiated during one cycle, the one chosen to fire shall be the one which most recently fired during previous cycles. Or one might choose the rule which has the most complex (= the most detailed) LHS pattern. Or one might say that no rule shall ever fire more than once. Or twice. Or N times.

Although it is perfectly possible to write a large Lisp program which employs a PS as a subroutine to achieve only a part of the overall program's purpose, production systems are usually found as programs in their own right, intended to solve any one of a possibly large class of problems. They therefore quite often come complete with their own top level and their own syntax (cf LSOLO, Chapter 8), the latter designed specifically to be self-evident and easy to use in the context of the kind of problem the PS is geared to solve. After all, there isn't much point in building a very clever system, one which can answer any question on a given subject and/or infer the answers it doesn't know, if every potential user of it is obliged to learn Lisp in order to make it work!

One famous production system, called MYCIN (Davis, Buchanan and Shortliffe 1977) is fed with data concerning patients' symptoms, and it delivers medical diagnoses. Such things are not, by the way, the first signs of the Machines Taking Over. I can't tell you whether or not that will ever be a possibility, although I suspect that the simple truth is that since we hold the whip hand we won't LET them take over. At the moment, a machine is just a machine, no matter how clever it may seem to be in some very limited field, and any such notion is just a load of romantic twaddle – not far above the level of the man who personalises his car or a ship, referring to it patronisingly as "she" and pretending to himself that it has feelings and desires of its own. For the seriously foreseeable future, "intelligent" machines will be merely tools – mechanical slaves, if you like – to be used as such without a moment's qualm and, outside their little fields of expertise, very dumb indeed. One day we may be able to create the electronic equivalent of, say, a brain-damaged child or a moron with an overall I.Q. of about 70. And then, as Aaron Sloman (1978) once said, if there is to be a moral question it concerns what we will do to them, rather than what they might do to us.

Besides being used for the diagnosis of faults – in human metabolisms, in cars, in electronic circuits and so on, production systems can be and are used for predictive purposes, such as weather forecasting. So far, the machines have proved to be no better at that than human experts are; and this is because meteorological knowledge, as coded into the production rules, is necessarily incomplete and imprecise. When, as in the Tower of Brahma problem, the rules can contain all the necessary knowledge with no vaguenesses and no possibility of unforeseen factors, the machine does not make mistakes. Hence the usefulness of programs like MYCIN to harassed doctors.

In this chapter you will see how to build a production system which is a problem solver. The class of problems it can handle are those encountered by children who are learning to subtract fractional numbers. The set of production rules will have to cover the operations necessary to perform these subtractions correctly, and are in fact the very same rules as are normally taught to the children. But the program becomes suddenly much more interesting when one considers it not as a problem solver but as a model of the process of fraction-subtraction: a model of the "algorithm" which a child has in his/her head. For, if you change a rule, or delete one, or add a spurious rule, the model will consistently make the same kind of mistake – such as always failing to get the right answer to problems where "cancelling" is required. Thus it becomes a model of poor little beleaguered Mary, who one day can get all her sums right, but the next day is "being lazy" and gets most of them wrong. Mary doesn't know why her system sometimes works and sometimes doesn't; still less does she understand why her teacher is pleased with her one day and cross the next, when as far as she (Mary) is concerned she has tried just as hard and has done just the same things each time. Clearly there is something important missing from the teacher's understanding of Mary's difficulties. A production-system based program employing the same principle has been used by Young and O'Shea (1981) to investigate "algorithmic" errors in schoolchildren's arithmetic.

Later, you will see how the same INTERPRETER can be given a different set of production rules, so enabling it to solve completely different types of problem.

There is one function you will need, which may not exist in your Lisp. It is called ATOMCAR, and as its name implies it returns the first CHARACTER of its atomic argument:

```
*- (atomcar 'foo)


F
```

Your Lisp may have an equivalent function, perhaps called GETCHAR or ORDINAL. Or, if you have EXPLODE, you can define it easily:

```
(defun atomcar (a)
  (car (explode a)))
```

If all else fails, don't worry – I'll tell you what to do about it when the need arises. You'll also need the four basic arithmetical functions PLUS, ZEROP, LESSP, and

REMAINDER (see Chapter 4). PRINC would also be handy, although not essential.

Have a look at this rather pointless function:

```
(defun ps ()
  (prog ()
    loop

    (and (equal wm '(a b c))                        <--LHS1
         (return (print 'done)))                    <--RHS1
    (and (equal (car wm) 'a) (equal (second wm) 'b) <--LHS2
         (setq wm (list (car wm) (second wm) 'c)))  <--RHS2

    (and (equal (car wm) 'a)                        <--LHS3
         (setq wm (list (car wm) 'b (third wm))))   <--RHS3

    (and (not (equal (car wm) 'a))                  <--LHS4
         (setq wm (list 'a (second wm) (third wm)))) <--RHS4

    (go loop)))
```

It has four production rules, each of which is represented by an AND. For any one of them, if all the conditions specified in the LHS evaluate to T, the rules "fires" and the RHS will be evaluated. (The blank lines are there just to separate the rules so that you can see them more clearly, of course. Lisp would ignore them.)

Now suppose that the variable WM is initially bound to:

(x y z 1 2 3 (f . g))

and suppose we call (ps).

Once into the LOOP, rules 1, 2 and 3 will not fire, but rule 4 will. So WM is reset to

(a y z)

On the next iteration, rules 1 and 2 will still not fire, but rule 3 will. So now WM is set to

(a b z)

Subsequently, rule 4 will not fire on this iteration. On the third iteration, rule 2 will fire, setting WM to

(a b c)

and neither rule 3 nor rule 4 will fire. On the fourth iteration, rule 1 fires, printing "DONE" and halting the program.

Notice that none of the atoms comprising the final state of WM is present in the original WM. The rules add these items, one by one as the PATTERN in each rule's left-hand side matches to the current state of WM – the latter, of course, standing for Working Memory – and they delete other items.

As I said, that was a pointless function. Merely to show you the basic idea behind a production system. I used the simplest possible pattern matcher (EQUAL) and I made sure by my choice of LHS conditions that only one rule could fire during any cycle. Now imagine using a similar program to solve the Tower of Brahma problem (Chapter 8). If the working memory always contained a representation of the current state of the problem, the exit-rule would be looking for the state in which all of the discs were correctly positioned on the target pillar. The other rules would all specify what changes should be made to WM (i.e. what disc should be moved where) at times when the exit-condition was not yet satisfied. By the time you have reached the end of this chapter you should be able to write yourself a production system to solve the Tower of Brahma problem.

9.2 The subtraction algorithm: part 1

Successful subtraction of one fractional number from another depends upon using the correct PROCESS to do so, and this process can be reduced to a series of steps each of which takes the program one stage nearer to the overall goal. Clearly, I'm talking about an ALGORITHM. I intend to adopt a bottom-up approach, considering the simplest cases of fraction subtraction first. At each stage I shall specify the algorithm as it then stands, and I shall represent that algorithm as a set of production RULES of increasing complexity. As the resulting model of the subtraction process grows, you will be able to see how and why the production system interpreter does what it does as it interprets the rules. You'll see that the production system interpreter "translates" in an analogous way to the LSOLO interpreter, from the language used to express the production rules into Lisp functions. When the interpreter is complete, you will be able to write new sets of rules which will enable it to solve different kinds of problems.

The simplest type of fraction-subtraction problem is that where the two DENOMINATORS are the same and where the result after subtraction does not need to be simplified by CANCELLING:

$$ \tfrac{7}{8} - \tfrac{6}{8} = \tfrac{1}{8} $$

(In case you've forgotten the meaning of the relevant terms, the NUMERATOR is the number above the "divided by" line (e.g. 7); the DENOMINATOR is the number below that line (8); and CANCELLING would be required if the answer came out as, say, four-eighths — which is equal to a half.)

This simplest form of the problem is solved by the algorithm:
1. if the denominators are equal, note the value of one of them;
2. subtract the numerators, and note the result;
3. return the answer as 2 divided by 1.

9.3 The Working Memory representation

WORKING MEMORY will initially contain a representation of the problem.

Exactly what that representation looks like doesn't matter a bit in principle – so long as the production system INTERPRETER can detect within it the various parts of the problem itself. The standard representation of the problem as above isn't too convenient in Lisp: we'd prefer a linear LIST to a two-dimensional "picture". So let's rewrite it in a linear fashion:

```
((7 / 8) - (6 / 8))
```

That looks better already. However, the slash-sign is a special character in some Lisps, so let's avoid any possible problems with that by using the backslash (if your keyboard hasn't got one, use something else which is not a special character to symbolise "divided by"):

```
((7 \ 8) - (6 \ 8))
```

The next thing to worry about is that we don't want the machine to be able to lose track of which of these fractions is which. So let's put an extra element into each sublist to label it:

```
(((fr 1) 7 \ 8) - ((fr 2) 6 \ 8)))
```

The extra element, as you see, is actually a sub-sublist, containing the atom "FR" for "fraction" and a suitable number to distinguish one label from the other. Notice now that the minus-sign is completely redundant. We're in the process of building a production system to perform subtraction, and if in the end our rules do the right things there will be no point in explicitly telling them to subtract. So:

```
(((fr 1) 7 \ 8) ((fr 2) 6 \ 8)))
```

In our production system's syntax, that list will mean "subtract, from the fraction seven-eighths, the fraction six-eighths". This is the kind of thing you would have to put into WORKING MEMORY so as to get the production system to work out and return the answer.

Yes, I know the syntax looks horrible. I'm sure you'd much rather be able to type something like

```
((fr1 7\8) (fr2 6\8))
```

and have the machine sort it out. And on larger Lisps you certainly could. In Chapters 5, 7 and 8 you had a taste of how it is possible to write a top level which will take any syntax you like and "understand" it to be Lisp. But, for the sake of readers who may be working with very simple Lisps indeed, please bear with the above – it's not so bad once you get used to it!

9.4 The first rules

Now look again at step 1 of the algorithm:

1. If the denominators are equal...

A production system works by pattern matching the left-hand side of a RULE against the contents of a WORKING MEMORY. And we know what the latter is going to look like at the start of the problem:

    (((fr 1) 7 \ 8) ((fr 2) 6 \ 8)))

The objective now is to write a rule whose left-hand side will match to that, and whose right-hand side carries some corresponding action. "Match" means that each of the elements of the list comprising the LHS of the rule must be "equal" to one or other of the elements in the list comprising working memory. Have a look at this:

    (((fr 1) =n1 \ =d) ((fr 2) =n2 \ =d))

It's a two-element list like working memory, and each of those elements certainly begins with the appropriate FR label. The backslashes correspond as well, so we're not far off. And you may have guessed already that the symbols beginning with "=" are variables which get bound to whatever appears in the corresponding position in working memory: =N1 to 7, =D to 8, and =N2 to 6. This is very similar to what MICRO-ELIZA did with its "–BIND–" variables. The variables themselves can of course be any atoms you like, provided they each begin with "=". The function ATOMCAR will detect these "=" symbols inside the matcher by looking at the first character of any atom. If your Lisp has no ATOMCAR, see section 9.6 – although you won't need it until you get to that point.

   The important points about the matching process is that it takes place from left to right, and that during the attempt to match any one rule against working memory no variable can be bound more than once. Thus, during matching of the first element of the above rule, the atom =D will get bound to 8. If during subsequent matching of the second element of the rule =D would have to be bound to something else (i.e. if the denominators were NOT equal), the match would fail.

   Therefore, the rule as written effectively says: "if there are two fractions in working memory, consisting of (a) some numer =N1 divided by some number =D, and some number =N2 divided by the SAME number =D..."

   That looks OK to me. So let's think about the right-hand side of that rule. The right-hand side of any production rule is an action of some sort, or a series of actions, and normally the effect of each action in the RHS is to "deposit" some new element into working memory. The second part of step 1 of the algorithm is:

    ...note the value of one of them.

which can be effected simply by putting the value of the atom =D, into working memory along with what is already there. It would, however, be sensible to LIST this value along with a backslash, so as to signify to later rules that it IS a denominator:

    (\ 8)

A convenient representation for the whole rule is:

    (<rule-name> <LHS> ==> <RHS>)

So the whole of the rule to handle the case of equal denominators is:

    (denominator (((fr 1) =n1 \ =d) ((fr 2) =n2 \ =d))
        ==>
        ((\ =d)))

The LHS has two elements; the RHS has only one. The name of the rule and the
"==>" symbol have no purpose other than to make the rule easier for we
humans to read. The program will ignore it. The interpreter will use handy little
accessing-functions to dig the relevant portions out of this structure so that it can
hand them on to the matcher; for example it might say something like:

    (and (match (lhs:of current-rule) wm)
        (mapc 'deposit (rhs:of current-rule)))

Right. That's the first step in the algorithm rewritten as a rule. When the rule
has fired, i.e. when its LHS has matched against equivalent elements of working
memory and therefore its RHS has deposited a new element, working memory
will look like this:

    ((\ 8) ((fr 1) 7 \ 8) ((fr 2) 6 \ 8))

Now the second rule:

2. Subtract the numerators and note the result.

The LHS of this new rule will be matched against working memory as before, so
that the actual numerators in the problem get bound to suitable "=" variables,
which the RHS of the rule can then subtract. And it is to fire only if the
"denominator" rule has already fired – that is, if the (\ 8) which the latter deposits
is present in working memory. So the LHS of the new rule is exactly like that of the
previous rule, but with a check added for the new =D element:

    (((fr 1) =n1 \ =d) ((fr 2) =n2 \ =d) (\ =d))

Remember that the bindings of =N1 and =N2 created by the first rule are now
lost, and must be re-created here as needed. But there is no harm in also
re-creating the =D binding even though this rule will not use it.

The RHS of this new rule actually contains as a part of its pattern a function to
effect the subtraction of =N2 from =N1. In order that the interpreter can KNOW
that it's a function (and not merely the first item in a sublist to be matched against
something similar in working memory), its name begins with the symbol @ (any
other character will do, of course):

    (numerator (((fr 1) =n1 \ =d) ((fr 2) =n2 \ =d) (\ =d))
            ==>
            (((@subtract =n1 =n2) \)))

The "right-hand side function" @SUBTRACT is evaluated BEFORE this element of the rule's RHS is deposited into working memory, so that what is actually deposited is:

```
((1 \))
```

As before, the final backslash serves to indicate that this element represents a NUMERATOR. This is the new state of working memory:

```
((1 \) (\ 8) ((fr 1) 7 \ 8) ((fr 2) 6 \ 8))
```

The third rule says:

3.   Return the answer as 2 divided by 3.

that is, the RESULT of 2 divided by the RESULT of 3. And those two results are already present in working memory. All that the LHS of the third rule has to do is select those two results by matching, and put some suitable new item into working memory:

```
(answer ((=n \) (\ =d))
    ==>
    ((answer is =n \ =d)))
```

So the working memory now is:

```
((answer is 1 \ 8) (1 \) (\ 8) ((fr 1) 7 \ 8) ((fr 2) 6 \ 8))
```

Since no cancelling is being attempted yet, it is now OK to write the rule to halt the system:

```
(halt ((answer is &x))
    ==>
    ((@print the answer is &x)
    (@halt)))
```

An "&" variable is like the "−MANY−" variable used in MICRO-ELIZA: it matches to any number of elements in working memory (and therefore must of course always be the last item in any LHS-element). So the LHS of HALT matches successfully, the RHS-function @PRINT prints the answer, and the RHS-function @HALT stops the recognise-act cycle so that the program halts. Here are the four rules together, and the initial state of working memory:

```
(setq ruleset
    '((halt ((answer is &x))
    ==>

        ((@print the answer is &x)
        (@halt)))
```

212

```
(answer ((=n \) (\ =d))
   ==>
   ((answer is =n \ =d)))

(numerator (((fr 1) =n1 \ =d) ((fr 2) =n2 \ =d) (\ =d))
      ==>
      (((@subtract =n1 =n2) \)))

(denominator (((fr 1) =n1 \ =d) ((fr 2) =n2 \ =d))
        ==>
        ((\ =d)))))

(setq problem1 '(((fr 1) 7 \ 8) ((fr 2) 6 \ 8)))
```

9.5 The interpreter

Right. Now let's see what the interpreter has to do in order to achieve what I've just described. Two points need to be stressed straight away: the contents of the working memory are not thought of as being ordered in any way; and it isn't necessary for any given rule's LHS to match to all of them. But it IS necessary that all of the patterns in a rule's LHS find their equivalents in working memory before the rule's RHS can fire. In other words, the LHS patterns

```
(a (b c) d)
```

would be expected to match against a working memory which contained the patterns

```
(d x a (y z) (b c))
```

but not against a working memory which contained the patterns

```
(d x (y z) (b c))
```

because that does not contain "a". Working memory is just a sort of grab-bag of bits and pieces of data, and if a rule's LHS can find ALL of what it is looking for in there, the rule fires and its RHS is executed.

On the other hand the production memory – the full set of production rules – may or may not be ordered. If it isn't, conflict resolution may well be required. Ours will be ordered, and there will be no conflict resolution.

9.5.1 The recognise-act cycle

This has to:

1. try to match one pattern (i.e. one element) of any LHS against each pattern (i.e. element) of working memory in turn;
2. repeat 1 for each element in any one rule;
3. repeat 2 for each rule in production memory;
4. repeat 3 until the halting-rule fires to stop the program.

That will translate into four nested loops, loop 4 being the outermost. Let's therefore consider them in reverse order. Loop 4 is also the top level function which you call when you want to run the production system. It takes two arguments: the production memory or RULESET, and the problem statement or initial Working Memory:

```
(defun ps (ruleset wm)
  (prog (halted rule&bindings)
    loop
    (setq rule&bindings (match-rules ruleset wm))
    (cond ((null rule&bindings)
           (print (list 'no 'productions 'match))
           (print (list 'final 'wm: wm))
           (return 'stopped))
          (halted (return (print 'halted))))
    (print (list 'wm: wm))
    (setq wm (append (fire rule&bindings) wm))
    (go loop)))
```

RULESET, as you'll have gathered, is bound to the complete set of rules (four so far), and WM is bound to the initial representation of the problem, again as above. To run the PS with the rules we've developed so far and on the only problem we have, you would type:

```
*- (ps ruleset problem1)
```

You'll probably want to be able to save these bindings along with the program itself, and most Lisps won't save bound values. However, most Lisps will save property-lists. So it's probably a good idea to put both the production memory and the initial working memory onto the property-list of some suitable atomic identifier; you can then save and re-load the entire system. You would subsequently run the PS via a call rather like this:

```
(ps (get 'problem1 'ruleset) (get 'problem1 'wm))
```

Or, of course, you could write a couple of extra lines into the top of PS to do the GETs for you, and simply call it as:

```
(ps 'problem1)
```

But such refinements are up to you. I don't suppose you need to be spoon-fed with them in this the last chapter of the book!

As you can see, most of PS consists of PRINT statements so that you'll be able to watch what is going on as it runs. It has two PROG variables: HALTED, which is set to T by the @ HALT function in the HALT rule but otherwise remains at NIL, and RULE&BINDINGS. The latter will resemble the VARIABLES of LSOLO, holding dotted pairs corresponding to all the "=" and "&" bindings created during the matching of a single rule's LHS. Its purpose, of course, is to allow any variables in a rule's RHS to be evaluated. For the convenience of one of PS's subroutines, it will also hold the actual rule concerned.

The bindings themselves will be created during the innermost loop, by the matcher proper.

So each time around the recognise-act cycle (i.e. each time around the loop in PS), MATCH-RULES will try to match the whole LHS, of each rule in turn, against the contents of working memory. If any one of the rules does match, its bindings as created during the matching of each of its individual elements will be stored en masse in RULE&BINDINGS, together with the whole of the successful rule itself. Further down the PS loop, the function FIRE will use these bindings to evaluate the rule's RHS so that the correct things are added to working memory. If NONE of the rules match, MATCH-RULES returns NIL so that RULE&BINDINGS also remains at NIL.

The COND specifies two conditions under which the recognise-act cycle should halt: if during a whole cycle no rule fires at all; or if during any cycle the HALT rule fires. The former condition is included for safety: it prevents endless cycling should the production system fail to solve a problem it is set.

MATCH-RULES is loop (3). As it iterates through the RULESET trying as above to match each LHS against the contents of working memory, it is to return the required list of the rule and its bindings if the matching of any LHS succeeds:

```
(defun match-rules (ruleset wm)
  (prog (bindings)
    loop
    (cond ((null ruleset) (return nil))
          ((setq bindings (match-lhs (lhs:of (car ruleset)) wm))
           (return (list (car ruleset) bindings))))
    (setq ruleset (cdr ruleset))
    (go loop)))
```

Notice the little access function LHS:OF, which – as its name implies – retrieves the LHS of the first rule in any current RULESET. Its purpose is to make the code more readable for us humans; we can worry about its (very simple) definition later on.

MATCH-RULES carries out one complete recognise-act cycle. If it gets right through the RULESET without managing to match any rule's LHS against working memory, it returns NIL. But if any LHS does match, it returns the desired list. Notice that the latter RETURN, in the second clause of the COND, ensures that only the first rule to fire in any one cycle is counted. This will obviate any possibility of more than one rule firing per cycle, and hence will also obviate any need for conflict resolution.

MATCH-LHS is loop (2). It takes the LHS of one rule as supplied to it by MATCH-RULES and tries to match each of its patterns in turn against working memory:

```
(defun match-lhs (lhs wm)
  (prog (lhs-bindings temp)
    (setq lhs-bindings '((no . bindings)))
    loop
    (cond ((null lhs) (return lhs-bindings))
          ((setq temp (match-pattern (car lhs) wm))
```

```
            (setq lhs-bindings (append temp lhs-bindings)))
         (t (return nil)))
   (setq lhs (cdr lhs))
   (go loop)))
```

As long as each successive pattern in the rule is shown by MATCH-PATTERN to
match some pattern in working memory, its bindings if any are appended onto
LHS-BINDINGS. If any pattern doesn't match, MATCH-LHS returns NIL at
once. MATCH-RULES will then re-iterate, calling MATCH-LHS again for the
next rule. But if they all match, the aggregate LHS-BINDINGS is returned to
MATCH-RULES. This returned value ultimately becomes, in PS, the value of
RULE&BINDINGS – and the PS halts if RULE&BINDINGS is NIL. Now, it's
quite possible that one day you may devise a set of rules one of whose LHS will
match perfectly against working memory, but won't need to create any bindings in
the process. In order to prevent the system from halting if that happens (because
of NULL RULE&BINDINGS in PS), LHS-BINDINGS is given an initial dummy
value. So if any rule's LHS matches working memory, whether or not that rule
created any bindings, MATCH-LHS returns non-NIL. The dummy value won't
do any harm: whenever the matcher – or FIRE, which handles the RHS of rules –
needs to retrieve the bindings, it will do so using ASSOC, as the evaluator in
LSOLO did; and since there can never be a legal variable called NO, its "value" of
BINDINGS will never be retrieved. But if ever you need to print out the value of
LHS-BINDINGS or of RULE&BINDINGS – for debugging, say – it will help
YOU to see what it going on.

   MATCH-PATTERN, loop (1), is even simpler:

```
(defun match-pattern (patt wm)
  (prog ()
  loop
  (cond ((null wm) (return nil))
        ((match patt (car wm)) (return lhs-bindings)))
  (setq wm (cdr wm))
  (go loop)))
```

It iterates through the patterns in working memory either until one of them is
matched by the LHS pattern supplied from MATCH-LHS, or until there is no
working memory left. Notice that LHS-BINDINGS is a global variable for all of
MATCH-LHS's subroutines, including the matcher itself.

   Those four loops together create the recognise-act cycle.

9.5.2 The matcher

The matcher is very similar to that used in Chapter 7 (MICRO-ELIZA). Its
purpose is to compare corresponding items in (a) a pattern comprising one LHS
element from a rule, and (b) a pattern comprising one working-memory element.
It has to check that they are "equal" in some way. If all corresponding elements in
the two patterns match, the overall match succeeds. If any one pair do not match,
the overall match fails. Clearly, these two patterns do match:

```
LHS:     (goal nil)
WM:      (goal nil)
```

These next two will match if the matcher can effect the binding of variables as MICRO-ELIZA's matcher does:

```
LHS:     ((fr 1) =n \ =d)
WM:      ((fr 1) 3 \ 4)
```

and so will these:

```
LHS:     (answer &x)          WM:      (answer 1 \ 2)
```

Every time it encounters either type of variable it must check with LHS-BINDINGS – the bindings created so far during matching of the current rule's earlier LHS patterns – whether or not the variable is bound already; and if so it must ensure that the corresponding item in the working memory pattern is equal to that variable's bound value. It achieves this via LEGALP, a predicate which returns T if the variable is unbound or if its value is equal to the working memory item, and otherwise returns NIL. Thus, when the matcher encounters =D for the first time during matching of the DENOMINATOR rule, LEGALP will return T because =D is unbound. When =D is encountered for the second time during matching of that same rule, LEGALP will return T if the denominators were equal in the original problem and NIL if they were not. LEGALP is quite simple, and we can leave its definition until later.

The matcher also has the job of allowing for the possible presence of LHS functions. These have not been mentioned before and are somewhat different from RHS functions. It is important to realise that LHS functions should be PREDICATES, whose arguments will usually be "=" and "&" variables. For example, in this case:

```
LHS:     ((\ =d) ((@needs-cancelling =n =d) \))
WM:      ((\ 6) (12 \))
```

the item (@needs-cancelling =n =d) has to match against the item 12 if the match is to succeed. That is, the entire LHS-function's call has to match a single atom in working memory. This implies that only one new binding – that of =N to 12 – can occur during the process; and that therefore any other variables used as arguments to the LHS function – such as =D – must be bound previously. And in this example that does happen, as you can see. Our matcher will assume that the new variable, if any, is the FIRST argument to the LHS function, and the latter will have to be defined with this restriction in mind.

Here is the definition of MATCH:

```
(defun match (p w)
  (cond ((and (null p) (null w)) t)
        ((null w)
         (cond ((and (null (cdr p)) (&variablep (car p)))
```

217

```
                    (setq lhs-bindings (cons (list (car p)) lhs-bindings)))
                  (t nil)))
            ((null p) nil)
            ((equal (car p) (car w))
             (match (cdr p) (cdr w)))
            ((atom (car p))
             (cond ((=variablep (car p))
                    (and (legalp (cons (car p) (car w)) lhs-bindings)
                         (match (cdr p) (cdr w))
                         (setq lhs-bindings
                               (cons (cons (car p) (car w)) lhs-bindings))))
                   ((&variablep (car p))
                    (and (legalp (cons (car p) w) lhs-bindings)
                         (setq lhs-bindings
                               (cons (cons (car p) w) lhs-bindings))))
                   (t nil)))
            ((and (listp (car p)) (ps-functionp (caar p)))
             (cond ((match (ncons (cadar p)) (ncons (car w)))
                    (apply (caar p) (expand (cdar p) lhs-bindings))
                    (match (cdr p) (cdr w)))))
            ((and (listp (car p)) (listp (car w)))
             (and (match (car p) (car w))
                  (match (cdr p) (cdr w)))))))
```

Don't panic. Take the COND clauses in order; they'll have to work on these possible kinds of LHS pattern:

```
((fr 1) =D =N)      (\ =D)      (answer is &rest)      (@lhs-fn =D =N)
```

and, like the matcher in MICRO-ELIZA, this version of MATCH calls itself recursively in order to deal with one element of any pattern at a time. MATCH will be looking to see if essentially the SAME elements occur in both the LHS pattern and the working memory pattern, these being what are fed to it from MATCH-PATTERN. Its formal parameters are: P to represent the LHS pattern; and W to represent the working memory pattern.

The first COND clause says "if I have reduced both patterns to NIL, they match". So T is returned.

The second clause copes with cases where an "&" variable occurs in the LHS pattern, and matches to nothing (as it is allowed to do) in the working memory pattern. If the "&" variable were &REST, it would put onto the list LHS-BINDINGS the equivalent of

```
(&rest . nil)
```

and, as you may remember from Chapter 3, that is the same thing as a LIST of &REST:

```
(&REST)
```

218

The mini-COND inside that second clause ensures that if working memory has been recursively reduced to NIL but some LHS items still remain, MATCH returns NIL – the match fails.

The third clause of the main COND does the opposite: if the LHS pattern has been reduced to NIL but there is still some remainder of the working memory pattern, the match fails.

The fourth main COND clause does the standard recursive-matcher trick: if the CARs of the two patterns are equal, it goes on to MATCH their CDRs.

The fifth clause checks to see if the CAR of the LHS pattern is an atom which did not match as above to the CAR of the working memory pattern. If so, it may be one of two things: an "=" variable or a "&" variable. So an inner COND dictates what shall be done in either case. An "=" variable is allowed to match to one atom of the working memory pattern only. So, provided that it is legal to do so an attempt is made to MATCH the CDR of the LHS pattern with the CDR of the working memory pattern. And if this attempt succeeds, it's OK to put the new binding of that "=" variable onto LHS-BINDINGS. And LEGALP, remember, returns T if the variable is unbound, or if it is bound to the corresponding working memory item.

An "&" variable is easier to handle, because it may match to any number of elements in the working memory pattern. So, provided again that it is legal to do so, the WHOLE of the remainder of the working memory pattern is put into LHS-BINDINGS as the value of the "&" variable, and no recursive call to MATCH is needed. If the CAR of the LHS pattern is anything other than an "=" variable or an "&" variable, MATCH returns NIL.

The sixth clause deals with LHS functions. If the current head of the LHS pattern is a list rather than an atom (if you haven't got LISTP, use (NOT (ATOM (CAR P))) instead, as shown in the Appendix), it checks to see if it is a PS-FUNCTION. The predicate is so named because it will be used later to check for RHS functions as well. If the current head of the LHS pattern is an LHS function, MATCH is called again to bind or evaluate the function's first argument; the function itself is applied to the list of its arguments; and then matching proceeds normally on the CDRs of both patterns. EXPAND retrieves any necessary bound values from LHS-BINDINGS.

And the last clause of the main COND simply does the recursive matching call in cases where the CARs of both patterns happen to be lists.

There. That wasn't so bad, was it? Now for LEGALP:

```
(defun legalp (key-pair bindings)
  (prog (present)
    (setq present (assoc (car key-pair) bindings))
    (return (or (not present)
        (equal (cdr present) (cdr key-pair))))))
```

KEY-PAIR will be a dotted pair created by MATCH out of the name of a "=" or "&" variable and its possible value as retrieved from the working memory pattern. And BINDINGS is, of course, LHS-BINDINGS, which might look like this:

```
((=d . 8) (=n1 . 7) (=n2 . 6) (no . bindings))
```

So the local variable PRESENT is initially bound to the result of ASSOCiating the CAR of the dotted pair with LHS-BINDINGS. If the variable has not previously been bound, this will be NIL, so the OR returns T. If it was previously bound, the OR returns T if the bound value from LHS-BINDINGS is the same as the value found in the working memory pattern.

The only major functions remaining are FIRE and EXPAND. FIRE is quite easy. It merely takes each element of the RHS of a rule in turn and applies EXPAND to it. The latter's job is to be an evaluator, replacing "=" and "&" variables in the RHS of a rule with their bound values from LHS-BINDINGS. And it also has to handle RHS functions. FIRE returns the result of this operation, deleting any NILs which may crop up, and PS CONSes it into the current working memory. So working memory acquires the patterns specified in the rule's RHS, with all variables replaced by their bindings and all RHS functions executed:

```
(defun fire (rule&bindings)
  (terpri)
  (print (list 'firing 'rule (name:of (rule:of rule&bindings))))
  (delete nil
          (mapcar '(lambda (action)
                     (cond ((setq action
                                  (expand action
                                          (bindings:of rule&bindings)))
                            (print (list 'deposited: action))
                            action)
                           (t nil)))
                  (rhs:of (rule:of rule&bindings))))))
```

NILs are possible because RHS functions are allowed either to deposit some new item into working memory or not. @PRINT, for example, does not. So @PRINT is defined so as to return NIL, which gets ignored by FIRE as above.

EXPAND itself works in a similar way to MATCH, but allowing for the presence of RHS functions in the the ACTION – i.e. in the RHS of the rule:

```
(defun expand (action bindings)
  (cond ((null action) nil)
        ((atom (car action))
         (cond ((=variablep (car action))
                (cons (cdr (assoc (car action) bindings))
                      (expand (cdr action) bindings)))
               ((&variablep (car action))
                (append (cdr (assoc (car action) bindings))
                        (expand (cdr action) bindings)))
               ((ps-functionp (car action))
                (apply (car action) (expand (cdr action) bindings)))
               (t (cons (car action) (expand (cdr action) bindings)))))
        ((listp (car action))
         (cons (expand (car action) bindings)
               (expand (cdr action) bindings)))))
```

All that is left is a handful of workhorse functions which are so simple that you could certainly define them without my help. But, for completeness, here they are:

```
(defun =variablep (element)
  (and (symbolp element) (equal (atomcar element) '=)))

(defun &variablep (element)
  (and (symbolp element) (equal (atomcar element) '&)))

(defun ps-functionp (element)
  (and (symbolp element) (equal (atomcar element) 'a)))
```

SYMBOLP checks that the element concerned is not a number. If your Lisp hasn't got it, but has NUMBERP, define it like this:

```
(defun symbolp (x)
  (and (atom x) (not (numberp x))))

(defun name:of (rule)
  (car rule))

(defun lhs:of (rule)
  (cadr rule))

(defun rhs:of (rule)
  (car (cdddr rule)))

(defun rule:of (rule&bindings)
  (car rule&bindings))

(defun bindings:of (rule&bindings)
  (cadr rule&bindings))

(defun adelete (element)
  (print (list 'deleted: element))
  (setq wm (delete element (copy wm)))
  nil)

(defun ahalt ()
  (setq halted t) nil)

(defun aprint args
  (mapc '(lambda (a)
            (princ (eval a)) (spaces 1))
          args))
```

These last three functions, all of them RHS functions, are strictly speaking part of the INTERPRETER group of functions. Other rulesets (see section 9.9) will use them as well. Notice that @PRINT is a FEXPR, so that you can give it as many arguments as may be convenient. And MAPC returns NIL, as is required in an RHS function which doesn't deposit anything into working memory.

9.6 Modifications for Lisps without ATOMCAR

If your Lisp has no ATOMCAR, you will need a different kind of test whereby the predicates =VARIABLEP, &VARIABLEP and PS-FUNCTIONP can distinguish those items in the rules. A simple solution is to define yourself the following three additional functions:

```
(defun def=variable args
  (put 'ps-aux '=variables args))

(defun def&variable args
  (put 'ps-aux '&variables args))

(defun defps-function args
  (put 'ps-aux 'ps-functions args))
```

These, as you can see, put the fact that certain ARGS are =variables or whatever onto a suitable property-list. They are all FEXPRs, so ARGS in each case can contain as many separate variable-names or function-names as you need. The way to use them is, for example:

```
(def=variable =n1 =n2 =d)

(def&variable &rest)

(defps-function @subtract)
```

Then the three predicates have to be redefined:

```
(defun =variablep (element)
  (member element (get 'ps-aux '=variables)))

(defun &variablep (element)
  (member element (get 'ps-aux '&variables)))

(defun ps-functionp (element)
  (member element (get 'ps-aux 'ps-functions)))
```

Then everything will work normally. You have to use the three new "DEF" functions to set up any new set of =variables, &variables and ps-functions – which means every time you want the production system to work with a new set of rules. Of course, you still have to write the ps-functions themselves: the above merely serves to indicate that they ARE ps-functions.

9.7 The subtraction algorithm: part 2

You have now written a fairly sophisticated production system interpreter. Quite large production systems have been built which do not have the facility either for "segment variables" – "&" variables, so called because they match to a whole segment of a working memory pattern rather than to just one item of it – or for LHS functions. Now that you understand the purpose of each symbol in a rule, and how they are matched against working memory, we can write the remainder of our model of fraction subtraction. The next steps in the algorithm say:

5. if the denominators are not equal, find their lowest common multiple;
6. divide the LCM by the first denominator and note the result;
7. multiply the corresponding numerator by this result;
8. repeat 6 and 7 for the other fraction;
9. the denominators now being equal, return to steps 1 to 4.

9.8 The remaining rules

Step (9) is already expressed in the existing rules. We shall need four new rules. Imagine that this time the initial working memory looked like this:

DENS-NOT-EQ detects the presence of unequal denominators and puts into working memory two "make alike" instructions: one to trigger steps 6 and 7 — and one to trigger them again for the sake of step 8:

```
(dens-not-eq  (((fr 1) =n1 \ =d1) ((fr 2) =n2 \ =d2))
              ==>
              ((make alike (fr 1))
               (make alike (fr 2))))
```

The effect of this on working memory is:

```
((make alike (fr 1))
 (make alike (fr 2))
 ((fr 1) 3 \ 4)
 ((fr 2) 2 \ 3))
```

The presence of both "make alike" instructions together triggers the rule which finds the LCM:

```
(lcm ((make alike (fr 1)
      (make alike (fr 2)
      ((fr 1) =n1 \ =d1)
      ((fr 2) =n2 \ =d2))
     ==>
     ((lcm (@findlcm =d1 =d2))))
```

which deposits the LCM into working memory:

```
((lcm 12)
 (make alike (fr 1))
 (make alike (fr 2))
 ((fr 1) 3 \ 4)
 ((fr 2) 2 \ 3))
```

Now come the two factorising rules for steps 6 and 7. The first (in order of execution) recognises the presence in working memory of one of the "make equal" instructions together with the LCM, deletes the former, and puts in its place a note of the "factor" by which the numerator of one of the fractions is to be multiplied:

```
(factor2 ((make alike (fr =x))
          (lcm =lcm)
          ((fr =x) =n1 \ =d))
         ==>
         ((@delete (make alike (fr =x)))
          ((fr =x) factor (@divide =lcm =d))))
```

Working memory now becomes:

```
(((fr 1) factor 3)
 (lcm 12)
 (make alike (fr 2))
 ((fr 1) 3 \ 4)
 ((fr 2) 2 \ 3))
```

The FACTOR is labelled to show which fraction it refers to.

The other factorising rule detects the presence of the new FACTOR and of the corresponding fraction FR 1. It deletes both, and deposits the new form of the fraction with its numerator multiplied by the factor:

```
(factor1 (((fr =x) factor =fct)
          ((fr =x) =n \ =d)
          (lcm =lcm))
         ==>
         ((@delete ((fr =x) factor =fct))
          (@delete ((fr =x) =n \ =d))
          ((fr =x) (@multiply =fct =n) \ =lcm)
```

And the new working memory is:

```
(((fr 1) 9 \ 12)
 (lcm 12)
 (make alike (fr 2))
 ((fr 2) 2 \ 3))
```

The two factorising rules then fire again in turn, dealing with the second fraction, producing two successive changes to working memory:

```
(((fr 2) factor 4)
 ((fr 1) 9 \ 12)
 (lcm 12)
 ((fr 2) 2 \ 3))
```

```
(((fr 2) 8 \ 12)
 ((fr 1) 9 \ 12)
 (lcm 12))
```

After that, DENOMINATOR, NUMERATOR, and ANSWER fire in sequence as before:

```
((\ 12)
 ((fr 2) 8 \ 12)
 ((fr 1) 9 \ 12)
 (lcm 12))

((1 \)
 (\ 12)
 ((fr 2) 8 \ 12)
 ((fr 1) 9 \ 12)
 (lcm 12))

((answer is 1 \ 12)
 (1 \)
 (\ 12)
 ((fr 2) 8 \ 12)
 ((fr 1) 9 \ 12)
 (lcm 12))
```

and the final stage is, of course, that HALT fires to stop the system.

Only one algorithmic step remains now: the cancelling step which in practice comes between steps 2 and 1 — or between ANSWER and HALT. If you were wondering why ANSWER and HALT were not combined into one rule, you now know! The step says:

1a) If the answer needs cancelling, do so.

Here's CANCEL:

```
(cancel ((\ =d) ((@needs-cancelling =n =d) \))
        ==>
        ((answer is (@cancel =n =d))))
```

The LHS of this rule matches to the third and second elements of the above final working memory, and clearly @NEEDS-CANCELLING should bind =N to 1 but return NIL so that the match fails and @CANCEL is not called at all. ANSWER would fire on that cycle instead. But if those third and second elements had been (2 \) and (\ 12), @NEEDS-CANCELLING would bind =N to the corresponding item in working memory – that is, to 2 – and CANCEL would supply "1 \ 6" as the answer. ANSWER would then not get the chance to fire (only one firing allowed per cycle). In either case HALT would fire on the following cycle.

Here are all the rules together, followed by the initial working memory:

```
(setq ruleset
     '((halt ((answer is &x))
             ==>

               ((@print the answer is &x) (@halt)))

       (cancel ((\ =d) ((@needs-cancelling =n =d) \))
               ==>
               ((answer is (@cancel =n =d))))

       (answer ((=n \) (\ =d))
               ==>
               ((answer is =n \ =d)))

       (numerator (((fr 1) =n1 \ =d) ((fr 2) =n2 \ =d) (\ =d))
                  ==>
                  (((@subtract =n1 =n2) \)))

       (denominator (((fr 1) =n1 \ =d) ((fr 2) =n2 \ =d))
                    ==>
                    ((\ =d)))

       (factor1 (((fr =x) factor =fct)
                 ((fr =x) =n \ =d)
                 (lcm =lcm))
                ==>
                ((@delete ((fr =x) factor =fct))
                 (@delete ((fr =x) =n \ =d))
                 ((fr =x) (@multiply =fct =n) \ =lcm)))

       (factor2 ((make alike (fr =x))
                 (lcm =lcm)
                 ((fr =x) =n1 \ =d))
                ==>
                ((@delete (make alike (fr =x)))
                 ((fr =x) factor (@divide =lcm =d))))

       (lcm ((make alike (fr 1))
             (make alike (fr 2))
             ((fr 1) =n1 \ =d1)
             ((fr 2) =n2 \ =d2))
            ==>

         ((lcm (@findlcm =d1 =d2))))

       (dens-not-eq (((fr 1) =n1 \ =d1) ((fr 2) =n2 \ =d2))
                    ==>
                    ((make alike (fr 1))
                     (make alike (fr 2)))))))

(setq problem1 '(((fr 1) 7 \ 8) ((fr 2) 6 \ 8)))
```

To make the rules work, these LHS and RHS functions must be defined:

```
(defun @subtract (x y)
  (difference x y))

(defun @multiply (x y)
  (times x y))

(defun @divide (x y)
  (quotient x y))

(defun @findlcm (dn1 dn2)
  (prog (n1 n2)
    (setq n1 dn1)
    (setq n2 dn2)
    loop
    (cond ((equal n1 n2) (return n1))
          ((lessp n1 n2) (setq n1 (plus n1 dn1)))
          (t (setq n2 (plus n2 dn2))))
    (go loop)))
```

@FINDLCM takes two arguments, DN1 and DN2. DN1 is successively added to one of two running totals N1, and DN2 is successively added to the other total N2. Whichever total is the smaller is augmented on each cycle, until the two are equal.

```
(defun @needs-cancelling (n d)
  (and (numberp n) (numberp d)
  (not (equal (prog (hcf)
                (setq hcf n)
                loop
                (and (zerop (remainder n hcf))
                     (zerop (remainder d hcf))
                     (return hcf))
                (setq hcf (difference hcf 1))
                (go loop))
              1)))))
```

@NEEDS-CANCELLING returns either T or NIL. HCF is initially set to the numerator of the fraction being tested, and is reduced by 1 each time around the loop. When it divides exactly into both N and D, it is returned. Notice that HCF MUST divide exactly into both N and D when it has been reduced to 1. So if it divides before then, cancelling must be possible.

```
(defun @cancel (n d)
  (prog (hcf)
    (setq hcf n)
    loop
    (and (zerop (remainder n hcf))
         (zerop (remainder d hcf))
         (return (list (quotient n hcf) '\ (quotient d hcf))))
```

```
(setq hcf (difference hcf 1))
(go loop)))
```

@CANCEL works similarly to @NEEDS-CANCELLING. It returns either the cancelled fraction if cancelling is possible, or the original fraction (though of course it will not be called in the latter case, so what it returns is irrelevant). Note that it returns a list, suitable for EXPAND to CONS "answer" and "is" into.

You can try out your complete production system on various other similar problems, such as

```
(((fr 1) 11 \ 12) ((fr 2) 5 \ 12))
```

and it should unfailingly produce the correct answers.

9.9 Exploring the model

Now that the production system (interpreter plus ruleset) can subtract fractions correctly, it is interesting as mentioned above to see the effect of making it do so incorrectly, as a child might do if he or she had somehow acquired the wrong algorithm for the process. An obvious example is to remove the CANCEL rule. You might alternatively like to try redefining @FINDLCM so that it ADDED the two denominators; or altering FACTOR2 so that it removed both "make equal" instructions at once, rather than only one. In all cases you'll see that the system fails on only some particular class of problem, just as a child might. Of course, if you want to be really scientific about it, you should run a survey of the errors real children make, and then try to alter your model so as to account for those errors. The proper methodology, using a production system similar to yours, is described in Evertsz (1982, 1983).

9.10 Other problems for the production system interpreter

You can use the same interpreter to solve many different kinds of problem. To a large extent, you are limited only by your own ingenuity in working out a set of problem-solving steps and then expressing them as production rules. Only the rules and the initial working memory have to be changed, of course; although you may as in the examples above find that you need to define a few LHS or RHS functions. But the interpreter itself remains just as it is for all problem-solving tasks. There follow a couple of simple examples just to give you the idea.

First, an LSOLO-type very simple inferencer:

```
(setq infer-rules
      '((halt ((answer is =a))
       ==>

             ((@print answer is =a)
              (@halt)))

       (check ((goal =id =rel =val)
               (=id =rel =val))
              ==>
              ((answer yes)))
```

```
       (chase ((goal =id =rel =val)
              (=id isa =ako))
              ==>
              ((@delete (goal =id =rel =val))
               (goal =ako =rel =val)))

       (fail ((goal =id =rel =val))
              ==>
              ((answer no)))))

(setq infer-wm '((mary isa woman)
                 (woman isa human)
                 (human isa mammal)
                 (mammal isa being)
                 (being has soul)
                 (goal mary has soul)))
```

And here, for those who don't fancy trying it alone, is the Tower of Brahma solution:

```
(setq brahma-rules
    '((halt ((target 1 2 3))
      ==>

               ((@halt)))

       (newgoal ((goal nil)
                 (biggest =n))
                 ==>
                 ((@delete (biggest =n))
                  (@delete (goal nil))
                  (goal (move =b (@peg:of =b) target))))

       (biggest ((goal nil))
                 ==>
                 ((biggest (@biggest start spare))))
       (move1 ((goal move =n =x =y)
               (obstruction nil))
               ==>
               ((@move =n =x =y)
                (@delete (obstruction nil))
                (@delete (goal move =n =x =y))
                (goal nil)))

       (move2 ((goal move =n =x =y)
               (obstruction =o))
               ==>
               ((@delete (goal move =n =x =y))
                (goal move =o (@peg:of =o) (@third-peg =x =y))))
```

```
(obstructing ((goal move =n =x =y))
             ==>
             ((obstructing (@biggest =n =x =y))))))

(setq brahma-wm '((start 1 2 3) (target) (spare) (goal nil)))
```

The program is interesting because it establishes its own intermediate goals as it goes along. So we don't have to provide it with one at the start. The corresponding algorithm is:

1. If all rings are on the target peg, halt;
2. If no goal exists in working memory, and if ring B is the biggest ring not yet on the target peg, establish the goal of moving ring B from its present peg to the target peg;
3. If the goal is to move ring N from peg X to peg Y, and ring N is unobstructed (that is, no smaller ring on top of it and no smaller ring on peg Y), move ring N from peg X to peg Y. Delete the goal from working memory.
4. If the goal is to move ring N from peg X to peg Y, and if ring O is the largest of the rings obstructing it (i.e. the largest of all the rings on peg X and peg Y), delete the goal from working memory and establish the new goal of moving ring O from its present peg to peg Z.

Here are the extra RHS functions this production system needs:

```
(defun @peg:of (ring)
  (or (and (member ring (assoc 'start wm)) 'start)
      (and (member ring (assoc 'target wm)) 'target)
      'spare))

(defun @biggest (pegA pegB)
  (apply 'max (append (cdr (assoc pegA wm))
                      (cdr (assoc pegB wm)))))

(defun @third-peg (pegA pegB)
  (car (delete pegA (delete pegB (copy '(start target spare))))))

(defun @biggest-obstruction (ring pegA pegB)
  (prog (data result)
    (setq data (append (cdr (assoc pegA wm)) (cdr (assoc pegB wm))))
    loop
    (and (null data)
         (return (cond ((null result) nil)
                       (t (apply 'max result)))))
    (and (less (car data) ring)
         (setq result (cons (car data) result)))
    (setq data (cdr data))
    (go loop)))

(defun @move (ring pegA pegB)
  (terpri)
```

```
(print (list '>>> 'move 'ring ring 'from pegA 'to pegB '<<<))
(terpri)
(prog (rings)
  (setq rings (cdr (assoc pegA wm)))
  (setq wm (delete (assoc pegA wm) (copy wm)))
  (setq wm (cons (cons pegA (delete ring rings)) wm))
  (setq rings (cdr (assoc pegB wm)))
  (setq wm (delete (assoc pegB wm) (copy wm)))
  (setq wm (cons (cons pegB (delete ring rings)) wm))))
```

And, just in case your Lisp hasn't got MAX, here it is:

```
(defun max (L)
  (prog (result)
    (setq result 0)
    loop
    (cond ((null L) (return result))
          ((greaterp (car L) result)
           (setq result (car L))))
    (setq L (cdr L))
    (go loop)))
```

9.11 Conflict resolution

As I've indicated already, there isn't any. MATCH-RULES ensures that only one
rule can fire per cycle. But of course this must be the correct rule. So the ordering
of the rules within RULESET is crucial. For example, reversing the order of
OBSTRUCTING and MOVE2 in the Tower of Brahma set would cause the
interpreter to cycle endlessly, firing OBSTRUCTING every time around. As a
general guide, the halting rule or rules should come first in the ruleset, much as the
halting S-expression comes first in an ordinary PROG loop; and a rule (such as
OBSTRUCTING) whose purpose is to set up the conditions for some other rule
or rules (such as MOVE1 and MOVE2) should come AFTER the latter. BIG-
GEST comes after NEWGOAL for the same reason. Conversely, a rule such as
FAIL in the inferencing example must come after all the other rules because it is
only appropriate for this one to fire if none of the others has fired during that
cycle.

9.12 An improvement

One improvement which is crying out to be made is a switch to turn all those
printouts on and off. The neat way to do it is to give PS an additional formal
parameter, perhaps called PRINTOUT or PROTOCOL. When you call PS, the
value supplied for this parameter will be T or NIL. Then each PRINT statement in
the three functions PS, FIND and @DELETE should be embedded in an AND:

```
(and printout (print (list ...)))
```

This will not, of course, inhibit the more desirable printouts coming from any
members of the ruleset.

Appendix

This Appendix comprises a section of text covering the use of INIT files, followed by an alphabetical list of most of the Lisp functions mentioned in this book. If a function isn't listed, it is one of the minimal subset (see Foreword).

INIT files

Any collection of functions or programs which are in some way associated with one another can normally be kept together in what is known as a FILE. Physically, the file will be a tape or disc reserved by you for that purpose. As you work through this book you will probably encounter several functions which you would like to have incorporated permanently as part of your Lisp; and certainly you will write some functions of your own which you would also like to add to Lisp. All programmers acquire their own set of favoured useful functions, or "utilities".

However, it isn't a good idea to try to squeeze a few extra definitions onto the end of your existing Lisp tape or disc. Even if you know exactly how to do that, it is conceptually tidier to keep the Lisp itself clean and uncorrupted, just as it left its maker, and to put your own functions into a separate file of their own. Such files are known as INITialisation files. The normal procedure is to load Lisp, and then to "initialise" it (in the sense of "start", rather than in the sense of "add a signature") according to your own preferences by further loading your personal INIT file. Other than that, the INIT file is just one more amongst the many tapes or discs which you will soon fill with Lisp programs.

On a typical microcomputer, a command to its operating system (consult your machine's manual) loads the contents of your Lisp tape or disc into the computer's memory. The Lisp prompt then appears, perhaps after a copyright announcement. Lisp is then ready to accept your instructions, and one of the possible instructions (this time, consult your Lisp's manual) will be one which enables you to LOAD another tape or disc: such as your INIT file. At the end of a session with Lisp, there will be a similar Lisp instruction which will SAVE the whole of the current contents of memory back onto a tape or disc – i.e. into a file. The contents of memory usually means your own programs and property-lists, which you have created during that session, but not Lisp itself – the SAVE command being clever enough to distinguish the one from the other. So loading this new file alone in future will usually not restore Lisp. You must load Lisp, and then your INIT or other file, just as before.

For your INIT file, you don't want all the junk of a whole session saved along with your prize new utility. The way to keep an INIT file tidy is:

Load Lisp.

Load your INIT file if it already exists.

Define your new function. Debug it. Carefully note down its definition on a sheet of paper (or print it out, if you are lucky enough to own a printer).

Clear your computer's memory (or switch it off, then on again in the normal way).

Reload Lisp.

Reload your INIT file, if it exists.

Type in the definition of your new function.

Save everything onto your INIT file.

A long-winded process. But unless your computer is sophisticated enough to let you edit the files themselves, there is really no alternative.

Alphabetic list of Lisp functions

For each function listed below there is an entry which is in essentially three sections: (1) guidance as to possible alternative names which your Lisp may give to the same function; (2) a simple test or series of tests which you can carry out to ensure that your Lisp's version of the function, or its equivalent function, really does behave in the way my version behaves; and (3) a definition of the function in terms of the above minimal subset, which if all else fails you can copy verbatim into your computer in order to provide the missing function. In the majority of cases these definitions are quite short and simple: by the time you reach the end of Chapter 3, you should know enough about Lisp to check them for mistakes on my part or for typographical errors. If you do need to define or redefine a function, what was said in the previous section on INIT files may well be useful. But first read the entries below on DEFUN and FEXPR.

When in the main text I ask you to check a given function in this Appendix, please find the corresponding entry below and do the following:

(a) Find out (from your Lisp's manual) if you have available a function with the same name, or with one of the likely alternative names I suggest.

(b) Carry out the test or tests I've given. Every test specifies what the computer should print out as the result of the test. If it prints out ANYTHING ELSE, whether or not accompanied by an error message, the function has failed the test.

(c) If any function fails its test, please try the test again (and possibly again), until you're quite sure that its failure can't be due to some typing mistake on your part (that is, make sure you get exactly the SAME failure – the same error message, or the same incorrect response – several times in a row).

If your function has the same name as mine and passes its test, you have done all that a reasonable person could do, and can safely go back to the main text. If your function passes its test but has a different name from mine, your best bet is probably simply to remember the difference. However, you may prefer (especially when you get more accustomed to handling Lisp) to rename the function so that it is identical to my version. In order to do that you will have to have understood the differences between the two main types of Lisp function: the EXPR and the FEXPR. You will also need to have read the entries below under DEFUN and FEXPR, because the definitions I give are necessarily written in MY Lisp, and will perhaps need to be slightly modified for yours.

If your function fails its test, or if your Lisp has no equivalent for a function which arises in the text, you're in a slight amount of trouble. Fortunately, this situation is extremely unlikely to arise before you have acquired sufficient Lisp expertise to be able to define or redefine the aberrant function. Every function listed below has a definition supplied: what you have to do is copy that definition into your computer when your Lisp tape or disc is loaded. As you do so, you will have to make allowances for any differences found below under the headings DEFUN or FEXPR. The function will then exist in your Lisp and will behave as I say it should. If you want to make the change permanent, so that you don't have to do the copying again each time you reload Lisp, refer to the section above on INIT files.

ADDPROP This is unlikely to be called anything else. But many Lisps do not provide it. ADDPROP is like PUT or PUTPROP (see below) except that it will allow more than one value to be placed under any one property. PUT puts an atom onto the property-list; ADDPROP puts a list – and will subsequently "add" new items to that list:

```
*- (put 'a 'b 'c)

C

*- (addprop 'a 'b 'd)

(D C)
```

The definition of ADDPROP is as follows:

234

```
(defun addprop (i p v)
  (cond ((get id prop)
         (put id prop (cons v (get id prop))))
        (t (put id prop (cons v nil)))))
```

AND I cannot imagine that any Lisp would have an AND which was called
something else. However, in some Lisps it returns T if it succeeds, and in
others it returns the value of its last argument.

Test for AND:

```
*- (and (equal 'x 'x) (equal 'y 'y) 'a)
```

T or A

Since in Lisp anything which is non-NIL is counted as T, an AND which
returned A in the test would always work in place of one which returned T.
The AND in this book returns T.

Here is a definition of an AND which returns T:

```
(defun and args
  (cond ((null args))
        ((eval (car args))
         (eval (append (list 'and ) (cdr args))))))
```

and here is one which would return A in the test:

```
(defun and args
  (cond ((equal (length args) 1)
         (eval (car args)))
        ((eval (car args))
         (eval (append (list 'and ) (cdr args))))))
```

Notice that both are FEXPRs.

APPEND This is very unlikely to be called anything else in your Lisp. My version
of APPEND will take as many arguments as you like. In some Lisps it will
only take two.

Test for APPEND:

```
*- (append '(a) '(b))
```

(A B)

Definition of APPEND (two functions together):

```
(defun append args
  (cond ((null args) nil)
        (t (*append (eval (car args))
                    (eval (cons append (cdr agrs)))))))
```

```
(defun *append (L1 L2)
  (cond ((null L1) L2)
        (t (cons (car L1) (*append (cdr L1) L2)))))
```

APPLY This is very unlikely to be called anything else in your Lisp. It takes two arguments: the name of a function and a LIST of the arguments to which that function is to be applied. For example:

```
(apply 'plus '(1 2))
```

returns 3

You need to check in your manual whether or not in your Lisp the first argument to APPLY (the function-name) should be quoted. APPLY cannot normally be used with FEXPRs.

Definition of APPLY:

```
(defun apply (fn args)
  (eval (cons fn (mapcar '(lambda (a)
                            (list 'quote a))
                         args))))
```

One point to take note of is that in some Lisps the first argument to APPLY (the name of the function to be applied) has to be quoted, and in other Lisps it does not. LAMBDA expressions in place of the function-name always have to be quoted.

ASSOC The only likely alternative name for ASSOC is ASSQ. The difference between the two is the same as that between MEMBER and MEMQ, and between EQUAL and EQ (which see). As you will know from Chapter 3, this difference rarely matters in practice.

Test for ASSOC or ASSQ:

```
*- (setq q '((a b) (c d) (e f)))

((A B) (C D) (E F))

*- (assoc 'c q)

(C D)

*- (assoc 'z q)

NIL
```

Definition of ASSOC:

```
(defun assoc (item L)
  (cond ((null L) nil)
        ((equal item (caar L)) (car L))
        (t (assoc item (cdr L)))))
```

236

Definition of ASSQ:

```
(defun ASSQ (item L)
  (cond ((null L) nil)
        ((eq item (caar L)) (car L))
        (t (assq item (cdr L)))))
```

CAR/CDR and their combinations. Some Lisps don't provide them, or will only allow two, rather than three, As and Ds between the C and the R.

Test for 3 As and Ds:

```
*- (caddr '(a b c d e))
```

```
C
```

Test for 2 As and Ds:

```
*- (cadr '(a b c d e))
```

```
B
```

Of course, a Lisp which allows three As and Ds must also allow two! The combinations are very easy to write. You simply expand the CADR or whatever inside the definition. Here are a couple of examples:

```
(defun cadr (L)      (defun caddr (L)
  (car (cdr L)))       (car (cdr (cdr L))))
```

If you do have to write such things, you may prefer to call them SECOND, THIRD etc. while you're at it, rather than the unreadable CADR and CADDR.

A source of obscure bugs is that some Lisps do not automatically assume that the CAR or CDR of NIL is NIL. So if ever your programs apply either of them – or any routine such as the two above which uses either of them – to NIL, you get an error. The way round the problem is to put in a check for NIL before applying the function:

```
...(and L (cdr L))
```

COMMENTS Unless your manual specifically mentions them, you will not be able to insert comments into your programs. But if there's nothing in the manual under COMMENTS, look under SEMICOLON – which is the Lisp COMMENT-CHARACTER.

Test for the comment-character:

```
*- (setq a 'foo)
```

```
FOO
```

237

```
*- a ;hello
```

```
FOO
```

The value of A was returned. Both the semicolon comment-character and the remainder of that line were ignored by Lisp.

The comment-character is not a function having a definition in the normal sense. Special allowances have to be made for it inside EVAL.

DEFUN Unfortunately, DEFUN is not only the most likely system function of all to be differently named in your Lisp: it is also the most likely to demand subtly different usage.

Your Lisp may use a different word for DEFUN. Likely alternatives are DE, DEF, and DEFINE. Please also check carefully in your Lisp manual the syntax (i.e. lexical shape) of the two items immediately following that word.

The customary syntax is that the DEFUN-equivalent is followed first by the one-word name of the function without any brackets around it, and second by a bracketed list of any number of words, including none. In the latter case this "slot" should be filled by an empty list, which is signified in Lisp by two brackets "( )" or by the word NIL. There will be further lists and words in the complete definition, but they are not important in this context. For example:

```
(de name (word word word ...)
    .....)
```

is normal. A possible but rare variation (notice the different bracketing) is:

```
(de (name word word word ...)
    .....)
```

In the vast majority of cases there will either be no difference at all between your Lisp and mine in this respect, or the difference will lie only in the actual DEFUN-word that is used. For now, and especially if you are still in the early stages of reading this book, I would advise you simply to remember the difference(s) whenever you see the word DEFUN. Later on, you will understand what is meant by the following.

To rename an EXPR. Suppose you have in your Lisp a function called FOO, which is to all intents and purposes the same thing as a function which in my Lisp is called BLAH. Suppose that you would prefer your FOO to be called BLAH, and suppose that it is an EXPR. This is how to rename FOO, provided that you allow for your Lisp's equivalent of DEFUN:

```
(defun blah (<formal variables of FOO or BLAH>)
    (foo <same variables, not in a list>))
```

DELETE In your Lisp, it may be called DEL, REMOVE, or some such obvious synonym. In my Lisp, DELETE takes two arguments: the item to be deleted and the list it is to be deleted from. In some Lisps a third argument is necessary: it is numeric, and specifies how many copies of the item are to be deleted from the list (assuming that there are duplicates in there). If your DELETE is like that, just remember to include a third argument of 1 every time you see DELETE, and all will be well. My DELETE removes only the first instance of ITEM that it comes to as it looks down the list.

IMPORTANT: In some Lisps DELETE surgically alters its second argument just as RPLACA and RPLACD do. See below.

Test for DELETE:

```
*- (delete 'a '(a b a c))

(B A C)
```

If your DELETE, without allowing a third argument, returned (B C), redefine it like this:

```
(defun delete (item L)
  (cond ((null L) nil)
        ((equal item (car L)) (cdr L))
        (t (cons (car L) (delete item (cdr L))))))
```

A version of DELETE which does get rid of all instances of ITEM from the list is:

```
(defun delevery (item L)
  (cond ((null L) nil)
        ((equal item (car L)) (delete item (cdr L)))
        (t (cons (car L) (delete item (cdr L))))))
```

Test for surgical-type DELETE:

```
*- (setq x '(a b c))

(A B C)

*- (setq y x)

(A B C)

*- (setq x (delete 'c x))

(A B)

*- y

(A B C)
```

If your Lisp returned (A B) in this test, you have a surgical DELETE.

239

For most purposes this doesn't matter much, but as Chapter 3 explains there are times when it could. If you prefer, redefine DELETE as above.

EQUAL EQ In larger Lisps, and in a few smaller ones, these two functions are subtly different (you'll find out what that means in Chapter 3). Unfortunately, but perhaps inevitably, in some smaller Lisps the two functions tend to get interchanged, so that what is called EQ should really be called EQUAL, and vice versa. The tests below will sort them out.

```
*- (equal 'a 'a)  or  (eq 'a 'a)

T

*- (equal '(a b) (append '(a b) nil))

T

*- (eq '(a b) (append '(a b) nil))

NIL
```

Notice that the second test and the third are the same test, using the two different versions of EQ/EQUAL. If your Lisp has both EQ and EQUAL, the functions should pass both the above tests. If your Lisp has only EQUAL, it should still have passed both tests by returning T in each case. If it returned NIL for the second test, it is really EQ in disguise.

If your Lisp has only EQ, and if it returned T in the second test, it is really EQUAL in disguise. For the purposes of this book that will never matter. You can rename it if you like (it's an EXPR) as shown here under DEFUN. Here is a definition of EQUAL:

```
(defun equal (a b)
  (cond ((eq a b) t)
        ((or (atom a) (atom b)) nil)
        (t (and (equal (car a) (car b))
                (equal (cdr a) (cdr b))))))
```

FEXPR Some system functions, and hence some of the definitions given in this Appendix, are FEXPRs. If you don't yet know what that means, you'll find out at the end of Chapter 1, and you'll see a FEXPR in action in Chapter 3. In general, if a function's type is not specifically stated, it will be an EXPR.

Being a different type of function from EXPRs, FEXPRs are defined differently. A frequent way of doing this is to use DEFUN, DE or whatever (see under DEFUN) followed by the one-word name of the function as usual. But the next item in the definition, rather than being a list as in the case of an EXPR, is another single unbracketed word:

Standard EXPR definition:

```
(defun name (word word word ...)
  .....)
```

Standard FEXPR definition:

```
(defun name word
  .....)
```

    Throughout this book, that single unbracketed word in the third "slot" of a function-definition is a sure sign that the function is a FEXPR.
    Some Lisps use two DEFUN-words, one reserved for EXPRs and one for FEXPRs (for example, DE may define an EXPR whilst DF defines a FEXPR). Others use their normal DEFUN-word, but expect you to insert the word "fexpr" immediately after the function-name. I'm afraid only your Lisp's manual can tell you exactly what you should do; but, once you've got the hang of it, it shouldn't cause you any trouble at all. Here, following the pattern suggested in the entry under DEFUN and with the same provisos, is how to rename a FEXPR:

```
(defun blah args
  (eval (cons 'foo args)))
```

GET This is classed as one of the "primitive" functions listed in the Foreword, but is included here because some Lisps give it alternative names. The name your Lisp gives to GET will certainly begin with "GET" – the most likely alternative being GETPROP. There is also an added complication in that the order of GET's arguments may vary from Lisp to Lisp. My GET takes the following arguments:

```
(get <identifier> <property> <value>)
```

but some Lisps reverse the order of the second two arguments:

```
(get <identifier> <value> <property>)
```

    It is easy to rename a GETPROP to be a GET if the order of GETPROP's arguments is the same as those of my GET:

```
(defun get (id prop val)
  (getprop id prop val))
```

    Redefining a GET whose second and third arguments are reversed is more tricky, because of course this BOGUS redefinition:

```
(defun get (id prop val)
  (get id val prop))
```

is recursive, with no halting condition! Your solution here is either to

REMEMBER that your GET takes its arguments in a different order from mine, or to redefine it to have a different name (GETPROP wouldn't be a bad choice!) and then to use that wherever I have used GET. The following would work:

```
(defun getprop (id prop val)
  (get id val prop))
```

LENGTH May possibly be called by some abbreviation such as LEN, but is not likely to have any really different name.
   Test for LENGTH:

```
*- (length '(a b c))

3
```

Definition of LENGTH:

```
(defun length (L)
  (and (listp l)
       (cond ((null L) 0)
             (t (plus 1 (length (cdr L)))))))
```

LIST This will not be called anything else, but is not to be confused with a function called LISTP – which does quite different things! LIST takes any number of arguments, and is a FEXPR.
   Test for LIST:

```
*- (list 'a 'b 'c)

(A B C)
```

Definition of LIST:

```
(defun list args
  (cond ((null args) nil)
        (t (cons (eval (car args))
                 (eval (cons 'list (cdr args)))))))
```

LISTP May be called PAIRP or CONSP (you'll realise why in Chapter 3). It is a predicate returning T if its argument is a Lisp list, otherwise nil:

```
*- (listp '(a b))

T

*- (listp '(a . b))

T
```

242

```
*- (listp 'a)
```

```
NIL
```

```
(defun listp (a)
  (and (not (atom a)) (not (numberp a))))
```

LOOP Your Lisp may just possibly have a PROG such as is defined in Chapter 3. But it is more likely to have an off-the-peg looping construct called LOOP, DO, WHILE or UNTIL. It will, if it exists, certainly appear in your manual under one of the keywords LOOPING or ITERATION. Common looping functions are:

```
(loop (while L)              (while L
      <do a few things>            <do a few things>
      (setq L (cdr L)))            (setq L (cdr L)))
```

As you can see, looping constructs like the above are fairly easy to understand. The two shown here are precisely equivalent. But unfortunately neither of them allows you to specify a returned value, nor to have locally-bound loop variables. For these reasons PROG is preferable.

MAPCAR MAPC May be called by any name beginning with "MAP". Unfortunately, most Lisps have more than one function beginning with "MAP", and as with EQ and EQUAL it is possible for the names to get interchanged. So please read the following very carefully before concluding that your Lisp has no equivalent of my MAPC or MAPCAR.

First, these "mapping" functions take at least two arguments, the first of which is the name of some other function FN and the second of which is a list. The "MAP" applies FN to each member of the list in turn. So FN would normally be a function which took only one argument. In some Lisps you need to quote FN as the second argument to a "MAP", and in others you do not. Your manual will tell you – but if FN is replaced by a LAMBDA expression it must always be quoted, in any Lisp.

Mapping functions cannot normally be used with FEXPRs.

MAPC differs from MAPCAR only in terms of its returned value: MAPC returns NIL, and MAPCAR returns a new list of the results of its successive applications of FN. In these tests, the FN is PRINT:

Test for MAPC:

```
*- (setq L '(a b c))
```

```
(A B C)
```

```
*- (mapc 'print L)
```

```
A B C NIL
```

Definition of MAPC:

```
(defun mapc (fn L)
  (cond ((null L) nil)
        (t (eval (list fn (list 'quote (car L))))
           (mapc fn (cdr L)))))
```

Test for MAPCAR:

```
*- (setq q '((a b) (c d) (e f)))

((A B) (C D) (E F))

*- (mapcar 'car q)

(A C E)
```

Definition of MAPCAR:

```
(defun mapcar (fn L)
  (cond ((null L) nil)
        (t (cons (eval (list fn (list 'quote (car L))))
                 (mapcar fn (cdr L))))))
```

MEMBER MEMQ May be called by some other name beginning with "MEM". MEMBER is (should be) defined in terms of EQUAL, and so inherits that function's properties. MEMQ should be defined in terms or EQ. Please see under EQUAL for what that means. Don't worry if your Lisp has no MEMQ: you can almost invariably use MEMBER in its place.

Test for MEMBER:

```
*- (member 'b '(a b c))

(B C)
```

Test for MEMQ (the same test, plus another):

```
*- (memq 'a '(a b c))

(B C)

*- (memq 'a (append '(a b c) nil))

NIL
```

The second test for MEMQ distinguishes it from MEMBER in just the same way as EQ was distinguished from EQUAL.

Notice that both functions are shown as returning either NIL or that portion of the list (A B C) which begins with the member-item B. In some Lisps you will get (C), that portion of the input list which FOLLOWS the item, instead. This almost never matters – but don't forget about it, just in case!

Definition of MEMBER:

```
(defun member (item L)
  (cond ((null L) nil)
        ((equal (car L) item) L)
        (t (member item (cdr L)))))
```

Definition of MEMQ:

```
(defun memq (item L)
  (cond ((null L) nil)
        ((eq (car L) item) L)
        (t (memq item (cdr L)))))
```

NULL NOT Most Lisps have both NULL and NOT for the sake of readability, although they are just different names for exactly the same function. Neither is likely to be called anything else.

Tests for NULL:

```
*- (null t)
```

NIL

```
*- (null nil)
```

T

Tests for NOT:

```
*- (not t)
```

NIL

```
*- (not nil)
```

T

If your Lisp produces error messages for either NULL or NOT but the other of the two seems to be OK, it is trivial to define either in terms of the other:

```
(defun null (x)        (defun not (x)
  (not x))               (null x))
```

245

OR OR could not reasonably be called anything else. However, in some Lisps it
returns T where in others it would return the first non-NIL value it found
amongst its arguments.
   Test for OR:

```
*- (or nil 'a)
```

T or A

Since in Lisp anything which is non-NIL is counted as T, an OR which
returned A in the test would always work in place of one which returned T.
The OR in this book returns T.
   Here is a definition of an OR which returns T:

```
(defun or args
   (cond ((null args) nil)
         ((eval (car args)) t)
         (t (eval (append (list 'or (cdr args)))))))
```

and here is one which would return A in the test:

```
(defun or args
   (cond ((null args) nil)
         ((eval (car args)))
         (t (eval (append (list 'or (cdr args)))))))
```

Notice that both are FEXPRs.

PLIST In some Lisps, the function which allows you to inspect an atom's
property-list is not PLIST but CDR. In either case the correct argument to
give is a QUOTED atom:

```
(plist 'foo)      (cdr 'foo)
```

Before attempting to test PLIST, please read the entry here under PUT.
Test for PLIST:

```
*- (put 'a 'b 'c)
```

C

```
*- (plist 'a)
```

(B C) or ((B . C))

   Actually, there are other possibilities for what is returned by PLIST,
because some Lisps keep all sorts of internal data on the property-lists of
atoms. But if your PLIST does not return NIL or an error message in the test,
and if amongst what is returned you can clearly see a list which contains B and

C, you're in good shape.

The test for CDR is the same as the test for PLIST:

```
*- (put 'a 'b 'c)

C

*- (cdr 'a)

(B C)  or  ((B . C))
```

If your Lisp has CDR rather than PLIST, you may like to define PLIST for yourself:

```
(defun plist (x)
  (cdr x))
```

PRINT The PRINT in my Lisp takes a single argument, and before printing it prints a carriage-return so that each separate print instruction appear as a new line of output. If the PRINT in your Lisp is different, don't worry about it. The only effect will be that the format of printed outputs may be slightly different from what I show them as being – perhaps all on the same line, rather than on separate lines. A trivial difference, which I'm sure you can handle!

PROG There are at least three other functions available in some Lisps which have similar names to PROG. They are: PROG1, PROG2, and PROGN. Sometimes these names get interchanged, so you need to check, as follows.

My PROG is used within some other function (as COND is) like this:

```
(prog (<list of variables>)
  <S-expressions>)
```

If your Lisp has a PROG-like function which DOESN'T require the list of variables, the function isn't PROG. Because of the possible confusion of names, you may like to use a name other than PROG for the function developed in Chapter 3. PROG is its correct name, but it wouldn't hurt to call it, say, PROGV – for PROG-WITH-VARIABLES – to distinguish it from any other PROG your Lisp may have. But please don't omit any of Chapter 3: it's important.

Test for PROG:

```
*- (setq x 1)

1

*- (setq y 2)

2
```

```
*- (prog (x y z)
    (setq x 'one)
    (setq z (list 'x 'y))
    loop
    (cond ((null z) (return t))
          (t (print (car z))))
    (setq z (cdr z))
    (go loop))

ONE
NIL
T

*- x

1

*- y

2
```

If your Lisp has no PROG, it will have by the end of Chapter 3!

PUT This is classed as one of the "primitive" functions listed in the Foreword, but is included here because some Lisps give it alternative names. The name your Lisp gives to PUT will certainly begin with "PUT" – the most likely alternative being PUTPROP. There is also an added complication in that the order of PUT's arguments may vary from Lisp to Lisp. My PUT takes the following arguments:

```
(put <identifier> <property> <value>)
```

but some Lisps reverse the order of the second two arguments:

```
(put <identifier> <value> <property>)
```

It is easy to rename a PUTPROP to be a PUT if the order of PUTPROP's arguments is the same as those of my PUT:

```
(defun put (id prop val)
  (putprop id prop val))
```

Redefining a PUT whose second and third arguments are reversed is more tricky, because of course this BOGUS redefinition:

```
(defun put (id prop val)
  (put id val prop))
```

is recursive, with no halting condition! Your solution here is either to REMEMBER that your PUT takes its arguments in a different order from mine, or to redefine it to have a different name (PUTPROP wouldn't be a bad choice!) and then to use that wherever I have used PUT. The following would work:

```
(defun putprop (id prop val)
    (put id val prop))
```

QUOTE Most Lisps allow the single-quote sign (= apostrophe) abbreviation for this function. It is inconceivable that anyone should ever produce a Lisp in which QUOTE was called something else, or in which the abbreviation for it was something other than the single-quote sign.
   Test for QUOTE:

```
*- 'tony
```

if this does NOT produce the response

```
TONY
```

you must have one of the very few Lisps which will not let you use the single-quote abbreviation. In that case, I'm afraid you're stuck with one of two alternatives: (1) get yourself a Lisp which DOES allow it; or (2) remember that every time you see the single-quote sign, either in my Lisp or in any of the other books on the subject, you must nest whatever is quoted, be it an atom or a list, within this:

```
(quote ... )
```

For example:

```
for 'tony            read (quote tony)
for '(x y)           read (quote (x y))
for '((a b) (c d))   read (quote ((a b) (c d)))
```

   To put it bluntly, Lisps without the quote-sign abbreviation are a pain in the neck!

REVERSE This is unlikely to exist under any diferent name.
   Test for REVERSE:

```
*- (setq q '((a b) (c d) (e f)))
```

```
((A B) (C D) (E F))
```

```
*- (reverse q)
```

249

```
((E F) (C D) (A B))
*- q
((A B) (C D) (E F))
```

Definition of REVERSE:

```
(defun reverse (L)
  (cond ((null l) nil)
        (t (append (reverse (cdr L))
                   (cons (car L) nil)))))
```

SEMICOLON See COMMENTS.

SET SETQ You may just possibly find that your Lisp allows SETQ (they all do) but not SET. Neither of them is at all likely to be called anything else. If the SET instruction at the start of Chapter 1 doesn't work, don't worry: read on and try the SETQ version. That one is certain to work unless you have made a mistake.

SET isn't used very often anyway. If you're sure it is missing from your Lisp, type in this definition:

```
(defun set args
  (eval (list 'setq (eval (car args)) (cadr args))))
```

Both SET and SETQ are FEXPRs.

REFERENCES

Most of the following publications are referred to in the text. All are highly recommended: they cover Lisp programming, Artificial Intelligence techniques, and the impact of Artificial Intelligence on other fields such as philosophy and education.

Allen, J. (1978) Anatomy of Lisp. McGraw-Hill, New York, USA.

Boden, M. (1977) Artificial Intelligence and Natural Man. Harvester Press, Falmer, Sussex, UK.

Charniak, E., Riesbeck, C. and McDermott, D. (1979) Artificial Intelligence Programming. Lawrence Erlbaum Associates, New York, USA.

Davis, R., Buchanan, B. and Shortliffe, E. (1977) Production Rules as a Representation for a Knowledge-based Consultative Program. Artificial Intelligence, Vol.8, pp 15-46.

Eisenstadt, M. and O'Shea, T. (eds) (1983) Artificial Intelligence: Tools, Techniques and Applications. Harper and Row, New York, USA.

Eisenstadt, M. (1982) Design Features of a Friendly Software Environment for Novice Programmers. Human Cognition Research Group Tech. Report No. 3. Open University, Milton Keynes, UK.

Evertsz, R. (1982) A Production System Account of Children's Errors in Fraction Subtraction. Computer Assisted Learning Research Group Tech. Report No. 28. Open University, Milton Keynes, UK.

Evertsz, R. (1983) Production Rule Models, in The Computer Revolution in Education. (Jones, A., Scanlon E. and O'Shea T., eds) Harvester Press, Sussex, UK.

Hart, P. E., Nilsson, N.J. and Raphael, B. (1968) A Formal Basis for the Heuristic

Determination of Minimum Cost Paths. IEEE Transactions on Software Science and Cybernetics, Vol.4, No.2, pp 100-7.

Knuth, D.E. (1973) The Art of Computer Programming. Vol. 3. Addison-Wesley, Reading, Massachusetts, USA.

Minsky, M. (1975) A Framework for Representing Knowledge. in The Psychology of Computer Vision. (Winston, P.H., ed.) McGraw-Hill, New York, USA.

Nilsson, N.J., Principles of Artificial Intelligence. Tioga Publishing Company, California, USA.

Raphael, B. (1976) The Thinking Computer: Mind Inside Matter. W.H. Freeman and Co., San Francisco, USA.

Schank R.C. and Riesbeck C.K. (1981) Inside Computer Understanding. Lawrence Erlbaum Associates, New Jersey, USA.

Siklossy, L. (1976) Let's Talk Lisp. Prentice-Hall, New Jersey, USA.

Sloman, A. (1978) The Computer Revolution in Philosophy. Harvester Press, Falmer, Sussex, UK.

Weizenbaum, J. (1965) ELIZA – A Computer Program for the Study of Natural Language Communication Between Man and Machine. Communications of the ACM, Vol.9, No.1.

Winston, P.H. (1981) Artificial Intelligence. Addison-Wesley, Reading, Massachusetts, USA.

Winston, P.H. and Horn B.K.P (1981) Lisp. Addison-Wesley, Reading, Massachusetts, USA.

Young, R.M and O'Shea, T. (1981) Errors in Children's Subtraction, Cognitive Science Vol.5, No.2.

Index

Note: entries in upper case are the names of Lisp functions. Mathematical symbols are entered alphabetically under the letter immediately following the symbol.